CRITICAL ACCLAIM FOR *AMERICA II*

"Informative and provocative . . . Louv may well have defined the America of the 1990s and beyond."
—*The New York Times Book Review*

"A thought-provoking book, one that will set you to thinking . . . a superbly inquisitive mind is sharing its insights with you."
—*San Diego Union*

"A brilliant tapestry of social analysis, personal interview, and undeniable statistical fact"
—ALA *Booklist*

PENGUIN BOOKS

AMERICA II

Richard Louv is a graduate of the William Allen White School of Journalism of the University of Kansas. He has been a contributing editor for *Human Behavior* and *San Diego* magazines and a special projects reporter for the *San Diego Union*.

AMERICA II

Richard Louv

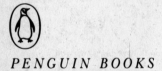

PENGUIN BOOKS

PENGUIN BOOKS
Viking Penguin Inc., 40 West 23rd Street,
New York, New York 10010, U.S.A.
Penguin Books Ltd, Harmondsworth,
Middlesex, England
Penguin Books Australia Ltd, Ringwood,
Victoria, Australia
Penguin Books Canada Limited, 2801 John Street,
Markham, Ontario, Canada L3R 1B4
Penguin Books (N.Z.) Ltd, 182–190 Wairau Road,
Auckland 10, New Zealand

First published in the United States of America by
Jeremy P. Tarcher, Inc., 1983
Published in Penguin Books 1985

LIBRARY OF CONGRESS CATALOGING IN PUBLICATION DATA
Louv, Richard.
    America II.
    Reprint. Originally published: Los Angeles: J.P.
Tarcher; Boston: Distributed by Houghton Mifflin,
c1983.
    Bibliography: p.
    Includes index.
    1. United States—Social conditions—1980–
2. Social values.   3. Social change.   4. Social conflict.
5. Quality of life—United States.   6. Nostalgia.
I. Title.   II. Title: America 2.   III. Title: America two.
HN59.2.L68   1985   306′.0973   84-25443
ISBN 0 14 007.560 7

Some names and identifying details in this book have been changed.

Page 329 constitutes an extension of this copyright page.

Printed in the United States of America by
R. R. Donnelley & Sons Company, Harrisonburg, Virginia.
Set in Baskerville

To my wife, Kathy,
and to my son, Jason

*It's this nomad people which the rivers and lakes do not stop. . . .
before which the forests fall and prairies are covered with shade, and
which, after having reached the Pacific Ocean, will reverse its steps
to trouble and destroy the societies which it will have formed behind
it.*

—*Alexis de Tocqueville,* **Democracy in America**

*Now I been lookin' for a job but it's hard to find
Down here it's just winners and losers and
don't get caught on the wrong side of that line. . . .
Everything dies baby that's a fact
But maybe everything that dies someday
comes back.*

—*Bruce Springsteen*

Contents

Introduction—Two Americas **xvii**

PART ONE: Home and Pain 1

Chapter 1. The Image of Elsewhere **3**

Chapter 2. Fueling Forces **10**

Chapter 3. The Dispersal of America **23**

PART TWO: Living in the Anticity 35

Chapter 4. Dreams of the Anticity **37**

Chapter 5. The Blob Gets a New Image **47**

Chapter 6. Laissez-Faire Lifestyle: The Anticity Unchained **66**

PART THREE: The Shelter Revolution 81

Chapter 7. The Coming of the Shelter Revolution **83**

Chapter 8. The Rise of Capitalist Communes **92**

Chapter 9. The Design and Selling of Condo America **109**

Chapter 10. Control Thy Neighbor **127**

PART FOUR: The New Eden   147

Chapter   11. Eden Redux   **149**

Chapter   12. In Search of Norman
Rockwell   **158**

Chapter   13. The New American Gothic   **176**

Chapter   14. The Price of Eden   **195**

PART FIVE: Working in America II   213

Chapter   15. You're on the Bus or You're
off the Bus   **215**

Chapter   16. The Company As Cult   **224**

Chapter   17. The Faith of
Entrepreneurialism   **241**

Chapter   18. Winners and Losers   **256**

**PART SIX: Somewhere over the
Postindustrial Rainbow   265**

Chapter   19. The Transforming Cities of
America I   **267**

Chapter   20. The Third Road   **286**

Selected References   **305**

General Sources and Suggested Reading   **317**

Index   **321**

Credits   **329**

Acknowledgments

A book comes not just from the labor of its author, but through the help of various midwives: editors, other writers, a host of sources, friends, and friendly critics. So, I wish to thank them for assisting in the birth (and also in the conception) of this book.

First, my gratitude goes to my wife, Kathy, who is a fine and natural editor and who helped in many ways to see this thing through, and to my son, Jason, who, though he can't yet read a book, one day will read here of the pleasure he gave me, which compensated for the isolation of writing. He's good company. I'm also grateful to Roz and Bill Frederick for their support and encouragement, and to my mother and brother for understanding during a difficult time. My researcher, Maribeth Mellin, was indispensable, not just for the many hours she spent in libraries and on the phone, but also for keeping me on track in rough terrain.

This book could not have been finished without the hundreds of hours invested by my editor, Millie Loeb, who is a very remarkable woman; nor could it have taken shape without the special vision of Jeremy Tarcher. Others at Jeremy P. Tarcher, Inc., who gave extra attention to the book include Laura Golden, Derek Gallagher, Linda Greer French, Thom Dower, and Kim Freilich. For copy editing, my gratitude to Penelope Suess. For lawyering, my thanks to Howard Behar of Los Angeles and Steve DeForest of Seattle.

The help of my agent, Mary Yost, was essential.

For the sharing of time and information, I'm particularly grateful to Robert Rodale, Louis A. Ploch, John Kasarda, Mary Duncan, Clark Reynolds, David Wolfe, Neal R. Peirce, Calvin Beale, and the many others whose thoughts appear in these pages.

The editors of the *San Diego Union,* Gerald Warren, Peter Kaye, and J. D. Alexander, encouraged the time and expenditures necessary to travel around the country to do the original series from which this book is drawn. By the end of the project, so many members of the staff were involved, one way or another, that it would be impossible to list them all here, but my special thanks go to city editor Marcia McQuern, who ushered in the series. Many other friends and fellow journalists assisted along the way, including David Boe, Steve Randall, Ralph Keyes, and Joel Garreau, who offered inspiration and warning.

Finally, I am forever indebted to Richard Kipling and Leigh Fenly for their help with the labor and delivery.

THE TWO AMERICAS

The America we know is dying, but a second America is rising from the body of the first. This second nation—America II—can best be seen in the South and West, but it exists, in varying degrees, in every state of the Union. It has a physical form: a very different kind of city; a radically changed rural and small-town life; a revolution in shelter; a new workplace. But the second America is also a state of mind: a powerful yearning for opportunity, for old values and new technologies, for refuge and escape.

This book is an exploration of what it's like to live in America II, or on the outskirts of it. It's about the people left behind, but mostly it's about the people who are moving, about condo dwellers and pot farmers, corporate utopians and private police, rural entrepreneurs and urban escapees, computer programmers and unemployed wanderers. It's about people trying to get control in an economic and social environment that seems out of control. It's about the search for home, the creation of new nests from the sticks and mud of our fantasies of what home should be. This book is about the unintended consequences of that search.

I've used the phrase America II as more of an experiential than historical categorization (to be historically accurate, it might well be the third America: agricultural, industrial, postindustrial, but most people do not think in these terms in their everyday lives). What we perceive is a break in our experience, the peaking of one America around the mid-1960s, its gradual decline, and the rise of a new America that is only now beginning to be identifiable.

America I is made up of all those steel workers and middle managers so bewildered by a society that, more each day, does not seem to need them. America I is once-vibrant big cities, big labor unions, auto workers, public swimming pools, railroads, New Deal politics, and the freestanding single-family home. It's a park in Seattle made from an old gasworks, where children now play and write their names on the steam valves and smokestacks of another age. America I is all those people left behind, outside the gates.

In contrast, America II is the rural shopping mall, condominiums and large, planned communities, private police forces and sophisticated residential security systems. America II includes ex-hippies and new "techies," desperate for what was and for what will be, fleeing with their computers (the new symbol of personal control) to small towns in New England and the Midwest. It's a countrified city and a citified country. America II is entrepreneurs working out of their homes and high-tech companies that have circled their corporate wagons, taking on some of the characteristics of cults. It's a national economy changing so quickly that even those lucky enough to have the sanctified skills feel threatened, as medieval princes must have once felt within their gates. And America II is the people from Oaxaca and the Yucatán who come north having heard that a dream still exists.

We are now two cultures. Like a quarreling parent and child, the fading America and the emerging America view the world in entirely different ways; they speak different languages. America I is steeped in tradition, the past trapped in the present, explosively dangerous in its frustration and distrustful of the new high technologies; America II is almost adolescent in its headstrong exuberance. It sees the nation transforming into something new and fresh; it perceives the future as a new technological frontier to be conquered and won.

This book began as a journalistic assignment, but over time it became something of a personal journey, an effort to come to terms with, or at least identify, some of the forces that are shaping the lives of my family, my friends, and so many millions of other people.

In 1981, as a reporter for the *San Diego Union,* my job was to cover long-range social and political trends. San Diego was and is an excellent place to do this; in the space of a few years it has progressed from being a rather sleepy Navy and tourist town to being the eighth largest city in the nation, a bellwether city plugged into the new information and service economy. For some time, the newspaper's editors had wanted a series of articles written on the Sun Belt, yet the Sun Belt seemed, for a variety of reasons, a conceptual framework whose time had passed. (There are at least a dozen demographic definitions, one of which even includes Seattle.) Further, the preliminary results of the 1980 census revealed demographic change that was much more complex and interesting than any solely regional explanation. So instead of looking only at the states of the southern tier, I decided to travel to the deltas of the migrant streams, with the idea that one could learn best where America is headed by going where Americans are moving.

As a result of that journey (and of subsequent travel), I have divided this book into six sections:

"Home and Pain": The America II migration patterns are undoing trends that have held steady for over a century. The number of families relocating is gradually dropping, but the power of migration to change the way we actually live has increased dramatically. As one demographer puts it, people seem "to be almost instinctively responding to overcrowding and seemingly intractable urban problems by seeking a more dispersed pattern of settlement." It's not just the fact that people are moving from one region to another that makes all of this significant but the reason they are moving: a powerful nostalgia, the rise of a counterculture-libertarian ethic, the hunger for personal control in a livable environment, and a paradoxical assumption that a sense of coming home can often best be had by moving away.

"Living in the Anticity": In a kind of urban "big bang," Americans are hurtling outward, creating what I've come to call "the anticity," an urban form strikingly different from the past. This new kind of urbanization is related to but quite different from the supercity or megalopolis that most urban experts believed represented the future. Instead of a wheel with a large central city at the hub, surrounded by rings of bedroom communities, the anticity is barely a city at all, but rather a spreading collection of much smaller wheels. The anticity is the successor not only to old industrial cities but also to the traditional suburbs as well. It replaces public with private services and has the potential for creating extreme divisions between different economic and racial groups.

"The Shelter Revolution": Along with deep demographic change has come a shelter revolution, a new kind of housing significant not only because of the architecture but because of its inherent political power. In a single decade, condominiums and planned communities have given rise to an enormous number of private minigovernments. These minigovernments now outnumber all the other elected local governments (cities, towns, counties), and many of them maintain the kind of control over people's lives that most Americans have never tolerated in the past. The growth in the number of condominiums and planned communities might well be considered a sideshow of American culture, except when one considers that housing construction starts are now dominated by these forms. The shelter revolution radically changes what it means to be a neighbor.

"The New Eden": A brand-new rural America is part of America II. This is one of the most important demographic and social developments in the history of the nation. As recently as the late 1970s, some social scientists considered the continued growth of large cities unstoppable, the rural eclipse ongoing. But the reversal in rural-to-urban migration is changing all the rules. The rural rush, as this section of the book describes, is creating a condoized, computerized culture not really rural and not quite urban. This new Eden offers enormous possibility for a better life, but it also offers what could potentially be the final destruction of nature and the small-town culture for which so many people yearn.

"Working in America II": The new economy feeds and validates the dispersal of America. Home and work are more intimately interwoven than at any time since Americans left the farms in search of urban opportunity, producing a new workplace and a new attitude toward work. Increasingly, entrepreneurialism is perceived, especially by the baby-boom generation squeezed by a shifting job market, as a way to gain control of their careers and obtain greater geographic freedom. In the new high-tech industries and beyond, the old corporate ethic and big labor unions are being supplanted by experimental new management styles designed to make the company a "family." The unintended consequences is a "buffering" psychology that may eventually do more to undermine economic security than create it.

"Somewhere Over the Postindustrial Rainbow": The final section deals with several implications for the future. For example, the fate of what remains of America I, particularly the older cities, may ultimately have much more to do with growth than with decay, but a kind of growth that makes current trends in America II seem mild in comparison. The nation is at a crossroads.

Categorizing social change is a risky business that calls for a few provisos. First, I am not a sociologist, so this book does not meet the requirements of that discipline. However, in the effort to understand the new America, I've borrowed a certain amount of jargon from social scientists and have added some of my own. The term *postindustrial* has, for lack of a better word, been used in these pages. Daniel Bell first introduced it in *The Coming of Post-Industrial Society,* published in 1973, and it has come to be an accepted way of describing the relative decline of manufacturing industry as the primary economic force in Western society, the rise of service and information industries, and the social shifts that go along with the new economics. He is an uncomfortable parent to the term (his original conception was more complex), but it has entered the language as one useful way of categorizing change. Second, no single book could adequately cover all the major areas of postindustrial social change. For example, I have not dealt in any depth with the crucial issue of immigration. As Bell writes, "No conceptual scheme ever exhausts a social reality. Each conceptual scheme is a prism which selects *some* features, rather than others, in order to highlight historical change." So it is with with *America II.*

Since Bell's book was published, much has been written about postindustrial change, and I owe a debt of gratitude to those who have paved this path, especially to Daniel Bell, Alvin Toffler, John Naisbitt, and Joel Garreau. But some of my concerns and conclusions are different from theirs.

My emphasis, ultimately, is on the America II social agenda: the growing privatization of public services, residential separatism by lifestyle and age, the widening wage spread, the conflict between the right to migrate and the rights of people in the attracting areas, and the potential despoliation of nature by those seeking nature. There is a light and a dark side to what we are becoming. Therefore, *America II* is an examination and critique of underlying values and social issues, especially those that threaten traditional democratic values. Americans, I've come to believe, aren't just creating the transformation, they're also beginning to question how best to share its burdens and benefits. This book is an attempt to take that next step, to look past the technological and structural changes to the social issues that will be dominant in the years directly ahead.

Finally, this book is a study in unintended consequences. I initially went looking for the Sun Belt and found instead an America whose form had changed radically from that of my suburban Kansas City childhood. In the beginning I was excited and impressed by what I saw: individuals seemingly grabbing control of their lives. But I gradually began to wonder about the unintended consequences—if, for instance, this search for control is constructing, in some corners of America II, the antithesis of control, a peculiarly vulnerable way of life. I began by reporting physical phenomena; I ended fascinated with the invisible web of American dreams, illusions, and possibilities.

PART ONE

HOME AND PAIN

*In the United States there is more room where nobody is than where
everybody is.*
That is what makes America what it is.

—*Gertrude Stein*

*One of the peculiarities of the white race's presence in America is how
little intention has been applied to it. As a people, wherever we have
been, we have never really intended to be. The continent is said to
have been discovered by an Italian who was on his way to India.*
—*Wendell Berry,* The Unsettling of America

*Every man, every woman, carries in heart and mind the image of the
ideal place, the right place, the one true home, known or unknown,
actual or visionary.*
—*Edward Abbey,* Desert Solitaire

THE IMAGE OF ELSEWHERE

They talk about it as if it were much more than an abstraction. They have no name for it, though when the word *home* is happened upon, they say that word strikes close, but it is a peculiar home, one that exists as much in the future as in the past.

A woman, a single parent, who lives in Beverly Hills, California, talks of her suburban childhood, and how her memories of that time somehow set the stage for the shaping of her own internal landscape: "I had a difficult childhood. I don't have many happy memories of our family life, but I have nothing but good feelings about the small town, which was really a suburb seven miles outside of Boston. Across the street from my parents' home was the Hurley Farm, which is now a subdivision. I used to walk through the woods to get to elementary school. The woods are all gone now, of course. When I lived there, whatever anxiety that prevailed—the cold war, drop drills in school—these weren't things that deeply troubled our lives. We felt safe. That was an era when parents didn't share their troubles with their children. Maybe that was the right thing to do, I don't know. I talk to people my age, in their early forties, and if they grew up in a house—not an apartment, but a home in a suburb—they talk about what it was like then, that enormous feeling of having arrived at the promised land . . . green grass, a certain safety. We may say a lot of critical things about suburbia, but an awful lot of us are trying to get back those feelings. And we can't seem to do it."

This woman has given the topic considerable thought. She hears so many of her friends talk of moving to a small town somewhere, "where the pace is slower, where people actually know and care about their neighbors, where life doesn't seem to be quite as frantic." She does not share their fascination with small towns. "Small towns, nice suburbs, maybe they're the same thing; maybe it's just our childhood we're looking for."

A few miles from her house, parts of Hollywood seem to be decaying almost as quickly as Detroit. Hollywood, of course, produced and still produces so many of the images and illusions of what home should be. At Universal Studios, a public tour tram whisks tourists past Beaver Cleaver's old house on the set of Mayfield, that most perfect suburb in a fictional small city, perhaps somewhere in the Midwest. "Leave It to Beaver" can be seen in reruns several times a day on multiple Los Angeles channels and has gathered a cult following around the country. (So has the "Andy Griffith Show" of the early 1960s, set in bucolic Mayberry, a fictional small town in North Carolina.) In a 1982 revival of "Leave It to Beaver," the grown-up Beaver, divorced and disappointed with his life, comes back to Mayfield with his two young sons. His mother has sold the old house to him and moved into a condo.

A former college roommate of mine, originally from a suburb of Topeka, Kansas, lives in a one-room apartment in a seedy section of Hollywood and, in the spring of 1983, was about to graduate from UCLA with a master's degree in business administration. On his little wood-plank desk, next to a row of paperback books popular among college students in the late 1960s, were stacks of letters he had written to large American firms, applying, unsuccessfully, for jobs. Out of his open window he could see the Los Angeles basin and the Los Angeles sky—one huge stretch of smog and overcrowding. "I went to visit a friend in Denver a couple weeks ago," he told me one day. "I sat there in his house for two days, way out on the edge of town, and looked out at the hills. The grass that covered the hills was brown from the winter. I remember there was just one bit of color, a stoplight, out in the middle of this expanse. I guess I'd just had it with being hemmed in, disappointed, exhausted. I stared at that stoplight, that one bit of color, and as the hours went by it all seeped into me again and filled me up—this feeling that I needed space and nature, like I grew up with. I guess I want to go home, but I'm just not sure where that is. Maybe I define home as a certain ratio of land to me. Here in L.A., the ratio is all wrong. It's just too much. Someplace like Boulder, that's just the right size." A few weeks later, he moved back to Kansas, in search of that mysterious ratio.

A beautiful phrase, coined by demographer Peter A. Morrison, captures what seems always to have drawn Americans: the "image of elsewhere." America, after all, was set up as an escape from the past. This chapter begins with examples from Los Angeles, instead of the more obvious places from which people are moving, because for so long Los Angeles represented the dream of opportunity, of space, of freedom. It still represents that dream for many people, especially Mexican and Asian immigrants. They account for the fact that Los Angeles was among the few large American cities to gain population in the 1970s. But for many people in L.A., the dream now lies elsewhere: in San Diego to the south, or Eureka to the north, or the Sierra to the northeast, or to the less populated regions of the mountain West and Midwest. In the American past, the image of elsewhere presented a bright and possible urban future. Now, as if on an early Kinetoscopic film, the image is flickering: first dim, then bright; changing.

With each day, the hunger for this image grows more urgent, particularly in those regions of the nation most radically changed by the coming of the postindustrial economy. In Boston and Philadelphia, Detroit and Chicago, Baltimore and St. Louis . . . in a dozen more big, industrial cities, people are aching for what they seem to have lost.

In New York City, a woman described her yearning to leave the fading America and move to a new one, one that somehow represented more of a connection to the past than the city in which she grew up. As she spoke, her dark eyes darted around her two-room wholesale shop, filled with racks of $300 antique-lace dresses. Five years ago, she started this business after a relationship ended badly. Healing her emotional wounds in Europe, she haunted antique stores in France. She thought about old things, things that last, things of warm familiarity, and so she began to collect lace: great wads of it, rolls of it stuffed in suitcases and boxes to take home. She sensed that she was not alone, that a wave of nostalgia was beginning in America. Now, in her little shop in a dingy brownstone next to a punk rock store that sells "urban guerrilla" T-shirts, she enjoys enormous success, including an anointment of publicity from national magazines. Movie stars wear the dresses made of her lace. But it's not enough. What good is all this success, she wonders, if she has to "run from my parked car to the front door of my shop—like out of the trenches? My purse was snatched. I got mugged; pushed into a doorway. I screamed, and I couldn't believe it was me—a noise like a siren came out of my mouth. I constantly think about moving to another part of the country. I mean it; all the time, literally." She thinks about the West, not Los Angeles but that part of the West that still resembles a frontier, albeit, a wish frontier: a frontier with solar panels and Indian art and Perrier water and waitresses wearing Danskin tops. "Maybe I could move to—what's that place that all the artists are moving to?—Santa Fe. Maybe that place could support what I do. I've got to get out of here. I'm tired of living in a war zone."

Home and pain.

Americanism, contend some sociologists, is an operative religious faith. If Americanism is a religion, then nostalgia is its liturgy. The word *nostalgia* was coined by a Swiss physician in the late seventeenth century from the Greek *nostos,* "to return home," and *algia,* "a painful condition." Nostalgia, the painful desire to return home, was thought at the time to be a disease, found especially among Swiss mercenaries then fighting far from home for a variety of English despots. The disease was thought to be caused by what one physician described as "the quite continuous vibration of animal spirits through those fibers of the middle brain in which impressed traces of ideas of the Fatherland still cling." Some physicians even posited that the disease was due to abrupt changes of altitude, an affliction of sentiment sometimes set off by the clanging of cow bells at rarefied atmospheres.

Nostalgia is no longer considered a disease, though it could certainly be thought of as a national condition. We are awash in nostalgia. In the Church of Reformed Americanism, ceiling fans and neon are everywhere. In San Diego private police dress up like Keystone Kops and patrol a renovated downtown district called the Gaslamp Quarter. In cities new and old architects have begun to soften the bleak lines of glass-box skyscrapers, favoring the vaguely "futuristic" humps and curves of 1930s art deco. In America II, we're nostalgic for the future, a future past.

Old heroes are being rehabilitated, such as Horatio Alger, Jr., whose entrepreneurial story of rags-to-riches inspired past generations. In 1982, the postal service issued a stamp commemorating Alger's one hundred and fiftieth anniversary. According to Ralph Gardner, author of *Horatio Alger or the American Hero Era*, this indicates "an obvious swing from cynicism back to the old virtues that made heroes as people again look for old virtues and heroes." As a culture hero, the entrepreneur was relegated to the back row during the late 1960s and most of the 1970s. Today the entrepreneur has been hustled back up to the front, dusted off, and handed some high-tech wares to sell.

In 1981, to the outrage of preservationists, designer Ralph Lauren announced a line of clothes called "frontier chic": Indian concha belts and squash-blossom necklaces, fancy down vests and rough-wear denims. A year later, *Newsweek* announced the coming of "country chic": up-scale clientele in Manhattan rushing out to bid on homespun linen sheets, Amish quilts, pine school desks, and "country" cabinets designed to hold home video equipment. Auctioneers report that collectors want their furniture to reflect age, even if the paint chips are circa 1981, not 1881.

The choir sings about the past. In 1961, country music sales amounted to less than $10 million; in 1980, country was worth $527 million. Urbanites who, a few years ago, looked down their noses at their country cousins, today enthusiastically prefer country and western music: the term *redneck* is now as much a compliment as it is an epithet. Indeed, nothing seems to sum up our contradictory mood quite as much as the sequin-studded urban partygoers, wearing their "bull rider" cowboy hats, bending and pawing over mirrors, snorting lines of cocaine. Even "new wave" bands, who prefer the regalia of robotics to western clothes (though one offshoot is called "country punk"), sing about the past—particularly about the 1950s and '60s. "Many of the new generation feel their lives were shaped by a period of irrevocable American decline," writes Craig Unger in *New York* magazine. "Born with high expectations, they are fed up with downward mobility. They embrace their suburban, shopping-mall culture with a mordant irony; they welcome technology as their savior and destroyer. . . . Like children in the attic, they rummage through . . . thrift shops, as if searching for the remnants of dreams that can never be theirs."

Social forecaster John Naisbitt calls the trendy attachment to the past "high tech/high touch." "Whenever new technology is introduced into society, there must be a counterbalancing human response," he says.

In the late nineteenth century, during the rapid onset of the industrial age, when power and people were shifting from a rural to an urban environment and foreign immigrants were streaming in, Americans were uneasy, fearful. They often blamed the new immigrants for the changes, and they longed for the past. "Nostalgia took the form of a yearning for an Anglo-Saxon republic and moral structure," explains Rabbi Marc Tanenbaum, interreligious director for the American Jewish Committee, quoted in *U.S. News and World Report*. "It was sort of saying, 'Stop the world; I want to get off.'" In part, the antiurban Populist movement of the 1890s was stimulated by these fears. Today, with a new rising tide of immigration, with decay and the coming of a postindustrial era, people are responding in much the same way. According to Ray Browne, a professor of popular culture at Bowling Green State University in Ohio, "there's a terror of technology, of social and economic conditions that we seem unable to handle. So we look back to times when things were simpler. A busy nation with its eyes on the future doesn't have time to think about where it's been—but if you lose momentum and aren't forced to look ahead, you think about what you left behind."

The baby boomers, those Americans born between 1946 and 1964 (one-third of our present population), seem the most attracted to nostalgia, and there is good reason. During the late 1950s and '60s, the dominating urge, especially for the baby boomers, was to head away from home. Home represented traditional values, and these values had seemingly failed. For so many in that time, the placid and affluent suburban neighborhoods could not be rationalized with the carnage in Vietnam, with assassinations and race riots, with the unhappiness of so many parents who appeared to have it all and yet were clearly discontented. Home, in Henry Miller's phrase, was the "air-conditioned nightmare." In any case, the nation was economically secure enough. One could always go home, always get a nine-to-five, if things got rough.

Then the economy began its long skid, and the single-family home, that symbol that had been viewed by so many young adults of the 1960s with such repugnance, was no longer within economic reach. For the first time a generation could not look forward to a more affluent life than their parents. And along with this was the growing suspicion that the search for personal fulfillment did not necessarily lead to a better life. Beyond personhood was community, and it could not be found. Community was the lowest of priorities to modern architects, with their love of glass boxes, and to developers, who slapped houses up as if they were so many milk cartons in a row. But the methods used by the counterculture to seek community did not work either: flashing the peace sign at passing muraled Volkswagen vans could carry them to 1969 and no further. Then came the pursuit of est and real estate, and the Moral Majority with its assurances of parental guidance and stern, traditional values. And finally, the hunger for home.

We could not go home again, but we could move to some fresh place that stood for something lost. We could surround ourselves with the molded, electronic, particle-board sensations of what we think is home. If we could not go home again, if home had been paved over or had never existed, then we could create it: It could be in the new countryside, in a new city, with a gabled roof and a prefab, polyethylene Victorian gazebo; it could be walled off, with its own private Keystone Kops; it could be a place of community or a place of repression; it could be in the West, the South, next door. It could be a paradise bought.

FUELING FORCES

The quest began in earnest in the 1970s. The unarticulated idea was this: you could fine-tune your inner self through meditation, divorce, running—or you could really run. Like the Pilgrims, the Mormons, and the pioneers who built houses of sod and faith on the Kansas plains, you could change your inner environment by changing the external. You could try, with some potential for temporary success, to satiate a gnawing hunger. You could move.

Americans had moved all through the 1950s and '60s, of course, wandering around the country, up the corporate ladder. There had always been the drift West, the California dreamers. But the nature of the nation's restlessness has changed dramatically. The actual rate of movement was slightly less in the 1970s and early '80s than in the '60s, but the effect of the movement is entirely different. The hunger for home, for control over our own lives, combined with massive technological and economic changes, is re-creating America.

Ever since demographers and social scientists began asking people why they moved long distances, the great majority of people who did so said the reason was simple: money.

Until 1970, most demographic studies noted that 70 percent of Americans who moved long distances did so in pursuit of a higher-paying job. But during the last decade, Americans began to answer the surveys differently. Suddenly economics did not appear to be quite so important. In the 1970s, only half of the people who moved said they did so because of a job. They were willing to take a cut in income, sometimes a substantial cut, for the intangibles of a livable environment, more civilized human contact, and access to unspoiled nature. In 1979, a University of

Illinois study found that only 24 percent of midwesterners who had moved from urban to rural areas had done so because they desired a new job. In comparison, 40 percent said that the reasons they had moved were related to the environment: they were escaping crime, busing, congestion, noise. "Some of the people I questioned said they were looking for nothing more than a quieter life," commented sociologist Andrew Sofranko, who conducted the study. "We detected a general feeling of disenchantment. They couldn't always come up with anything; they just wanted out."

Indeed, that could be the catchphrase of the 1970s and early '80s: they just wanted out. One poll illustrated that wanting out was not confined to the people of Pittsburgh or Detroit, but included 29 percent (in the late 1970s) of California's residents. Of that percentage, more wished to move to Oregon than to any other place. It is instructive to note that 29 percent of California's population is double the current population of Oregon.

In 1981, more than a third of all residents of cities of 50,000 or more would move to the country if they had a chance, according to a survey conducted for the National League of Cities by the Gallup organization. The study found little difference by city size in the percentage who said they would leave: 36 percent of the respondents in small cities (50,000 to 250,000 residents) said they would; 32 percent in medium-sized cities (between 250,000 and 1 million residents); and 38 percent in large cities (1 million or more residents). Of the reasons for wanting to move, crime (mentioned by 24 percent) came in first. Among the other reasons given were overcrowding (especially by people who lived in suburbs and medium-sized cities), unemployment, pollution, poor school systems, and the presence of "undesirable groups." The study's findings were remarkable, not just for ranking the reasons for increased migration to the country, but for suggesting that suburbs no longer fulfill their original purpose: the American dream of living away from the city while still enjoying urban amenities.

Certainly not all these people were ready to pack up and head for the hills. What they were expressing was a persistent national yearning for more dispersed living. Given a choice, free of economic constraints, millions of urban Americans said they would prefer living in a rural area, a small city, or even a large city with lower density. For most Americans, though, these desires re-

mained unrealistic and unrealized; the big, high-density cities
were where the jobs and the money were. But something had
been unleashed: a new ability to choose where and how to live,
to have both lower density and better job prospects. This does
not mean that rural life is necessarily the ultimate destination.
The small town is, for many people, not so much a real residential
goal as it is a symbol of safety, nature, community, family life, the
past.

PAVING THE WAY TO AMERICA II

The new ability to choose where to live was brought about, in
part, by advances in telecommunication and small computers,
but there are other, less flashy and more important, reasons.
Prior to World War II, the north central region and the northeast
contained most of the country's industrial advantages: deep-
water ports, intricate inland waterways, good highways in the
cities and between them, extensive railroad systems, nearby rich
coal deposits, a relatively well-educated work force, and the majority of the nation's consumers. As recently as 1960, these regions dominated industry with two-thirds of the nation's
manufacturing jobs, mostly concentrated in or near the core
cities of the largest urban regions.

The shift of power and people out of central cities, and out of
the north central region and the northeast, began because of a
complex pattern of heavy federal investment in the South, the
West, and in rural areas, plus progrowth attitudes and industrial
boosterism, lower wage rates, fewer unions, and, to a degree, the
shift of investment capital (including union pension funds) to
these regions. All of this began long before the personal computer or fancy satellite dishes started showing up in remote
woodlands. It began with federal investment in the nation's roads
and, especially, in the interstate highway system during the Eisenhower era. President Eisenhower pushed for a better national
transportation system, to open up vast new markets to manufac-
turers in the northeast and north central states, and to provide
for the quick transport of troops and munitions and the speedy
exodus of people from major population centers in the event
of war.

Not only did the highways allow companies to ship goods to
out-of-the-way places, they also made it possible for companies

to move to these places. New four-lane highways laced the South and West, and new farm-to-market roads created faster-pumping bloodlines between the cities and the countryside. Distance was no longer a barrier to selling or manufacturing goods.

With the interstate highways came a shift from railroads to trucking. This meant wider distribution of nationally standard-ized consumer goods. Regions that had been considered too hot or too remote were further opened up by the spread of central air-conditioning, the rise of southern and western universities, the extension of state college systems into smaller cities and rural areas, and the introduction of cable television in areas far from big cities.

A stockbroker could live in Dallas and have the *New York Times* delivered before 8 A.M. A person could live in the backwoods and, in all likelihood, drive down to the corner market and pick up some Perrier.

Without the jet, such cities as Phoenix, Atlanta, San Jose, Den-ver, and Houston, far from traditional financial centers of the northeast and upper midwest, could not have grown as rapidly. Improved air transportation has improved dramatically not only in the large cities of the South and West, but also in the more remote regions of the United States. Tucked away in the Tetons, Jackson Hole, Wyoming, for instance, now has its own jet port.

Changes in manufacturing technology were just as important in the dispersal of the nation's people and power. A good assem-bly line layout requires horizontal flows, which demand more land, and land is cheaper in exurbia, in most areas of the South and West, and in rural America. Many of America's largest com-panies, including AT&T, IBM, Union Carbide, and General Elec-tric, have already moved production or administrative and research facilities to regions beyond central cities. Moreover, production technology now centers on lightweight materials (aluminum and plastic instead of iron and steel), fewer movable parts, and increased use of miniaturization and electronics: all technological changes in manufacturing that mean plants can concentrate on small parts of products, parts that are more easily and cheaply shipped. Computer and communication technology allow a remote head office to communicate almost instantly with scattered branches, factories, warehouses, which means that a firm can function with smaller inventories and less working capi-tal. Thus the countryside and the technology could offer what the cities could not: large expanses of low-cost land, efficient high-way systems for transportation, and an instant communications network.

The sources and distribution of the nation's energy also underwent major changes. Beginning in the early 1960s, northern industrial plants converted from coal to oil and natural gas for production and plant heating; southern states were closer to domestic sources of oil and natural gas, so rates were lower there. This was crucial, especially after the Arab oil embargo and price decontrol of oil and natural gas. The boom in the Rockies was fueled by rich deposits in coal, oil, oil shale, tar sands, natural gas, uranium, copper, gold, silver, lead, beryllium, and molybdenum.

So, many of the same technological, governmental, and structural fueling forces contributed to the rise of southern and western cities and the emergence of small cities, small towns, and rural areas all over the nation. They were cut, as it were, from the same cloth.

Next came new technological linkages that made population deconcentration not only desirable but inevitable: the telecommunication revolution removes most advantages for centrality in business administration and research and development. Headquarters and branch offices may retain contact through two-way cable TV, conference picture phones, rapid facsimile teleletters, and computer networks. The ability of companies and individuals to trade information electronically is suddenly making the jet itself seem a bit archaic.

THE SEARCH FOR CONTROL

Technology and economics are making population dispersal practical, but just as important are the more ephemeral social forces pushing and pulling us toward America II. More than anything else, we seem to want control over our lives. A 1982 report by the Justice Department entitled *Violent Crime by Strangers* noted that polls found an increasing awareness and fear of crime, particularly of street crime by strangers, "even though the rate of violent victimization by strangers remained stable." The unexpected stranger, the shot in the dark, these are the real nightmares of American life. If one can move to a fresh city, a place where the sun illuminates the corners, or to a small town or high-security condo, then, the perception is, one can get control. The study reported that one of the advantages of living in a small town, if it can be considered an advantage, is that you are more likely to know your attacker.

Certainly race is associated with the crime issue, and here again perceptions count more than reality, since urban blacks are more likely to be the victims of crime than whites. White flight is no myth, however. According to the Joint Center for Political Studies, between 1968 and 1980 there were 77.8 percent fewer white students in large city school districts in Detroit, 45.7 percent fewer in New York City, 66.3 percent fewer in Cleveland. And yet the motivations to move are more complicated than just racism or fear of crime: blacks are leaving the old cities too, in record numbers. Both whites and blacks often report that they are attracted to the South or to small towns because they perceive—rightly or wrongly—that racial attitudes are now more tolerant outside the big cities than within them. Writer Maya Angelou, who is black, recently explained why she moved back to the South in 1981, to Winston-Salem, North Carolina: "One of the reasons people have fought for the South is because it's gorgeous . . . it's exciting. There are the worst and best of human beings to be found there. It is overt—racism is overt or friendliness is overt. It's not hidden, encased in those namby-pamby words like 'We must get together' . . . you know, people say 'I hate your guts' or 'My goodness, it sure is lovely to meet you, why don't you just come on right over,' and they mean right then. . . ."

The new impulses moving us are really a new slant on old values, something more complex and interesting than what is usually called the nation's growing conservatism. Americans have a growing feeling of personal helplessness. Pollster Louis Harris found in March 1983 that nearly two-thirds of Americans feel alienated from those who run the United States—a disturbing 62 percent, compared to 29 percent in the first Harris index on the subject in 1966. The percentage of people who believe they are "left out of things going on" jumped from only 9 percent to 48 percent. While some people act on this feeling of alienation by becoming more politically involved, especially through political action committees, a growing number of people simply withdraw.

A new American ethic is emerging, what U.S. Deptartment of Agriculture demographer Calvin Beale calls the "counterculture/libertarian" movement, a cross between a counterculture regard for the environment, the leisure ethic, and a conservative, almost libertarian, focus on self-reliance. Generally, this way of looking at things holds that someplace safe, secure, under control can be found or created—and that government is not going to provide it. Beale originally used the phrase to describe some of the wild and woolly sorts who had headed for the hills (the pot farmers of Humboldt County, California, for instance), but it can be useful in describing the motivations and actions of other groups as well. This ethic, given a wider interpretation, seems to cross all economic classes, from the back-to-the-landers, to conservatives who move to small towns in New Hampshire, to people who move into high-security condos, to entrepreneurs who head for antigovernment, unzoned Houston.

There is considerable irony in this antigovernment, antitaxation attitude, since government itself, both big and little, paved the way for the exodus to the South, the West, and the countryside by constructing the highways and roads; building colleges, dams, office buildings, and parks; and financing huge water and defense projects. But much of what moves America II is the urge to leave bigness behind: big cities, big corporations, big government, and big fears.

The search for control is not just a desire for protection, but an intensified pursuit of happiness and leisure. Vacation homes are no longer affordable only by the wealthy. The subdivision of rural land for vacation houses exploded in the 1960s and early '70s, with as many as 150,000 vacation houses built every year. During this same period, retirement communities began to spread outside Florida and the Southwest.

Among the people most affected by the counterculture/libertarian ethic are elderly Americans. Says Calvin Beale, "The whole environmental movement that developed in the 1960s, plus some of the antimaterialistic views of the youth movement, changed the unwillingness of people to move to or to stay in rural areas." And they were more willing, too, to move to increasingly self-contained retirement communities, or to leisure-oriented cities of the Southwest. "They quietly listened to the back-to-the-earth, quality-of-life rhetoric—and when it came time to retire, they had the income to do something about it," contends Beale. "We were surprised by something else, as well. We knew we were going to have more retired people in the 1970s and '80s. What we didn't expect was that older people would have such good incomes and pensions, giving them mobility. And we certainly didn't realize how many people would be retiring younger."

More older workers are retiring early, even though a law was passed in 1978 guaranteeing the right to work longer. As of February 1978, fewer than 12.5 percent of U.S. workers remained in the labor force once they reached the age of sixty-five, a proportion that has dropped steadily since 1950, when the figure was 26.7 percent. The continuation of this trend has surprised many experts, who expected concern about inflation and recession to keep seniors on the job. Another factor in the liberation of seniors was that the average retirement age for employees of the federal government dropped from sixty-four to fifty-nine in less than a decade.

Older Americans have been for some time destroying the myths and stereotypes so often attached to them. Although many seniors, especially in the shadow of supply side economics, are worse off than ever before, a significant percentage of the "gray wave" is, because of accumulated affluence and changes in attitudes, better off, younger in attitude, and determined to make the most of life. They are redefining the notions of what it means to be old. In one psychological study, most older Americans rated themselves as "highly optimistic."

So, in their post-hippie vans and Winnebagos, retirees and elderly Americans led the way to small towns and leisure-oriented cities in the sun. They were the first to move into condominiums and large planned communities, the first to adopt the new nests.

This is not just the psychology of footloose and affluent seniors. Developers have discovered a new market, the preretirement household, made up of working people who are looking for a more carefree, more physically active way of life, who want smaller houses that are easier to take care of and easy access to outdoor recreation. This new leisure-oriented market, as one marketing chief said, "want to live a little. They're not intent on leaving something to the kids after they've gone."

The acceptance of the jet as a necessity, not a luxury, is a good illustration of the almost frenetic pursuit of happiness. Though air travel sputtered a bit during the recession, Americans have experienced in the past decade a complete change of attitude toward air travel. In 1979, according to a panel of social scientists brought together by the trade magazine *Travel Weekly* and Boeing

Aircraft, more than half of all American adults took at least one 200-mile trip that included air fare or paid accommodations—a jump of 16 million people in just one year. Americans that year took 276 million trips, an increase of 66 percent. While some of that explosive growth can be credited to the greater number of working women, social researcher Daniel Yankelovich looked closely at the social motivations. What he determined was that our motivations for travel have changed. New values born in the 1960s and propagated in the '70s had shifted many Americans away from self-denial and toward self-gratification. Travel, according to Yankelovich, is no longer considered a luxury: the need to escape is considered a right. According to a Census Bureau survey, with higher incomes, fewer children, and more women working, many American families may be more able now than in the past to assign high priority to environmental qualities when deciding where and how to live—at least during nonrecessionary times. Something else quite curious and paradoxical has happened to how we decide where to live. Women are now more willing to relocate to get a promotion or a better job than men are. Merrill Lynch, the investment company, reported that 6 percent of its employees who were moved in 1980 were women, twice the percentage of 1978. A study by Boyden Associates showed that single and divorced female executives were the most mobile, and that men are more willing now than in the past to move in order to advance their wives' careers.

At the same time, for many men the Holy Grail of upward corporate mobility has lost its sheen. At IBM, corporate moves were once so frequent that employees claimed the company's initials stood for "I've been moved." But IBM's work-related transfers are down from 5 percent in the mid-1970s to a current 3 percent. Inflation, soaring interest rates, and the demands of dual-career marriages have all worked to slow down job related movement.

These social changes contribute to two movements: a fever to stay at home, if where you live fits your notions of home, or to move to a newly fabricated home. At first glance, these two movements appear contradictory. However, they both contribute to national deconcentration. These impulses, rooted in the same ground, do not just shift the nation around (as with the parents of the baby boomers), but help reshape it into new forms. As *Business Week* reported in 1981: "How industry responds [to the resistance to corporate moves] could alter traditional ways of doing business—and living—in the United States as well as determine the fates of individual companies." Declining mobility will actually speed up the decentralization of the U.S. economy, according to the article,

> as companies build new, electronically linked plants near untapped labor sources, to the increasing detriment of the cities. For the United States as a whole, the mobility crunch will speed the economic decentralization set in motion by the revolution in data communications and the economy's growing orientation toward service and high technology. If people cannot or will not move to jobs, many jobs will move to them. Electronics companies, which regard product transportation as a minor concern, have already set up satellite operations in rural areas to tap resident work forces . . . ,

since the bulk of Americans who are moving to new areas are heading for small cities and towns—and also because housing and relocation costs are usually so much cheaper in less populated regions.

This new emphasis on quality of life over corporate needs has some management experts worried. They fear that employees who are allowed to put down roots in a community will "lose a sense of corporate identity, loyalty, and job worth." Uprooting executives and transferring them around the country had in fact been a manipulative tool to ensure "corporate community." One new way of corporate coping with the search for home: in a number of cities, companies are forming "spouse employment networks" that trade information on jobs that might suit the wives and husbands of transferred employees. Other coping mechanisms: some companies, IBM included, are now giving greater autonomy to regional branches; others, such as Hewlett-Packard, use management methods that make the company a relatively gentle home and family.

As the recession of the late 1970s and early '80s wore on, the mobility of Americans again picked up. A study by Employee Transfer Corporation found that the proportion of employees willing to transfer had returned to the 1977 level. Staying home, in tough economic times, can be a real luxury, especially when the corporations have figured out that what we really want is to be moved somewhere that looks more like home than where we now live.

THE NEW ECONOMY

Overlaying all of these technological, structural, and values changes is the new economy, which compels many Americans to migrate, to be a part of the new America, sometimes whether they want to or not.

As almost everyone knows by now, we are changing rapidly from a manufacturing society to an information society. The extent to which this is radically changing where we live and how we live is remarkable. In 1950, approximately 17 percent of the work force held information jobs. Today, 58 percent work in information, in jobs that relate to creating, manipulating, marketing, and distributing information or information machines.

The agricultural age took a millennium to develop, the industrial age, a century, but the information age is forming in a matter of a few years, and then shedding its skin again and again. These new jobs and new technologies, arriving at a time of massive social confusion, fill us with both dread and excited anticipation. "In a matter of a few years," writes Daniel Yankelovich, "we have moved from an uptight culture set in a dynamic economy, to a dynamic culture in an uptight economy."

The homeless and the unemployed—many of them shoved out of declining industries not just by recession, but by structural changes in the economy that will last long after the recession ends—wander around the country sleeping in tent cities or under decaying freeway overpasses, looking for the kinds of jobs that have seemingly disappeared. At the same time, what appears to be a new class, the Postindustrials (those people with the sought-after skills and education), are decorating their electronic cottages with the latest hard-disc drives, data base management systems, projection TVs, and high-tech security apparatus, and going to work at thriving electronics companies—almost always located in the South, the West, or in strips of high-tech research and industrial park on the fringe of, or well beyond, the cities. The West and the South have emerged as the major growth poles of the U.S. economy, and dispersed pockets of prosperity in small towns and rural areas are flourishing in almost every state. All of these new magnets offer cheaper, less unionized labor pools. They attract the hot industries, the energetic entrepreneurs.

The faltering economy of America I, caught between old industries and new ones, helps push people out—especially the independent-minded ones. The drain of self-reliant individuals from the older industrial cities may be the most hidden and pervasive impact of the migration. A study of job movement in the 1970s by the Massachusetts Institute of Technology showed that job markets in older industrial cities were less affected by the desertion of big corporations than by their inability to produce and nurture small, self-sufficient entrepreneurs. On the average, about 8 percent of all jobs in any community disappear every year, mainly because companies fail or lay off workers. Surprisingly, the loss rate is fairly even all over the country—Houston, in other words, loses about as many jobs each year as Philadelphia. But cities in the South and West simply create new jobs at a faster pace than they disappear. "The main thing that happens is that entrepreneurs move and create new jobs in new places," according to David L. Birch, director of MIT's program on neighborhood and regional change. This means that hardy individualists, able to create jobs where there were none before, are a vanishing breed in America I.

The new economy offers both opportunity and insecurity; the engine inside America II is powered as much by one as the other. Today steel mill workers may be displaced, but tomorrow some types of skilled workers or middle managers (especially from the overcrowded baby boom generation) could be next, replaced by an electronic work station or a robot. Even the Postindustrials have a gnawing feeling that the transforming economy is like a blizzard or a tornado: unpredictable, beyond control, or, more precisely, controlling us. We long for independence, self-reliance, protection. This feeling began to grow long before the recession of the early 1980s. M. Harvey Brenner, a professor at Johns Hopkins University, studied the ups and downs of the national economy between 1940 and 1973, and their relation to personal health. His study showed broad and direct links between downward fluctuations in the economy and physical and emotional illness. Brenner calculated that an unemployment increase of 1 percent, or about a million people, when sustained for six years, could be statistically linked with increases of 36,887 in total deaths, 4227 in mental hospital admissions, and 3340 in state prison admissions. His study also showed that this pattern has existed for at least 127 years, and that it has intensified in recent years. Another study, done at the University of Minnesota and Williams College, has shown that members of the baby boom generation, who had come to expect so much, are particularly vulnerable to these fluctuations. They exhibit this vulnerability especially through higher rates of suicide.

Our health rises and falls with the health of the economy. We are increasingly vulnerable to even the most subtle economic fluctuations—in a time when large chunks of America, which not long ago represented power and security, are rusting away. It is no wonder that so many of us are rushing off to bright new areas of the South and the West in search of high-tech salvation, trying desperately to get out in front of the power curve; or that others are heading for the countryside, to grasp at least a sense of self-reliance and insulation; or that so many hunger for the safety of home, the protection of childhood.

THE DISPERSAL OF AMERICA

The most evident result of all this social and economic yearning and compulsion is the physical dispersal of America and the nation's reassembly into new forms.

In 1971, William McGill strode for the first time into the boardroom of the American Telephone and Telegraph Company, on the twenty-sixth floor of a grim, old Wall Street building. As he remembers it today, the room was a study in understated power: rich wood paneling and red leather chairs. Screwed into each chair's high back was a small brass plate bearing a director's name. He lowered himself into one of the chairs. A former chancellor of the University of California at San Diego and president of riot-torn Columbia University, he had recently been elected to the AT&T board of directors. He looked around at the august assemblage, which included such barons of commerce as William Hewitt, president of John Deere & Company, and Mil Batten, president of the New York Stock Exchange.

A leather-bound book that charted the monthly progress of AT&T was placed in front of each director. The contents were not available to academicians, who, at the time, were confident that the growth of America's industrial cities was unlimited and the rural eclipse ongoing.

McGill opened the book. Roughly in the middle was a map that depicted the growth of new telephone usage around the country. He was amazed by what he saw: a gradual but very evident shift of business telephone activity toward the southeast, Southwest, and Rocky Mountain states.

Like a camp follower with good economic instincts, Ma Bell

was following power and business and people right out of the older cities.

"My God," McGill exclaimed. "Look what's happening to the country."

The other directors nodded.

"Of course," said board chairman John DeButts, arching an eyebrow. He pointed to the map. "Didn't you know? That's how we make our investment decisions."

McGill did not know it at the time, but he was looking not only into the future of the nation but into his own future as well. Nine years after his first AT&T board meeting, McGill was chairman of the President's Commission for a National Agenda for the Eighties, a commission that suggested that the dispersal of America was the wave of the future, the day of big, concentrated cities was over, and the national future, demographically, was to be much more complex and powerful than just a shift of telephone hook-ups to the southeast, Southwest, and Rocky Mountain states. The audacious authors of the McGill commission's 1981 urban report went so far as to suggest that the nation could no longer assume that centralized, industrial cities would perform the full range of their traditional functions for the larger society. In later discussion, one academic attached to the commission said, "For 99 percent of man's history, he did not live in cities. They are brand-new social inventions. Probably the best thing that could happen to our older cities that reflect nineteenth-century conditions is that they shrink in population, that they decant."

Such talk outraged many of the nation's big-city mayors, especially New York City mayor Ed Koch, who told a *Playboy* interviewer that the suburbs were "sterile" and described rural America as "a joke. . . . (laughs) You have to drive twenty miles to buy a gingham dress or (laughs louder) Sears Roebuck suit (cracks up)." The *New York Times* quoted Koch as saying, "People invented cities early on because they thought that was the place to live. What we have to do is rejuvenate them." What the McGill commission was suggesting, he added, was that people "go out and reinvent the wheel." A lot of Americans are doing just that.

One day in 1982, George Poulos, of the St. Louis Building Inspection Service, noticed that houses on the city's North Side were vanishing, literally overnight. House thieves were tearing down the century-old buildings in a few hours. The bricks and plumbing, Poulos surmised, were finding their way into new houses, condominiums, and trendy restaurants in the South or the West, or, perhaps too, out in the changing countryside. Not only was St. Louis losing its population to America II, but its buildings as well.

St. Louis, a city originally built for fur trappers, was skinned; more than a quarter of its central city residents were gone. The list of shrinking central cities reads like a roll call of battle casualties: Philadelphia, Pittsburgh, Chicago, Baltimore, Milwaukee, Minneapolis, Detroit, Seattle, Louisville, and Kansas City, among many others. Thirty of the fifty top central cities fell in population in the 1970s. In just one decade, New York City, the biggest loser, lost enough people to populate the city of San Diego. Cleveland and Detroit lost almost a quarter of their residents. If current losses continue at the same pace, Washington, D.C.—which lost 100,000 people, 16 percent of its population—will have no residents at all in only fifty years. The future, *American Demographics* magazine predicts, will look like this: "By day, the District will be jammed with powerful officials. By night, visitors will flood the restaurants and hotels; but no one will actually live in the District —except perhaps a handful of the rich and a few holdouts from earlier years." Today, about one-third of all metropolitan residents live in areas of decreasing population. Urban America, as one of the members of the McGill commission pointed out, "has left town."

DECONCENTRATED AMERICA

America is deconcentrating, changing from a dense, concentrated, manufacturing-oriented society to a dispersed, deconcentrated, service-oriented society. The same deconcentration is happening throughout the developed world: Canada's prime minister, Pierre Trudeau, worries that his country is becoming "a loose confederation of shopping centers." This transformation includes three basic movements of people: the interregional movement to the South and West; the continued growth of suburbs, some of them far beyond the traditional edges of metropolitan areas; and the dramatic turnaround from urban growth to rural growth. The transformation also includes an ancillary movement of new immigrants, especially Hispanics and Asians, a wave rivaling the great European immigration to America just prior to and after the turn of the century.

Growth in the so-called Sun Belt, an uneven growth at that, was only part of a much larger transformation, a structural breakdown into smaller parts, a deconcentrated America.

The shift of population west and south is, of course, the most familiar component of the new America. During the 1970s, the West and the South captured fully 90 percent of America's population increase, with the West showing the fastest rise in the number of both rural and urban dwellers. Every western state except Montana and Washington grew at more than double the national rate. Of the fifty fastest-growing counties in the nation, fully twelve were in Florida. An average of about 45,000 new residents moved to San Diego each year in the 1970s, moving it from fourteenth to eighth on the nation's Top 40 list of cities. San Jose grew by a third, leaping from the twenty-ninth largest city to seventeenth. But the real action was outside California. Other western states pulled up alongside California's rate of growth, and then passed it. Texas now boasts three of the nation's ten largest cities, Arizona grew by over a half, and sparsely settled Nevada grew by 63.5 percent.

Roy Borgstede, a computer mapping specialist with the Census Bureau, plotted America's march west by locating the United States' exact center of population, defined as the point where the country would balance perfectly if it were a flat surface and every person on it had equal weight. During the 1970s, the imaginary point crossed the Mississippi River and came to rest in a tract of wooded land near a small pond forty-five miles south of St. Louis, in Jefferson County, Missouri, which had an almost 40 percent population increase in the 1970s. By any measure, this was a demographic milestone, a clean break from the past.

For a few months, the exact point was unclear, leading Claude Cook, an insurance agent, to worry that the center would be found in one of the town's two large sewage-treatment lagoons north of town. An entrepreneur at heart, Cook joked that he might "try for the boating concession to take tourists out to see it." Some of the citizens of Jefferson County thought it fitting and proper that the new population center bears the name of Thomas Jefferson, who idealized a deconcentrated, decentralized nation, and had arranged the Louisiana Purchase with that in mind.

Suburban growth, which gained its first surge of momentum in the 1920s, then exploded following World War II, has entered a new stage. Indeed, some of the older suburbs—surrounding New York, Boston, Pittsburgh, Newark, and Buffalo—are losing population right along with the central cities. Originally designed as bedroom communities for people working downtown, these suburbs are actually part of America I. The newest suburbs, however, even those around some of the cities that have lost considerable population, are growing at an increasingly rapid rate. For instance, Minneapolis–St. Paul lost 14.2 percent of its population in the 1970s, even as the surrounding suburbs gained 20.4 percent. The newest suburbs are extraordinary not only because of their apparent economic independence from large cities, but because they often extend far beyond the fringes of large cities and older suburbs. The line between what is suburban and what is rural becomes increasingly fuzzy.

The movement of people beyond the cities into rural areas, and farther out to isolated small towns, is considered another clean break with the past, a historic reversal that caught most demographers and social scientists completely off guard.

Ever since 1820, people have been moving from rural America into the cities. For the first time in 1910, the "typical" American lived in an industrialized city. During most of the twentieth century, the small town withered, drained by the migration to the cities and suburbs. Cities, it seemed, would never stop growing. In 1969, a prominent urban economist testified before the House Ad Hoc Subcommittee on Urban Growth that "once a city gets above a quarter of a million, it seems to grow forever," while smaller cities recede into economic crisis. As late as 1979, Dr. Arthur P. Solomon, director of the Joint Center of Urban Studies at Harvard and MIT, said that a series of trends—the economic squeeze, the energy crunch, and the growing number of households with two working adults and fewer children—appeared to be keeping people closer to the urban centers and slowing the process of suburbanization. Rural America was seen as a place of sharp contrasts: booming agribusiness and poor, dying towns. For many of these towns, it appeared, the last picture show (as a popular movie of the 1970s dramatized) had been shown.

There had been signs along the way that the urban spell was actually fading: the growth of distant suburbs, and the fact that by 1975 less than half of all suburban workers commuted to a job in the central city. With the release of preliminary figures from the 1980 census, it became clear just how many people were moving to greener pastures. Today, the population growth rate in the United States is higher in rural and small-town communities than in metropolitan areas. During the 1970s, almost 3 million more people moved out of the large urban centers than into them. Nearly two-thirds of all nonmetropolitan counties gained immigrants, compared with one-tenth in the 1950s. Although popular wisdom predicted the energy crisis would push people into high-density cities, the rural rush was especially prevalent in the counties with the least population.

The rural rush is happening in every region of the nation, even in the northeast. The question of the 1980s, says the Agriculture Department's demographer, Calvin Beale, is "How do you keep them down in Paree once they've seen the farm?" One popular destination is northern Idaho, a region of clear lakes and pine and spruce. "Even on the day that Mount St. Helens erupted and everyone was warned to close their businesses and stay indoors because of falling ash, a man from California knocked on my door wanting to buy land to build on," said George L. Shaw, himself a former Californian, who owns Idaho Panhandle Realty. "I sold him some that very day." Even urban cults are moving to the country, because they can have more control over their members. Coeur d'Alene, the county seat of Kootenia County, one of the five fastest growing counties in Idaho's northern panhandle, had a population increase of 40 percent in a decade; half of the police officers in Coeur d'Alene came from the Los Angeles Police Department. While St. Louis plummets in population, the nearby Ozark mountains are booming; some counties that were virtually deserted in 1960 are now so crowded with ex-urbanites that much of the region is suffering air and water pollution. Indeed, Archer City, Texas, the dying little town where Peter Bogdanovich shot *The Last Picture Show* in 1972, has come roaring back with new oil money and changing social attitudes. Instead of pool tables, one finds Pac-Man and Asteroids Deluxe machines, and, just outside town, backyard dish antennas pointing toward the sky, beaming in Colorado and New Mexico ski reports.

A NEW WAY OF LOOKING AT AMERICA

Until recently, the north-south shift, resulting in the Sun Belt, has been the easiest way to conceptualize population change in the

United States. However, the new trends, taken together, do not represent a single, prosperous, monolithic Sun Belt.

The Sun Belt (a term Kevin Phillips coined in 1969, in *The Emerging Republican Majority*) is a conceptual framework whose time has passed. Indeed, the term *Sun Belt* is thought by an increasing number of social scientists, demographers, and historians to be sloppy regionalizing.

A distinctly defined Sun Belt cannot be found: its location is ephemeral at best. According to the U.S. Census Bureau, the Sun Belt extends from Delaware south to Florida, and includes rainy Seattle. *Fortune* magazine includes all of Virginia in the Sun Belt, and splits California somewhere near Fresno, while *Sales & Market Management* magazine threw in all of California but excluded Virginia. Others have defined it as a political entity. In 1980, the *Atlanta Journal and Constitution* declared that the Sun Belt could boast a voter majority—true only if the Sun Belt includes the entire South and West census regions, containing everything from the Rockies to the northwest and from the Chesapeake region to the Deep South. "As yet," writes Bradley Rice in *American Demographics,* "no one has nominated Alaska as a Sun Belt state."

"Wrong, Mr. Rice," counters the *Wall Street Journal,* pointing out that John Shannon of the Advisory Commission on Intergovernmental Relations concludes that "the Sun Belt is the sunny side of the street from a fiscal standpoint. It should include Alaska."

Indeed, the Sun Belt can be measured more by what it does not take into account than by what it includes. For instance, the phrase *Sun Belt* tells us little about population deconcentration, a force that describes the dispersed cities of the Sun Belt as well as the thriving small electronics and publishing towns of New Hampshire; a shift of people and industry into that state from Massachusetts parallels the shift from the northeast to the South and West. Nor does it take into account the movement out of California into the north central plains states, states with few large cities, low unemployment rates, low wage rates, and miserable winters. Nor does the Sun Belt framework include the renaissance of pockets and corners of some older cities, a transformation that leaves these cities with fewer people, but more households; with less industry but taller, glassier (though not necessarily classier) buildings; with neighborhoods of intensified decay and misery right next to revived and gentrified, high-tech expressions of the upwardly urbane. In the transformed older city, one urban America loses its magnetism and decays, while another urban America, which also has lost population, eats quiche in a shiny new twenty-first floor condominium office or a gentrified Victorian mansion. This new urban America, no matter where it is located geographically, looks a lot like the fabled sun belt.

Economists, interested more in prosperity than population, have suggested the replacement terms *growth belt* or *money belt*. But no belt of prosperity can be delineated that wraps around a single belly that includes Houston's barons of laissez-faire capitalism and the rural poor of Mississippi. These conceptual belts contribute more to regional indigestion than to accuracy.

How then should we perceive the changing structure of America? Joel Garreau in *The Nine Nations of North America* provides one useful model. He sees the United States, Canada, and Mexico as comprising nine distinct economic and cultural regions, rival power blocs with separate loyalties, interests, and future plans (MexAmerica, for example, combines the southwestern United States and northern Mexico). In addition to this important way of looking at America, however, there needs to be a cross-regional way of understanding demographic change.

One of the more unusual and useful attempts to define the Sun Belt was published in the *Journal of the West* in 1979. Professor Carl Abbott used rapid population growth as the primary criterion. Abbott's belt would exclude such states as Louisiana, Tennessee, Mississippi, Alabama—states normally thought to exist in the Sun Belt—but include several states above the thirty-seventh parallel: Washington, Oregon, Nevada, Utah, and Colorado. What this definition has to do with the sun is left to the imagination, but it does point in the right direction, toward a complex, dynamic, and cross-regional web of change, the most notable characteristics of which are the rate of population growth, where that growth is occurring, and the new forms of community it is creating.

The sum of the major population shifts—regional population movement, continued growth of the newest suburbs, and the rural rush—is greater than the parts. The sum represents the blurring of the lines that previously have divided cities from suburbs, suburbs from small towns, and small towns from countryside.

THE INTERNATIONAL CONTEXT

Though there are some peculiarly American aspects to deconcentration, we are not alone in our wish for less density. We just happen to be out ahead, accomplishing, largely unintentionally, what much of the rest of the world would like to do.

In the less developed nations, migration into cities continues at an alarming rate. In 1950, only 25 percent of the world's people lived in cities. By the year 2000, it is estimated that 70 percent of the world's people (one out of three of them children) will be living in cities that are already struggling to feed and house the populations they have, according to studies presented in 1980 to a United Nations conference. Supercities such as Cairo, Mexico City, and Athens continue to grow, creating almost unlivable environments. The absorption by Athens of 37 percent of Greece's population is a national crisis close to disaster. The city offers too few jobs, is wracked by land speculation, and is enveloped in noise and pollution. The problem of Athens's growth could be tantamount to the collapse of the Greek countryside.

To deal with the continued concentration of people in large cities, the governments of some developing nations are adopting methods of conscious population deconcentration. These methods often look quite similar to the new forms of population distribution happening in the Untied States, except that in the United States, government has generally resisted the dispersal—with the exception of the New Town movement, to be described in a later chapter. For example, Thailand is fostering "regional urban growth centers" to save Bangkok. The Philippine government has tried to defuse exploding Manila by resettling urban dwellers around the ouskirts of the city in prefab condominiums clustered around community centers. Cairo, where every bit of unused space in the city is occupied by squatters, gained 6 million new residents between 1966 and 1976; in 1981, the government embarked on a plan to build satellite towns around Cairo to relieve the city's congestion and to preserve agricultural land. But still the economic migrants are flowing into the cities, forced out of the countryside by landlessness, joblessness, and poverty. Their fate in the cities is usually no better, crowded as they often are into nightmarish shantytowns.

Throughout the Communist world, governments have been trying to force people out of concentrated cities and into the countryside—more for political than ecological reasons. (One of the objectives of the *Communist Manifesto:* "Combination of agriculture with manufacturing industries; gradual abolition of the distinction between town and country by a more equitable distribution of the population over the country.") And yet, of the Communist countries, only China has been moderately successful in holding down city populations, and then by imposing exceedingly stringent and repressive controls on people's freedom of movement. According to a study by Roland J. Fuchs of the University of Hawaii and George J. Demko of Ohio State University, the Socialist people movers have located industry and housing in underdeveloped areas; demanded worker registration with police, work documents, and involuntary transfers; and imposed geographic bans on new industrial development in concentrated cities. The populations of Czechoslovakia, East Germany, Hungary, and Poland remain highly concentrated in big cities. Between 1958 and 1978, more Soviet citizens moved out of Siberia than settled in it. Cambodia succeeded in moving people out of the cities by a forced march. Most of them died. Unlike the developing and Communist nations, much of the developed world has moved over some great demographic hump.

In the 1970s, Belgium, Denmark, France, the Netherlands, and West Germany all experienced a gradual shift of population away from the highly industrialized core regions. Canada, Finland, Iceland, Italy, Japan, Norway, Spain, Sweden, and the United Kingdom followed, with a significant drop in net migration toward the core regions after 1970. The shift is even being felt in Paris. A French poll found that until twenty years ago many French people dreamed of living in Paris. Now 85 out of 100 maintain that they would never choose to live there, and 60 out of 100 Parisians would like to move elsewhere. Throughout much of the developed world, as University of Pennsylvania demographer Daniel Vining says, "the century-long migration towards the high density core regions is over."

The United States, which, with its own peculiar context, represents the most extreme and important case politically and

economically, appears to be out in front of a vast change throughout much of the developed world.

William McGill, sitting in his modest office at the University of
California, San Diego, where he is now an adjunct professor of
psychology, thinks often of the day he stared with disbelief into
the AT&T book of numbers, and how the board chairmen lec-
tured him "like an exceptionally stupid student." And he wonders at the economic, technological, and emotional hungers
loose in the nation that have led to such dramatic changes in
where and how people live. Staring out his office window across
the groves of academe and eucalyptus, at the high-tech buildings
and tanned students, he says, "As a commission, we got in trouble because we said what was true. Civilization is a compact, and
the terms of that compact can change. This is one of those turning points in history. And it cannot be stopped."

Deconcentration holds enormous potential for good, for reshaping the way we live, for reassembling our communities in more
human scale. Yet, once population dispersal is accepted as a fact
of American life, a whole new agenda of social issues arises.
Certainly the fate of those people, especially the poor, left behind
in the old cities, is on that list. But the most troubling issues on
the new agenda may have more to do with the creation than with
the decay. The most important issue may not be deconcentration
itself, but the new ways of life arising out of that deconcentration,
the reassembly of America into new forms: a new kind of city, new
kinds of shelter and workplaces, a new kind of small town and
countryside.

The chief psychosocial issue of America II is one of affiliation.
Most of us need a feeling of belonging, a sense of being protected. We need to feel a part of a group, a community, or a
company. Groups allow us a certain equilibrium, an ability to
weather ordinary and future shocks. One of the tenets of psychia-
try is that if group affiliation is destroyed and no new group offers
membership, we are more likely, under stress, to develop behavior disorders, depression, violence. Past decades have seen the
gradual breakdown of traditional ties and networks of family,
neighborhood, church, and town. This breakdown is partly at-
tributable to a factory and corporate system that brought about
urbanization, greater worker mobility, and the general feeling
that individuals were as replaceable and specialized as the widg-

ets they manufactured. The cultural and sexual revolutions of the 1960s and '70s further devalued or transformed the traditional affiliations. Today, given an atmosphere in which public education is devalued and egalitarianism out of favor, one social effect of our hunger is to protect ourselves by circling the wagons. The more vulnerable we feel, the more we fragment into smaller living and working units, or whatever it takes to create the feeling of insulation and safety and home. The real question of America II is whether the new forms of affiliation create further social fragmentation and isolation, or a new feeling of community and economic security.

PART TWO

LIVING IN THE ANTICITY

If you don't want to live in the city, pick a spot ten miles beyond its outermost limits—and then go fifty miles further.

—Frank Lloyd Wright

Railway-begotten giant cities . . . in all probability [are] destined to such a process of dissection and diffusion as to amount almost to obliteration. . . . These coming cities . . . will present a new and entirely different phase of human distribution. . . . What will be the forces acting upon the prosperous household? The passion for nature . . . and that craving for a little private imperium *are the chief centrifugal inducements. . . . The city will diffuse itself until it has taken up considerable areas and many of the characteristics of what is now country. . . . The country will take to itself many of the qualities of the city. The old antithesis . . . will cease, the boundary lines will altogether disappear.*

—H. G. Wells, 1902

I don't know. Sometimes I wish I could go to culture. But, I can't help it, I'm here and this is what I have. I have the shopping malls. I have, I don't know, here I am and I've got to make what I want here, and maybe when I get older I can make more of my life, but I don't know.

—teenage girl at the Oak Park Mall, Overland Park, Kansas; quoted in "CBS Reports: After the Dream Comes True"

DREAMS OF THE ANTICITY

For most of us, the shape of the city seems a remote concern, best left to planners, politicians, and developers. Yet, at some undefinable point, the cities we have shaped begin to shape us. A postindustrial urban arrangement is emerging, and it is going to change our lives. It is most visible in the West and the South, but is quietly spreading, in clusters and nodes, all over America. The seeds for this new growth were in the mind of Thomas Jefferson, and its roots are in the culs-de-sac of suburbia. It has been coming for a long time.

Almost since the birth of the nation, Americans have expressed a deep anticity sentiment. We were from the beginning of two minds. The city was either Sodom and Gomorrah or the New Jerusalem; it was part of a new economic pattern that would undermine the foundations of republican government or it was order on the frontier; it was a place of learning and culture or a place where natural man—restricted by an essentially artificial environment—could not comprehend his place in the universe. Added to the moral quandary was the scientific view that the city was essentially unhealthy: residents of cities were more likely to be struck down by yellow fever and other epidemics. Thomas Jefferson described cities as "pestilential" and as "sores."

Jefferson was one of the first to propose a new city design, a deconcentrated city that was, well, not a city. After the Louisiana Purchase, in an obscure act of his presidency, Jefferson devised a plan to remove disease-spreading vapors from American cities, especially New Orleans:

Such a constitution of atmosphere being requisite to originate [yellow fever] as is generated in low, close, and ill-cleansed parts of town, I have supposed it practicable to prevent its generation by building our cities on a more open plan. Take, for instance, the chequer board for a plan. Let the black squares only be building ones, and the white ones be left open, in turf and trees. Every square of house will be surrounded by four open squares, and every house will front an open square. The atmosphere of such a town would be like that of the country, insusceptible of the miasmata which produce yellow fever. I have accordingly proposed that the enlargement of the city of New Orleans, which must immediately take place, shall be on this plan.

The scheme was never applied to New Orleans, although Jeffersonville, Indiana, was initially designed in the Jeffersonian fashion. So was Jackson, Mississippi. In both cities, the empty squares soon filled up. But the idea stuck—the idea of a city that is not a city.

In Jefferson's time, the metropolis was not yet a fact of American life. Preindustrial cities were commercial in nature, dedicated to trade. Most people lived and worked in the same building. (Ben Franklin's printshop and home, in the same small building, can still be seen in Philadelphia.) These early American cities, with their zigzagged streets and varied, open architectures, were pedestrian cities; residents enjoyed a lively street life and were, socioeconomically, fairly well integrated. But extremes did exist, with beggars and propertyless laborers living out at the far edges of the cities, and the affluent and influential living in the center, port districts.

After the Civil War, these compact commercial cities began to grow, filling up with the massive movement of European immigrants and rural people pushed off the farms and into urban life by a rapidly changing economy. "We cannot all live in cities," wrote Horace Greeley, the editor of the *New York Tribune*. "Yet nearly all seem determined to do so." The commercial cities, dependent on trade and anchored to waterways, began to transform into industrial cities.

The industrial cities and their very early suburbs were dependent on manufacturing. They were powered not just by coal, but by oil and the steam engine as well. Because of this, population was anchored to power-generating plants and to the rail routes.

Where there was no track, there was no suburb. Distinct socio-economic patterns began to appear. The preindustrial pattern was reversing. In just two decades, in some cities (Detroit is one example), the poor and the affluent switched places. The center cities became factory districts near rail and water outlets, with segregated, crowded, working-class housing districts located within walking distance of the factories; the middle and upper classes began their exodus to the outer edges of the cities, to the new suburbs.

The industrial city, in its purest form, was actually short-lived; it was replaced, after the turn of the century, by the corporate city. Corporations began to locate their headquarters in the central cities, which were, between 1910 and 1920, growing twice as fast as the suburbs. With the introduction of the electric elevator in the 1880s came the sudden growth of downtown skyscrapers. In the early days of the corporate city, laborers and factories were still concentrated downtown, but labor conflict and the combustion engine changed all that. In 1911, Henry Ford introduced the Model T; three years later there were more than 600,000 cars on the American road. Manufacturing plants, liberated from the rails, began to decentralize, first within the cities, then in satellite industrial cities. Some historians contend that the decentralization of manufacturing was caused as much by labor unrest in the central cities as by cars and trucks: satellite industrial suburbs such as Chester, near Philadelphia, Lackawanna, outside Buffalo, Chicago Heights, and East St. Louis grew before the truck was a factor. One employer in the early part of this century called labor organizing "a veritable fever" that broke out among his workers every time the strikers paraded past his plant. By deconcentrating labor into more isolated communities, industry could counteract labor agitation.

Whatever the exact mixture of social unrest and new technology, by the 1960s the process was complete. The downtown districts of the old industrial cities were transformed into central business districts, surrounded by empty manufacturing areas, and the old working-class neighborhoods were now ghettos in decline. Outside the central cities lay suburbia, racially segregated and segmented into residential, commercial, and industrial zones.

THE SUBURBAN ROOTS OF THE DREAM

Slowly the suburbs began to resemble the antithesis of the Jeffersonian dream. Sociologist Bennett M. Berger, who, with his long, graying hair and small, rimless glasses, resembles Ben Franklin, was one of the early experts on suburbs, studying them in the mid-1950s, when many of the intelligentsia wished they would just go away. "In the mid-1950s, part of the dream was space, elbowroom," he said, sitting in his cramped office at the University of California, San Diego, set in the midst of America II. "The dream was real. The people I studied were working-class people looking for space to bring up a family. These factory workers had an average eighth- or ninth-grade education. A lot of Okies, Arkies. The suburbs of San Jose, for them, were a paradise gained. A washer, a dryer. The American dream fulfilled. They didn't aspire beyond that. Two studies have been done since mine, and these people still haven't changed their values. They're still UAW Democrats. It was space they aspired to. One of the things about urban life is that a lot of people are congregated in a very small place. Your status depends on space. The more space you command, the more status you have. In the early days of suburbanization, the three-bedroom, two-bath house, so different from a one-bedroom, one-bath apartment, was the place to live. It was yours! Enough space to live!"

As far back as 1925, social critic Harlan Paul Douglas had suggested that there was something at work here other than just the advent of the automobile age. Douglas suggested that the move to the suburbs was related to a desire for family privacy and independence, that suburbanites thought of themselves as "a chosen people separated from their fellow men." The dream was for that little place in the country with its own piece of green. The dream was (and still is) based on the pastoral ideal: the Jeffersonian notion that life has more meaning when the living is done close to nature, and that democracy thrives when people are self-sufficient. Our daily lives are enriched by this vital myth in its various forms, from Henry Nash Smith's idea of America as "the garden," to F. Scott Fitzgerald's image of "the fresh green breast of America," to Frederick Jackson Turner's premise of free land beyond the frontier as the nation's source of prosperity and virtue.

Berger contends that Americans have never bothered to create the urban equivalent of the appeal of rural individualism, and so the pastoral dream still has a lock on us. Berger has written that the rural commune movement of the 1960s echoed the early suburban rush and the pastoral myth that seems to have haunted Americans from Jefferson on down: "There is a sense in which the collective analogue of a person's self-image is the myth or myths that a culture invents about itself." The pastoral myth drives Americans, and yet their real lives no longer have much to do with it. We can wear our Frye hiking boots to the office and putter in the fifty-foot pastures of suburbia, but our lives are dissociated from the myths we dream of. "Well, what of it?" writes Berger. If American culture has somehow "failed to create an industrial or technological equivalent of the myth of rural virtue and self-sufficiency, and if the available stock of institutionalized fantasy does not enrich one's daily life, isn't an irrelevant fantasy life better than none at all? Isn't a 'false consciousness' better than an empty or barren or cynical one?"

It may be difficult to translate Jefferson's pastoral myth into current reality, but there is a modern-day counterpart for the urban diseases he found endemic to concentrated city life. Stress is the twentieth century's yellow fever, its "pestilential sore." In 1979, crosstown Manhattan traffic crept along at an average 6 miles per hour; by 1982 it had slowed to 5.2 miles per hour. In downtown Miami some 40,000 vehicles compete each day for about 32,000 parking spaces. In Jersey City, a check-out line at one twenty-four-hour supermarket often stretches from the register to the back of the store. The result, says Samuel Leff, a New York anthropologist who has studied urban overcrowding, is that "stress builds up and leads to a lot of diseases."

As for suburbia, its very success—and the stresses this success has brought about—has destroyed it as the pastoral ideal. All those GIs returning after World War II flooded, with their families, into quickly built housing tracts devoid of form. These bedroom communities, segregated from work, with no real Main Streets, spread across the landscape, destroying the nature that had been sought. As the authors of the 1968 President's Task Force on Suburban Problems stated: "In the rush to provide facilities that so many citizens wanted, suburban land has been cut too fine and built up too thick, and what should have been shapely towns have grown formlessly until the suburban sprawl has destroyed the sense of community and sense that the citizens could control their own environment." Suburbia became the symbol of conformist society, tending to destroy, as Lewis Mumford put it, "the value of both environments (rural and urban) without producing anything but a dreary substitute, devoid of form and even more devoid of the original suburban values." Says Berger, "Jeffersonian independence became bondage to the long commute . . . and bored and harried wives, and teenage children who would almost always prefer to be somewhere other than home," and to white-knuckle traffic jams, decrepit commuter trains, encroaching air pollution, and disappearing woods and fields. Presto, the country is no longer the country, and the dream is smothered by the crowd.

The collected evidence of the effect of population density on human beings is inconclusive. Environmental psychologists have shown that people are quite capable of living together at much higher densities than they do now, so long as the environment guarantees some peace, quiet, and privacy—environmental attributes disappearing quickly in today's automobile-dependent urban milieu. Some forms of social stress brought on by physical isolation are every bit as harmful as those related to constant contact with other human beings. America is not even all that densely populated. Though three-quarters of the population of the United States lives on just 16 percent of the nation's land, urban and suburban America are not dense compared to the rest of the world. Our population-to-land ratio is only about one-seventh that of Western Europe; the density of some of our smaller cities resembles that of rural Asia.

Even so, increased density does not match our national mythology, the dream of wide open spaces. According to the 1980 census, the nation's population increase over the last thirty years has meant that population density increased by more than half. That does not sit well with a people raised on stories of Daniel Boone, who moved farther into the wilderness every time a few new neighbors infringed on his elbowroom. Rand Corporation demographer Peter A. Morrison contends that "it's not over-population—it's the people." Our environmental problems come, he says, not from density or overpopulation, but from the sharp rise in living standards: from 1960 to 1970, while population rose 13 percent, the consumption of goods and services rose 20 percent, energy usage increased nearly 50 percent, and miles driven rose 40 percent. We are competing for space and time not just with one another, but with the products of our culture. However, Americans share a sense of manifest destiny about the pastoral dream, which now represents to some a simpler life, and to others room to stretch our consumption.

The suburbs fulfilled the dream only temporarily, but the dream survived.

THE DREAM CONTINUED

Jefferson was among the first of a long line of dispersalists to believe that piling ourselves up into high-density cities is not only unhealthy, but essentially un-American. The most prominent and respected contemporary representative of this school of thought is Lewis Mumford, who for decades has been the nation's foremost scholar in the field of technology and urban problems. In a prescient statement before a Senate urban affairs subcommittee in 1967—a time when all social problems, including the decay of central cities, seemed curable with government largesse —Mumford counseled against pouring money into the big, concentrated cities. The statement was remarkable, in its time, both for what it opposed and for what it proposed. All the "colossal mistakes," he said, that had been made during the last quarter century in urban renewal, highway building, transportation, land use, and recreation had been made by qualified experts and specialists; they had left the great urban areas worse off, with less of a sense of community and neighborhood, than when they began to work their "cures." Just as he opposed massive urban renewal, Mumford did not accept "megalopolis," a shapeless sprawl fusing strips and blotches of large cities into supercities. In the 1960s, some experts were saying that the megalopolis was dynamic and inevitable. That, according to Mumford, was "a silly idea." Mumford suggested:

> Surely it is time that there was a general realization of the fact that we must deliberately contrive a new urban pattern; one that will more effectively mobilize the immense resources of our great metropolises without accepting the intolerable congestion that has driven increasing numbers of people to seek . . . at least a temporary breathing space in less congested suburban areas. The new form of the city must be conceived on a regional scale. Not subor-

dinated to a single dominant center but a network of cities of different forms and sizes, set in the midst of publicly protected open spaces permanently dedicated to agriculture and recreation. In such a regional scheme the metropolis would be only the first among equals.

This is the organic type of city that the technology of our time, the electric grid, the telephone, the radio, television, fast transportation, information storage and transmission, has made possible. . . . But most of our planning authorities still remain like a scratched phonograph record, with the needle stuck in the old metropolitan groove.

Now, in the 1980s, some demographers say the shape of cities is reforming almost naturally into a potentially more humane, energy-efficient pattern. This new postsuburban pattern, say these urban analysts, is very different from the old style of city. It is closer to Mumford's dream than to megalopolis. This new form, say its enthusiasts, allows people to live far away from central cities; to work near where they live instead of commuting. It encourages the growth of a new kind of postsuburban, postindustrial, self-contained small town. The old labels—urban, suburban, exurban, rural—are breaking down, replaced by the emergence of new settlement patterns fueled by new technologies, but also by the same pastoral dream that gave birth to the suburbs.

When we spoke, Berger was in a particularly fatalistic mood about all of this, about what he considers a crucial flaw in the way we go about shaping our cities and suburbs and towns, a flaw that has more to do with basic values and our national mythology than with any clearly defined plan:

"In my own life, I've never seen how to merge my fantasies and the way I live. Like most of my class I have a townhouse and a rural piece of property, three and a half acres in the redwoods and fern, overlooking the ocean in Mendocino County. Deer running through, hawks, and buzzards. I hired some hippies to help me fix it up. Every time I go up there to commune with nature I realize it's not that I'm unique, but that I'm acting out a class phenomenon. Speak to anyone at Harvard—it's a feature of my class and time, it's the privileged who do that. It's nice to be privileged.

"Our mythology doesn't have any relevance to the lives we live. I'm a professor in a large bureaucracy, but in thinking about myself I imagine a life . . . it's got to be a small ivied college in a small town with me as Mr. Chips. But that's not my life. I'm immersed in a huge bureaucracy that I hate, one that takes care of me very well."

He stopped and looked out the small square window, a portal through thick concrete. The office was on the seventh floor of a grey monolith that looked, from the outside, more like the national headquarters of an insurance company than an ivory tower.

"This creates a terrible schizophrenia in our society."

The past is prologue. Out on the brown hills visible from Berger's concrete portal, the new postindustrial metropolis—part urban, part suburban, part rural—is assembling.

If you drive north from San Diego, you can see the new settlements spreading in thin patches along the brown hills. Only a few single-family homes have been built on this stretch. On these hills are clusters of condominiums and electronics companies. For every patch of development there is a long stretch of grass or chaparral. A University of California library sits on one hill, a box balanced on one corner; and in the far distance, here and there, are bursts of glass and concrete. Farther to the north are the squat hives of condoized, instant small towns, with names selected to conjure up visions of frontier California, of the isolated Spanish outposts: Rancho Bernardo and Rancho Santa Fe, Mission Viejo and Laguna Niguel. The new outposts are self-sufficient, in their way, with their own shops and private recreation facilities; some of them have their own office parks, some have electronic surveillance networks and private security forces; some are surrounded by walls. Along the highway, fortresslike mirrored-glass corporate headquarters rise from the open grassland. A string of brightly colored dune buggies buzzes past, headed for the desert to dig long trails across the sand—new cowboys, riding through this hallucinatory frontier.

The first industrial cities may have seemed, to the eyes of prairie farmers and small-town merchants, just as strange as this new arrangement does to those of us who grew up thinking that cities and suburbs looked a certain way. But we are beginning now to see and understand this new antiurban arrangement. The pastoral dream is recrystalizing, reforming itself into a new shape, a new postsuburban, postindustrial urban form stretching hundreds of miles into the countryside, attuned to shopping malls, airports, and freeways, with housing and workplaces clustered together within a low-density milieu; with mixed zoning, urban villages, walled communities, and frontier values. The cities have literally been turned inside out. This new form can be seen at the low-density edges of such cities as Kansas City, Atlanta, Cleveland, and a host of other urban areas. The Capital Beltway encircling Washington, D.C., as urban analyst David Leven says, "has become the real main street" of that metropolis, with twelve regional shopping centers strung along the beltway, and 800,000 people moving to and clustering around these new "downtowns" in a single decade. In addition to the rise of these new shadowy forms outside the older urban areas, whole new cities are rising—such as San Diego, Denver, Albuquerque, Houston, and Phoenix—that missed the industrial stage; they are assembled almost entirely from the postindustrial fabric, places not really urban or even suburban, at least in the way we have defined cities and suburbs in the past.

If the older cities and suburbs defeated the dreams that had made them, we'll try again. We'll take another shot at Jefferson's aborted plan for a city that is not a city.

The anticity.

THE BLOB GETS A NEW IMAGE

Arizona State Senator Alfredo Gutierrez's secretary was talking about a UFO sighting reported in the morning paper. Out in the desert the night before, a busload of Phoenix Bible students on the way home from a revival had seen strange red lights falling from the dark heavens. The singing of angels, or what sounded like it, had come floating in across the arroyos. The mystery remained unsolved.

Gutierrez, however, was worried about another kind of invasion. He was angry at the President's Commission for a National Agenda for the Eighties, chaired by William McGill. A few weeks earlier, the commission had suggested the federal government encourage the continued migration of millions of Americans out of the old, pent-up industrial cities to sprawling postindustrial cities of southern and western states.

The door to his inner office burst open. He ran past his secretary, late for a caucus. If Phoenix is the shape of things to come, I wanted to ask the senator, does the future work?

"No time to talk, no time," Gutierrez said, running toward the hallway. "Too many people coming down here. I'll say this: ought to load the members of that commission on a flatbed truck and send 'em all to New York. Permanently."

"Slow down," advised a physician who had been waiting to see Gutierrez, "you'll have a heart attack."

"I'm healthy, I'm healthy," Gutierrez called out as his voice faded away down the corridor.

The invaders have been arriving for some time now, from such alien places as Michigan and New Jersey. Through the 1970s, Arizona was the fastest-growing state in the nation. Phoenix is now the ninth largest city in the nation, leading Dave Hicks, a columnist for the *Arizona Republic,* to muse, "Phoenix has just passed a milestone. It is consummately easier to raise nine fingers than eleven." Arizona's population, now approaching 3 million, may quadruple by the year 2000, possibly reaching 12 million. All this in a state whose biggest city has weathered only a hundred summers—with barely the last twenty air-conditioned. Just about everyone in the Southwest, despite his or her claims of a laid-back lifestyle, is in a hurry. In 1980, U.S. Home/Suggs Division, based in Phoenix, constructed an 1810-square-foot house from scratch in Glendale, Arizona. Total construction time: nineteen hours and thirty-seven minutes, including pouring the floor slab. Their goal had been twenty-eight hours. They beat the previous record by about fourteen hours. Even during the housing recession, Arizona's developments kept spreading out across cropland and desert. On the highway between the Phoenix metropolitan area and its southern node, Casa Grande, the billboards announce dozens of new developments out beyond the fringes: Ahwatakee, Sun Lakes (with a $4 million country club for "active adult living"), Arizona City ("36 miles out of Mesa"). They zip by while radio station K-LIFE plays "your favorite nonrock hits," songs from the 1930s and '40s, "the music the others have forgotten." More than 95 percent of the people moving to Arizona are white, middle class—self-described escapees from urban decay and crime in the old northern cities. Though the in-migration began with retirees, most of the new residents are now younger people; the number of Arizonans in their twenties and thirties nearly doubled in the last decade, many of them attracted by thee high-tech industries moving here. Thirty-eight percent of Arizona's manufacturing sector is high technology, compared with only 7 percent nationally.

The frenetic migration is transforming Arizona into a twenty-first-century state, bringing unforeseen stresses to the residents and the environment. In some regions of the nation, this kind of sprawl has been cause for alarm, but not, generally, in Phoenix. Some Arizonans worry that the migration, out of control, is giving birth to one big blob, like the gooey science fiction monster of the 1950s that consumed everything in its path. The blob, they worry, is going to eat Arizona. But the blob, of late, has been given a new image; it is, according to its enthusiasts, metamorphosing into a new paradigm for urban life. Sprawl is in the eye of the beholder. "When the Phoenix bird really began to rise, it took off like a rocket," wrote Phoenix mayor Margaret T. Hance in 1982. "We exploded in area . . . now spreading over almost 350 square miles. Some planners have reacted negatively to what they see as 'urban sprawl.' If that term is translated to 'compatible, low-density neighborhoods,' it explains one reason why we now have more than 800,000 residents."

Phoenix, by most accounts, is the nation's best example of the shape of the new recreation-oriented, low-density settlement pattern beginning to emerge across the nation. Most civic leaders point to the bright vision of Arizona's future put forth by Arizona Tomorrow, Inc., a local civic group that decided in 1977 that the growth of Arizona needed some guidance. The group enlisted the help of the Hudson Institute of New York, an independent think tank that has helped the governments of Japan, France, and Denmark plan for the future. The Arizona Tomorrow study, in which futurist Herman Kahn participated, has become the state's blueprint for the future. According to the report, Arizona is "one of the first precursors" of a revolutionized societal structure in America and throughout the Western world. According to Paul Bracken, a Hudson Institute researcher who wrote the final draft, rather than people settling where industries are, industries are settling where people are. "Lifestyle considerations and values," according to Bracken, "will determine technological expansion and growth, making a sharp break with the historical pattern of industrialization that has shaped today's America."

Among the keys to this new city is the low density. New York City, which covers 300 square miles, has ten times as many people as Phoenix on less land area. Even with Phoenix's miserably designed and maintained roads and highways, it takes the average resident just twenty-two minutes to get to work, compared to an average of thirty-eight minutes for New Yorkers. "Phoenix is one of the lowest density large cities in the entire world," according to the Arizona Tomorrow report, "with over 40 percent of its area being open space. If only 10 percent of the state were to be developed at this low density, Arizona could house 26 million persons. At the density of Los Angeles, certainly not a high-density city by eastern standards, 70 million persons could reside in 10 percent of Arizona." In each case, a completely empty area the size of West Germany would be left over for recreation, an enormous land bank consisting of federal and state lands, national forests and parks, and Indian reservations—"plenty of desert, forest, and mountains left over for everyone."

In this new society, small towns and rural areas will be the "national centers of action for the next fifty years." Arizonans will "live on their own terms": desert living with energy-efficient air-conditioners, water fountains, swimming pools; getting back to nature with motorized houseboats on Lake Powell; a wave-generating machine for "surfers"; hiking in the wilderness. (This kind of recreational rationale for city life is a new development; instead of attracting people because of their cosmopolitan ambiance, as was the case with traditional cities, the new cities promote primarily their nonurban features—Albuquerque its Sandia Mountains within minutes of downtown, Atlanta its nearby Chattahoochee National Forest, Denver its collection of surrounding small towns in the Rockies, Knoxville the Great Smokies, and Salt Lake City, San Diego, Tampa, and Tucson their own special access to nature.) According to the Arizona Tomorrow report, the whole state of Arizona is becoming a playground for a new kind of urbanite. The report describes "totally new urban forms" rising out of the desert: a proliferation of "movable towns," such as the huge clusters of recreational vehicles that already exist along the Colorado River. Arizona's fastest growing demographic group will be the "variable population": people who live in Arizona part of the year, often in mobile homes and campers, who sometimes double and triple the populations of outlying areas during the winter. The size of this population may, in fact, force a "reconsideration of the very definition of what it means to be a city."

"It's not that people are abandoning the city; it's that they're inventing a new and better kind of city," says Gary Driggs, president of Arizona Tomorrow and also of Western Savings and Loan in Phoenix. Driggs views Phoenix as the prototype of what he calls the "new city." Here is his description:

"This is just part of the ongoing evolution of the city. It's happening all over the country, but especially here. It's simply easier to put a new electronics plant where the land is cheaper, like down along the Superstition Freeway near Tempe or Casa Grande. Drive down there and close your eyes and open them again and you're in Orange County, California. I just drove to Toronto and the same thing is happening there—and they have (in contrast to Phoenix) good mass transit, subways. It's a worldwide trend. Industrial parks in campus-style environments way beyond the edge of a city. Instead of a long commute every day, people have a short commute to their office in the suburbs. And they've got immediate access to outdoor recreation: their horses, the desert, and the mountains, right there. That's the emerging Arizona lifestyle, which is going to be the dominant American lifestyle. It's not that people are abandoning the city, it's that they're inventing a new and better kind of city.

"But people are nostalgic for the old-style city that was developed through 1920; in effect, what you had then was a modern transportation method, the railroad, and you had a fifteenth-century vehicle, the horse. And that's what society was structured around. The biggest stores and factories and the best hotels were all near the railroad stations, and a lot of the most elegant residents lived there; and the poor people commuted *in*. The poor were to be inconvenienced, the rich accommodated. But the truck changed all that. With the arrival of the truck there was no longer any premium on being close to the railroad station. It's the truck, not the auto, that has changed the cities. Once you have a truck, the last place you want your warehouse is in the center city. You want it away from a highly congested area because it's easier to get a truck into a shopping center; it's a pain to get it into a store downtown. But civic leaders are trying to replay the last century, trying to repeal the truck. They say the new city doesn't have a heart, but you can't hardly save anything in downtown Phoenix because [laughter] there wasn't much of anything there in the first place."

THE EVOLUTION OF SPRAWL

What is happening here, this rather new way of looking at sprawl, is important not just to Arizona. What is arriving comes in two forms, two siblings: first, the seemingly random anticity growths outside nearly every city in the nation; second, these new cities like Phoenix that are made up almost entirely of the new sprawling form. The reason the new urban form is more visible in cities of the South and West is that most cities in these regions missed the industrial age and so could be constructed from scratch to fit the needs of decentralized plants and office parks.

In the world of urban analysis, a notable shift has occurred: automatic disdain for sprawl has given way, among many experts, to a new interest in what some call the "polynucleated" form: vast urban areas with no dominating center, but rather many centers, often with lots of open space in between.

The giant regional shopping mall has become the hub of this new urban village, its Main Street. Part of what defines America II is the final dominance of the mall culture. Most of us think of malls as appendages to the city, not having much to do with the civic central nervous system. But in America II, it is as if the appendages now dominate the body; the head and the torso having shrunk away, the arms and legs now swell with muscle and strength, reaching out. Despite the recent renaissance of life in gentrified city neighborhoods, mall culture now dominates the nation's urban social and commercial life. Since the 1950s, almost 20,000 shopping centers have been built—currently they produce more than one-half of the nation's annual retail sales, and serve as the homogenized community centers for beauty contests, art, boat, and auto shows, and local craft fairs. The covered mall is a shelter from the society that produced it. In a suburb of Los Angeles, sufferers of pulmonary disease have formed a club that meets at a covered mall; there, in a less-polluted environment, they conduct races for exercise, pulling their oxygen tanks behind them. A regional mall in the suburbs of Cleveland even includes a cemetery. The boosters of the new city, in Arizona and around the United States, share no such worries.

The most important concept in understanding the metropolis of the twenty-first century, writes Charles Leven, Director of the Institute of Urban and Regional Studies at Washington University, is that the "old" cities were designed to maximize production, but the new city is determined spatially to maximize consumption. Writes Leven: "Most of the new metropoli will contain several million people within a few decades. . . . There will be a general convergence in the size distribution of places." In size, the new metropolis is going to be very large by present standards—100 to 300 miles across. This increase in size will allow people to live at different scales simultaneously.

At least spatially, the urban world of 2010, as Leven sees it, may look much more like the world of 1910 than that of today; and by 2010 the old metropolis will be replaced as an organizing concept, in most people's minds, by the new metropolis. He writes that much of the time, people will live "in a quite limited-range community, more limited than at present." Much of their lives—living, working, most shopping—will go on in a small urban area of only two to five miles across; a kind of village inside a city whose physical borders are only vaguely defined. People will travel outside their little urban clusters mainly for the purpose of consuming such specialized goods and services as exotic antiques or (Leven adds, perhaps tongue-in-cheek) "organ transplants or watching professional sports." Further, the new metropolis will be so stretched out across the landscape that its subcommunities will be too distant for regular commuter movement between them. According to Leven, this distance will produce an uncongested environment

> so that every time one walks out his or her front door, he or she is not living at the scale of a giant metropolis: one will be able to live in a village that is part of a large metro system, rather as Los Angeles *once was.* It would still be like that today if it had not put all the "suburbs in search of a city" right next to each other. . . . Los Angeles is becoming the last of the old metropoli.

What will happen to the old cities? The old metropolitan form will, in all likelihood, disappear; the old cities will continue to lose population, but as they lose it they will come to look much like the new metropoli. The second- and third-ring suburbs may, according to Leven, do poorly in the adjustment, because being relatively high-density bedroom communities, they lack the proper mix of workplaces and residences. But the more dispersed outer suburban and exurban rings will do well; population will continue to move outward, clustering around the shopping malls and office parks. The old downtown will actually do quite well, but not in the form that we have known it; it will be just another hub—an office park kept company by high-rise condominiums and gentrified townhouses.

LOOKING FOR THE URBAN VILLAGE

The urban village, suggested by Charles Leven as well as Lewis Mumford, Jane Jacobs, and a host of other critics of urban development, is one of the key elements in the reformation of urban sprawl and the formation of the new metropolis. The urban village, in concept, is a place in which work, residence, and recreational opportunities are in balance. It is an old idea, but its support by developers and public officials is new. The idea is to create small towns inside, on the fringes of or even beyond the metropolitan area; instead of a single downtown, dozens of urban villages: regional shopping centers with night entertainment, offices, department stores, light industry, all acting as magnets for new residential areas, especially condominium developments.

Arizona's Governor Bruce Babbitt is an enthusiast of the urban village. His press aide describes him as "a smart kid." At forty-three, he looks more like a young collegian working on his doctoral dissertation than a governor. Of course, he became governor by accident. After the resignation of one governor and the death of a successor five months later, Babbitt (a crusading attorney general with a mob-sponsored price on his head) was awakened at 7:30 one morning in 1977 and informed that he was governor. Sometimes mentioned as a potential Democratic presidential candidate, Babbitt has set his sights on establishing in Arizona the new urban form, one he hopes will be a model for the nation. As cochairman of the Council on Development Choices for the 1980s, an independent, bipartisan thirty-seven-member council of developers and public officials launched in 1980 by the Urban Land Institute, Babbitt has established himself as one of the nation's leading proponents of the new city form, specifically, of the urban village.

One hot afternoon, in his office overlooking Phoenix, Babbitt, in shirt-sleeves, spoke with enthusiasm about the concept:

"Since World War II, the dominant zoning concept was that you had to rigidly segregate industry from housing. That concept has meant more commuting, more roads, more energy costs. The fact is, though, that we're now entering an entirely different era. An increasing number of workplaces—the electronics industry, for instance—are utterly compatible with residential areas, actually enhancing them. There's no longer any reason that you can't have an industry next door to your house, if it's the right kind of industry."

The idea, essentially, is to accept urban sprawl, but guide it: acknowledge the American impulse for low-density living by allowing the city to deconcentrate away from the urban center, but, as it moves out, reconcentrate it into urban villages. These relatively high-density "small towns" within the larger, low density metropolis could (ideally) be separated by open, green space.

Rather than a great amorphous blob growing outward without regard for human social needs, the new metropolis, with its urban villages, could offer real, prearranged neighborhoods—small towns within the spreading city. If an urban village functions properly, the theory goes, transportation choices—car pooling, van pooling, bicycling, and walking—would cut down car use. Bus or light rail routes could connect these villages. Babbitt's notion is to plan for the new urban version of the pastoral dream. His council's report stressed that the urban village concept is already happening, even without government guidance.

Indeed, something out there wants to be born. The sprawling new anticities in Arizona and around the nation are trying to find themselves, congealing into clusters and nodes and urban villages. On August 2, 1981, the *Los Angeles Times* ran a story with a wonderful headline that asked: "Orange County Urban Hub Found?" Is there, the *Times* article asked, a "downtown" Orange County? Several Orange County developers, like a committee of Stanleys claiming to have discovered Livingston, announced that yes, they had found the region's downtown, a clearly defined metropolitan center beginning to assemble like a convention site for wandering Bedouins. The center is 2240 acres marked off by freeways surrounding one of the state's largest shopping centers (with 185 stores in about 2 million square feet of space). Also present (constructed in just over a year) is 1 million square feet of new office space and a growing concentration of county residents. The discovery of this downtown was a wonderful thing for these developers; they felt validated.

Aurora, Colorado, is another example of this new, centerless creation, an urban village trying to form. In an article for *Rocky Mountain Magazine,* writer David Chamberlain described Aurora as an "unsung suburban immensity on Denver's eastern borders" that had grown by a staggering 135 percent in the past twelve years, accounting, in 1979, for nearly half of all the population growth of the rapidly growing Denver metropolitan area. Aurora, that year, was the third-fastest-growing middle-sized city in America—a thousand migrants poured in each month, and the administrative branches of Citicorp, GTE, Western Electric, Exxon, and AT&T relocated there. Chamberlain described this growth as "the frontier ethic by comprehensive plan. . . . [Aurora is] one of those my-God-look-what-they've-done places—flat, treeless, eventless, home to a wild conflict of subdivision 'styles' that invoke themes, places, things, and even states of mind that bear only the most fanciful relationship to Aurora and none at all to each other . . . homes that pretend to be located in England, in France, in New England, in China (or at least in Chinatown; it depends on how you want to classify an apartment building designed to look exactly like a Chinese restaurant)." The city is so devoid of a central citiness that one resident dialed a 911 emergency number to report a fire in his subdivision, and did not know that he lived in Aurora. Like Orange County, Aurora is intent on finding itself. The city has no downtown, so the Aurorans are building one—around the Aurora Mall, a 600-acre "city center" as big as downtown Denver.

In Arizona there has been more effort to consciously locate the new downtowns, and then mold them into real, functional urban villages. Phoenix plans to have eleven urban villages by the year 2000, placed in relatively rural areas, in the suburbs, and in the central urban core. Each of these will have an identifiable, pedestrian-oriented core and a clearly identified boundary. One of the Phoenix area's natural urban villages that Babbitt points to with pride is Scottsdale, a community of about 80,000 on the eastern fringe of Phoenix, "the West's most western town," as the residents like to call it. The *Wall Street Journal* called it "one of the most innovative communities anywhere, with a city government that manages to provide, at minimal cost, a lot of things you don't find even in much larger cities."

Scottsdale, in the America II style, looks both backward and forward, encouraging a neo–Wyatt Earp style in dress and architecture, while securing a grant from the National Science Foundation to contract for the services of a "city technologist," whose first assignment was to adapt solar power to public buildings. The city's style of social services provides grand fun for these largely affluent, increasingly elderly transplants from the East. While cities of the northeast are cutting children's food programs, in wealthy Scottsdale you could enhance a party by stopping off at your nearby community center to check out a "funpack," a big container stuffed with games and sports equipment—free, courtesy of Scottsdale. If there's a fire, well, just call Rural-Metro, one of the most unusual fire departments in the nation. Scottsdale contracts this private company, which designs and builds some of its own trucks and uses exotic equipment like the Snail, a robot fireman that clanks heedlessly into the heart of a blaze to put it out. And instead of featherbedding its firefighting staff, Scottsdale complements it with twenty-nine auxiliary firemen called "fire wranglers," city employees, trained in firefighting, who leave their desks to cover a blaze when alerted by a belt-worn beeper. The cost to the city is thirty-five to fifty-five dollars a month per person, depending on the number of fires. While the trash piles up in New York, Scottsdale's sanitation department is so highly mechanized that the garbagemen don't have to get dirty; their air-conditioned, radio-equipped "Godzilla trucks" are operated by one man, who grabs big plastic trash containers with the truck's hydraulic claws, dumps them, then puts them gently back. And if you're having a fight with your spouse, the local police will bring along a "crisis intervention specialist" and a trained social worker who will try to patch up the quarrel. In fact, the police department (one-third of the department is made up of lower-paid civilians) was able to drive crime down 5 percent in 1975, compared with a nationwide increase of 12 percent.

The reasons for all this successful innovation? First, money is pouring in, along with the migration, along with tourism dollars. Second, the town has been quite proficient in dining at the federal trough—despite its conservatism and faith in private enterprise, Scottsdale is one of the smallest towns in the country to employ a full-time "grants planner." And third is the urban village concept, which happened in Scottsdale long before there was such a term for the idea that a small place can be controlled better, with less attachment to old traditions. "The big cities, counties, and state governments are almost paralyzed," the *Wall Street Journal* quoted City Manager Frank Aleshire in 1977. "The bureaucracies are terrible: buildings full of people passing papers. But a town like this can still be managed . . . partly because Scottsdale is still small enough to be responsive."

THE SKEPTICS: A BLOB IS A BLOB IS A BLOB

In Arizona, what appears to be happening so far is not quite the idealistic futureworld that so excites the young governor—at least for anyone except the affluent.

Affable Dr. Don Schaller, who had advised Senator Gutierrez to slow down, is medical director of Arizona Health Plan, the largest health maintenance organization in the state, and has thought considerably about the difference between reality and illusion in Arizona.

"I'll tell you, everybody's into health down here. You can't drive without hitting a jogger," he said, tugging on his white beard. He was sporting a string bolo tie and the air of native wisdom. "There's a lot of mythology about this place, and a lot of disappointment. For years folks have been coming down here for their allergies. They get here and there's a year-round growing season, and they're surrounded by farms, desert dust, pollen, and air pollution. Then there's the social isolation. Arizona is great for a group health program like ours. We've enrolled 70,-000 people in eight years, not only because they've severed their attachments with family docs back east, but also because once they get to Arizona, they often stay mobile, moving every nine months or so. So they never settle on one doc. People come down here to get away from stress, which in some ways is worse here —maybe because of the lack of attachments, the anxiety of rootlessness, which people kind of deny."

Bob and Lonnie Stedry, Nebraska natives, moved to Phoenix with their son, Gabe, after Bob finished a Navy stint in San Diego. They bought a home in a new housing tract called Country Meadows, in Peoria, a small city on the outskirts of Phoenix. Country Meadows is surrounded by a high wall of brown cement blocks. Inside, each yard is surrounded by another wall. Within this maze, built on what once was a cotton field, the Stedrys feel a growing sense of social isolation. They live in a compound, not a neighborhood. Even the stunning view of the nearby mountains is hidden behind the walls.

Bob worked for a brief and frustrating time as a sales rep for a stocking company and as a hospital administrator in the Midwest, but now he is a self-employed entrepreneur who quite happily makes his living remodeling homes in Sun City, a nearby planned community populated by retirees who have flocked down from the northeast and Midwest. Sun City is also surrounded by a wall.

"The walls around Sun City and around our neighborhood say a lot about Phoenix," he said. He is a young man with thick, callused hands. He was barbecuing steaks in his walled-in backyard. "Everybody's trying to keep something or somebody out. The neighbors don't communicate much. If Gabe loses a ball over one of the walls, it's gone forever."

Bob smiled as he turned a steak. "Everybody's so much into recreation and leisure that they don't have much time for each other. When we came here, the real estate people strongly suggested we buy a house in a particular section of Country Meadows because it was 'good for kids.' The developers didn't call what they did segregation, but that's what it was. Segregation of the young from the old."

Could it all turn out differently from the sunny predictions of Arizona Tomorrow? Even this glowingly enthusiastic report does foresee some "alternative futures": increasing traffic congestion, the "growing concentration of a politically self-conscious urban underclass." Indeed, minorities and no-growth advocates are, according to the report, Arizona's greatest potential problems: "With both the non-Indian and Indian populations growing in Arizona, the two societies may be on a collision course." The report warns that "the growing use of national welfare standards and court opposition to local obstacles for welfare could make Arizona . . . as attractive as the northeast" to welfare recipients, resulting in a "mass migration of the poor to Arizona." If no-growth advocates prevail, the report warns, needed housing and public facilities would not be built, even though people would continue to move to Arizona. Phoenix and Tucson then could, as the report puts it, "be ringed with hundreds of thousands of motor homes. The Colorado River area could mushroom into an enormous mobile squatterland. . . . California was unable to stop the immigration of the Okies in the 1930s," the report continues. "Even state police barricades at the border had very little effect as thousands and thousands poured into the state. Harassment tactics were employed that would not be possible today." During the recent recession, the poor indeed began to show up, camping on the edge of town, sleeping in their cars. The city administration, troubled by the sight of the newly arrived poor picking through garbage cans, declared the trash city property.

Representative Earl Wilcox, a Chicano leader, believes harassment of the poor—those already living in Phoenix—has already begun. Wilcox was born thirty-two years ago in South Phoenix, a neighborhood that Mayor Margaret Hance calls "a forty-mile-square pocket of poverty" larger than the entire area of many eastern cities. About 125,000 people live there, in sections that are mainly Hispanic, black, and Indian. Despite its problems,

Wilcox calls it one of the last "real neighborhoods with real social institutions" in Phoenix.

Bulldozers are now tearing down much of South Phoenix, making room for an airport expansion and new industries coming down from the north. About 10,000 people are being relocated, and that number eventually may reach 50,000. Parishes and other institutions with ties that stretch back three or four generations are breaking up. While some civic leaders see this as progress, pointing to the fact that the city's suburbs are more accessible to minorities than suburbs in the northeast, Wilcox and his ally Senator Gutierrez share a contrary view. They maintain that the forced breakup of the Hispanic community is leading to social disintegration, violence, and racial strife as Hispanics are forced out into the suburban areas among newly arrived Anglo populations. Police estimate that there are twenty-six active gangs on the suburban west side, where many of the Hispanic families move. "A lot of these people come from families who have lived in this neighborhood for three or four generations. They've spent their whole lives in this neighborhood. They end up living in trailers in their relatives' backyards out in the suburbs," said Wilcox. "They're paid off by the city, a few thousand dollars, and told to move on."

The roar and dust of bulldozers filled the air as Wilcox drove past cement slabs where homes had existed a few days before. Some of the people here are determined to stay, no matter the cost. As the airport spreads, the decibels rise and the jets passing overhead make one's teeth clatter. The vibration caused by this noise has begun to crumble some of the older adobe structures, but the people have built cement block walls inside their homes for protection from noise and collapse.

Wilcox does not accept the rationale that the incoming high-tech industries are going to provide jobs for the poor, not without massive training programs. Nothing, he says, can replace the heart of the Hispanic community, shredded and scattered in the suburbs.

He stopped the car and sat staring at a new power station.

"That's where my family's house was," he said softly. "That's where I grew up."

The poor are not the only obstacle to the spreading anticity. It takes room for this kind of development to flourish, lots of room—and water. Under Babbitt's leadership, valuable water rights are being radically shifted from agricultural use to industrial and residential use. (Babbitt's rise was due in part to the incoming migrants, who see him as their ally.) Arizona is using water at twice the natural replenishment rate. In fact, when it comes to the state's future growth, the bottom may quite literally fall out. At least 200 fissures are twenty-five feet wide, and one is nine miles long. Tucson is one of the largest cities in the world to obtain all of its water from underground wells. A fourth of its water drilling rigs are downtown, sucking water from directly beneath the business district. The water table is falling ten to twelve feet each year, so each year the wells must be drilled deeper. When water wells reach below 100 to 150 feet, geologists warn, land begins to collapse. Some of Tucson's wells are already reaching below the 100-foot level. A recent study shows that the ground in some parts of northern Phoenix is sinking at a rate of six inches a year.

Part of the water that is needed will arrive by the late 1980s through the Central Arizona Project (CAP), a system of canals, reservoirs, and aqueducts, channeling Colorado River water to Arizona. The issue is clouded by several lawsuits, including one lodged by Arizona's Indian tribes, that claim rights to the entire CAP supply. Most experts, though, contend that Arizona will have plenty of water to support new residents, chiefly because of state policies that are wresting water rights from farmers, who for decades have used 95 percent of the available water. In 1980, Babbitt, along with city, mining, and agriculture officials, battled for six months to adopt a groundwater code that would require conservation. The effort followed then-president Jimmy Carter's demand that the Central Arizona Project proceed only if Arizona reformed its groundwater code. The legislation, which will be phased in over the next thirty years, will require farms to adopt such new technologies as drip irrigation and laser beams to level fields in a way that avoids evaporation. Under this legislation, intended, like Babbitt's plans for the new urban form, to be a national model, if farmers take more water than they are allocated, the state will lock up their pumps and impose criminal penalties. As of the day the bill was signed, there is an absolute ban on all new agricultural development in urban areas. If the goals of the legislation are met, experts believe, most farms in the Phoenix and Tucson area will be gone in ten years, replaced by industrial parks, malls, and housing developments leapfrogging into the sunset. The response of farmers has been mild. "There's been no real fuss, although we feel the controls on pumping groundwater are unconstitutional and will eventually be thrown out," says Joe Cluck, director of Arizona Agriculture Management Corporation, which manages farms—and also sells them to developers for exorbitant amounts, more than the farmers could have earned through their crops.

Those who oppose the spreading anticity have some difficulty expressing their opposition, since so many of them are from somewhere else. A few years ago, poet Edward Abbey wrote a magazine piece called "The Blob Comes to Arizona," describing the slow destruction of the desert, allowing that his presence was itself a contradiction:

> I was among the first of the displaced refugees, after the War, to give up on the swarming East. And so when Arizona began to grow, as they call it, it was as much my fault as anyone else's. Like the man and his wife who moved from Des Moines into Phoenix last night, each of us wants to be the last to arrive. Each wants to be the final immigrant. If we could we'd raise a glass wall about ten miles high somewhere along the one-hundredth meridian.

Robert Hurt, like Gutierrez, questions the wisdom of encouraging more in-migration. Hurt, a dentist who moved from Chicago to Arizona in 1963, is now chairman of Ask Before You Tax, an antidevelopment citizen action committee. Asks Hurt: "How can you hold out the environment as an attraction for incoming people if you're destroying it at the same time? You can't encourage growth and still preserve the air—which is going to be worse than in Los Angeles."

I posed this question to the accidental governor. He sat back and considered for a moment. "A little-known fact in Arizona is that I'm sort of a native of Los Angeles," he told me. His family made its wealth largely through the operation of Indian trading posts near Flagstaff. "When my family first came here, it was so difficult to travel through some of the geography of Arizona that Los Angeles was a day closer to Flagstaff than Phoenix. So my family grew up with one foot in L.A. I used to think L.A. was an example of everything gone wrong in a city, but I've come around," he said, sinking lower in his chair. "I'm a fan of L.A., a city that works fairly well. The decentralization of L.A. has created a certain kind of diversity in its separate cities and extraordinarily alive subcultures. I don't find it depressing."

The difference between Los Angeles and the new city form, as Babbitt sees it, is that "the salad days of the freeways are over, and the communications revolution is just beginning to accelerate." Babbitt is convinced that the new city is entirely different from the old—different even from Los Angeles. He placed his hands behind his head and slid down even further in his chair, stretching out his long legs. "This new world," he said, "is already forming."

It stretches outward, in every direction, like vines from some other, waterless planet, clustering in splotches here and there, scattering its seeds in the desert.

A long time ago, sixty miles south of what is today Phoenix, the flourishing Hohokam civilization constructed a sophisticated irrigation system and a three-story ceremonial house, now slowly dissolving back into the sandstone. Before the first Spanish explorers arrived, the civilization mysteriously disappeared. Centuries later, a Southern Pacific Railroad crew came through, halted work because of the searing heat, and pitched camp; the settlement was called Terminus. That name was later changed to Casa Grande, after the big house the Hohokam had left. Throughout most of the twentieth century, it was a tiny desert town, dependent on agriculture and migrant workers from Mexico. What water that could be found was used by the farms. But now Casa Grande, next to one of the CAP canals, is one of the "urban villages" that Babbitt and the state government have slated to receive much of the incoming population. The new economic winds have brought companies that build computer frames, video display terminals, and bits and pieces of the space shuttle.

Twenty-five major companies have moved to Casa Grande in the last decade. The town is well situated (at the crossroads of two major highways and close to Phoenix) to become part of the peculiar new metropolitan life beginning to show up around the nation. Casa Grande is sheltered from urban malaise, and offers relaxed regulations, a highly favorable tax structure, and a nonunionized labor force. The population, as a consequence, has boomed. In 1960, Casa Grande had only 5000 residents; in 1981 it had 18,000. The population is expected to double in the next decade. As in much of the rest of Arizona, water rights are rapidly being shifted from agriculture to industry. Just outside Casa Grande, near the new stone sign announcing this metropolitan node in the desert, is a huge turquoise-colored water slide, erected on a long brown stretch of sand, standing almost alone —a little bit of Disneyland in the land of the Hohokam. From the highway you can hear the squeals of children.

Don Kramer, the laconic president of the Casa Grande Chamber of Commerce and publisher of a string of electronically linked small-town Arizona papers, has few fears about the future —not as long as the people and the water keep coming. "We're doing fine, growing at a good, solid pace," said Kramer, as he wheeled his aging Pontiac past sparkling new industrial parks blooming like mushrooms in the emptiness. A shopping mall is on the way. "All this is like planting a seed. You water it, give it nutrients, a warm climate, and maybe it grows." Overhead, an eagle or a buzzard circled. Kramer stopped his car in front of a long condominium development surrounded by empty space. The Pontiac's air-conditioner hummed. "Don't know what exactly it is that makes people want to come here all of a sudden. More and more people just want to get out of the big cities, including Phoenix. Maybe they want some, well, elbowroom." He pulled his mustache and turned on the car radio; a chorus of women were singing about real estate, something about selling "your house on Mars (East Mars)" and moving to Arizona.

"Take me to your Realtor," they sang.

LAISSEZ-FAIRE LIFESTYLE: THE ANTICITY UNCHAINED

Like their nineteenth-century predecessors, the new postindustrial cities are being shaped by migration and by laissez-faire capitalism. Over time, in part because of the realities of millions of people living in close proximity, the governments of the old industrial cities gradually accepted a certain responsibility for the welfare of their citizens, even the poorest of them. Inherent in the anticity's vague, deconcentrated, sprawling shape is a governmental lack of focus, an eased sense of responsibility. The new urban form allows clusters of relatively affluent people to avoid contact with groups less well-off than themselves. In the new cities (and the developing rural areas as well) local leaders and incoming businesses have generally agreed that taxes should be kept competitively low, that environmental regulations and zoning should be eased, and that expensive governmental social services should be avoided. Deconcentration means decentralized political power. Picture a parent whose brood, once easily controlled, has moved out of the house and is now scattered over the countryside; the parent, even if he or she wants to, can no longer enjoy the same power or, in some cases, prestige.

No urban area in the nation illustrates this better than Houston, the anticity unchained, a composite of the new city form and the antibureaucratic revolt deep inside America II. Arizona is at least trying to guide some of the growth, but Houston is a city with virtually no zoning. It claims the least amount of control over growth patterns of any city in the United States—and possibly in the Western world. Ada Louise Huxtable of the *New York Times* has written, "Houston even requires a new definition of urbanity." What is most important about Houston is not the city itself, but that the rest of the nation is gradually becoming more like Houston.

But Houston offers no apologies.

"Depending on your point of view, Houston is either a subtropical paradise or a subtropical disease," said social psychologist Richard E. Ryan, whose office is in one of the hundreds of campuslike glass-and-steel-and-landscaped office parks sprinkled through the piney woods of this part of Texas. The bearded Ryan was charging around his office, wearing a tie hand-painted with winged unicorns, puffing furiously on his Sherlock Holmes–style pipe. "What we've got here is the free-enterprise lifestyle, a kind of gonzo capitalism."

As vice president of Tarrance & Associates, the largest pollster in Texas, Ryan keeps track of social and political trends in what has become America's most vibrant state. Texas now claims three of the nation's ten largest cities: Houston, Dallas, and San Antonio. "Is Houston the city of the future?" asked Ryan rhetorically. "Maybe. The free-enterprise lifestyle is a wild alternative to the urban system most of us grew up in. The idea that the city should take care of people is only partially grasped here. In Houston, you wall yourself off in a private enclave. You get services if you pay for them—private police, private fire departments, private garbage collectors. And if you don't have the money, you suffer. That may sound cruel, but in Houston the wild entrepreneurism makes this an exciting place."

Ryan is not alone in his enthusiasm. Barry J. Kaplan, an urban historian at the University of Houston, characterizes American culture as a "business culture." Houston is the epitome of what America can do, says Kaplan, if left unfettered by taxation, zoning codes, and other regulation. Houston's growth is, indeed, phenomenal. With 1.6 million residents, it is the nation's fifth most populous city, and the fastest growing major city in the nation. Houston's economy blasted off in the 1960s as an important aerospace center, Space City, USA. Then, in the 1970s, most of the big New York–based oil companies moved their headquarters to the energy-rich Houston area, bringing thousands of well-paid engineers and executives. Wave after wave of migrants and industries flooded into the region, drawn by the expanding economy, low taxes, few regulations, and unparalleled industrial boosterism. In ten years, the city gained 900,000 people, almost doubling in population. Houston now boasts the tallest U.S. building outside of New York and Chicago.

What began (and continues) as primarily a migration of skilled Postindustrials widened in the late 1970s to include thousands of lower-skilled workers pushed out of America I by the changing economy. And, at least until recently, the idea that unfettered growth and a privatized government pay off in jobs rang true to the hopeful men sitting on the steps in front of the Houston YMCA, just before the oil glut hit. Among these new migrants from the northeast there is a sense of disillusionment and antibureaucratic rebellion against the government social programs, unions, and giant corporations that have, they feel, failed them.

A twenty-eight-year-old house painter from Detroit told me: "I didn't even get a chance to unpack my car. Had a job before I found a place to stay. Stopped for coffee and after three calls I found a job. This guy even gives away baseball tickets! I'm makin' less down here as a painter, but at least I've got a job. Who the hell needs a painter's union?" Another fellow, twenty-four, was from Battle Creek, Michigan, "where they make cereal, all that garbage like that." Two years ago he was laid off by Battle Creek Exercise Equipment Company. He remained there, unemployed except for a training program sponsored by the Federal Comprehensive Employment and Training Act (CETA). He worked eight weeks as a service station attendant. "Then they closed the gas station." He went to the Battle Creek public library, where he discovered that the help-wanted portion of the *Houston Post*'s classified ads was bigger than the entire Battle Creek newspaper. He found a job in a printshop two days after he arrived in Houston. "They're training me in bookbinding, running copiers. I'm getting a lot of overtime," he said, and shrugged. "This is a lot better than CETA, which is cutting back anyway. Here, I feel sort of like a pioneer."

Since these men arrived in Houston, a worldwide petroleum glut has put something of a hitch in the city's swagger; but the unemployed keep coming. They pile up, even more than in Phoenix, in tent cities outside of town, or move on to other promised lands like Denver, or go home, or set up a ramshackle roadside business. A trip down one of Houston's freeways tells it all. Former auto workers from Michigan pull their station wagons or vans up on the center divider, throw up a few boards and open instant businesses offering "real Texas Bar-B-Q," steamed shrimp, cut-rate clothing, birdbaths, "Indian" rugs flapping in the breeze. Then there are the more permanent setups: a law office housed in a mobile home in the roadside mud ("We specialize in divorce and real estate"); more lavish barbecue joints, smelling of charcoal and septic tanks. Long lines of billboards wind through the trees like corrugated snakes. High-tech industrial parks; prefab model "dream homes," set up on stilts for good freeway visibility; walled-off housing developments for the upper middle class such as Roman Forest, which has a freeway entrance bracketed by huge Roman columns and a triumphal arch; and Diamond Lil's Burlesk ("live girls") next door to a bait shop ("live minnows").

No apologies.

A huge and famous billboard above a used-car lot declares: "Owner Has Brain Damage." The lot's finance manager, dressed in urban cowboy garb—gold neck chains, Stetson, and cream-tipped boots—says, "Everybody needs wheels down here, so we advertise up in Michigan and Ohio. A lot of the guys coming down get off the Greyhound bus, hitchhike out here, and put their last cash down on a car." He leaned forward in a confidential way, "Hey, I can make you rich. I can't keep pickups on the lot. You buy some pickups in San Diego and ship 'em out here. If I could get a hundred, I could sell 'em in an hour."

The price of all this growth is municipal anarchy. Urban experts consider the city's transportation system to be among the nation's worst. Houstonians warn you not to get too aggressive on the freeway; someone is likely to pull out a gun and "blow you away." A particularly popular bumper sticker reads, "Drive 70, Freeze a Yankee." Even the city's graffiti has something to say about the traffic—phone booths along the freeway are covered with the scrawled phone numbers of wrecking companies, put there as advertisements by tow-truck drivers. "People think nothing of driving over the curbs and across the ditch to get around traffic," Ryan told me. Tarrance & Associates polled Houstonians during the gas crisis of the 1970s. Only 40 percent said they would adjust to the shortage by changing their driving habits, compared with 60 percent in much of the rest of the country. "The pickup is the new horse. It's part of the psychology around here, the psychology of rebellion, the cowboy ethic of lonely independence. Every damn Yankee who moves here buys a cowboy hat and adopts the psychology."

Houston's libertarian, laissez-faire spirit is even attracting gays, who might otherwise not venture into wild and woolly Texas. The Montrose section of Houston is one of the fastest growing gay enclaves in the nation. On the fringe of downtown Houston, it is a good example of one result of no zoning: an urban village prospering on the unfettered entrepreneurialism. This used to be a residential neighborhood, but now the previously run-down single-family houses have been converted (with no red tape or consideration of dividing residential from commercial) to a mix of multifamily buildings, restaurants, and shops.

I wandered into Montrose one day during its annual street celebration, the Montrose Art Festival. The favored clothing style would not be seen in *Gentleman's Quarterly:* bull-rider Stetsons, jeans, bare chests, fair imitations of bowed legs. One barechested fellow wearing a cowboy hat charged past a saloon offering "totally nude girls," surrounded by a yard full of skulls of goats and deer and steers. Oddly out of place, a group that looked like Tom Joad and his Okie family were weaving through the gay parade, eyes down, picking up aluminum cans and placing them in a wooden box. Nearby, a fight broke out; two young men were beating each other, their beer cans rolling toward the Joads. Helicopters circled overhead.

In one corner were Larry Nicholas, his wife, Sue-Anne, and their three kids. The family had recently moved to Houston from Los Angeles. Here they were, sitting on kitchen chairs behind a makeshift table, on which was spread out for sale a selection of homemade baskets and bunches of eucalyptus leaves. Larry Nicholas had a look in his eyes—a blazing look. He was in his early twenties, with a left-over-from-the-'60s demeanor. He was gleeful as he ruffled through a stack of bills: "I was born and raised in California, around Norton Air Force Base. They say California is shaky; tell 'em to come to Montrose, Texas. I worked carneys up and down California and I ain't never seen anything at all like this. I came for the money—made $500 today!" He and his wife were ecstatic. This place is reminiscent of Haight Ashbury in the 1960s, except that today they're stoned on money. "There's no money in California," Larry explained. "Look at it this way: L.A. is at its peak, but Houston's just beginnin'." Sue-Anne, with a baby on her knee, joined in, smiling: "I thought I was movin' away from crazy people. I didn't know! Rented a house in Montrose, didn't realize all this."

"Am I gonna stay?" said Larry. "Damn *right* I'm gonna stay!"

Larry stood up and thrust out a bunch of eucalyptus leaves. "Here, take this—it's from California. It'll remind you of us!"

What matters, in the laissez-faire lifestyle, is the frontier spirit, which is everywhere in Houston. The absence of zoning is, apparently, essential to that spirit, especially for people without a lot of capital. Indeed, in a zoning referendum in the 1960s, the strongest support for nonzoning came from the minority and low-income neighborhoods, who, as former city planner Dick Bjornseth points out, "realized that if they had zoning it might limit some of their small-business opportunities." For someone who is not particularly affluent or well-trained, entrepreneurialism in such an unregulated environment is a more realistic option than entrepreneurialism in, say, Philadelphia, where the city government (a liberal one, which ostensibly cares much more for the poor than does Houston's government) has banned downtown street vendors. The reason: street vendors are untidy, and too competitive with downtown shopowners.

THE PRIVATE CITY

Houston's entrepreneurialism is exhilarating, if messy. At least those at the lower end of the economic ladder have a chance to be capitalists. But there is a darker side of the anticity, a physical and social price.

The city's helter-skelter development has created severe water problems. Part of Houston, built on a swamp, sank several feet as groundwater was pumped out for public use. Tropical storms frequently unload portions of the Gulf of Mexico on the city. The water floods over the concrete slabs of development that seem to be in all the wrong places. "Do you think that any attempt is made to hook up all the new housing developments to each other via storm drains? Hell no!" social psychologist Ryan cried, waving his pipe in the air. "And the crime rate is getting ridiculous. In downtown Houston, the cops average a twenty-five-minute response time to get to—for the love of God—an armed robbery!" In 1980, there were 172 more murders than during the previous year; 383 more rapes; 11,058 more burglaries; 88,400 more people—and only forty-two more policemen.

Other major cities, when faced with such growth, have stepped in to impose order on the chaos. But not Houston.

In the offices of Houston's mayor and city council, the chairs are threadbare, the carpets thin with shiny patches. With its low taxes, the city has a hard time approximating traditional municipal services. The buses are perpetually broken down. Last year, the city's sanitation workers walked off the job—not for higher wages, but because their trucks were in such poor repair. Mayor Jim McConn, a heavyset ex-builder, dramatized this by enrolling the National Guard in what he called "the mayor's war on garbage." He donned a chrome-plated army helmet, hopped in a jeep along with his bodyguard, and led a caravan of twenty garbage trucks through the city. At one point, McConn stood up, thrust out his fist, and declared, "We're not going to give in to garbage." Some of his opponents began wearing buttons that read: "Shoot a Trash Can."

In 1981, Richard Ryan's polls detected a growing disgruntlement about the poor city services and the traffic. Houstonians still want something done, but they do not want higher taxes.

"People never gonna change," said the chain-smoking Mayor McConn, sitting in his office. "They're always gonna demand more services and lower taxes." (I interviewed him shortly before his defeat by the city's controller, Kathy Whitmire.) All in all, McConn, who sported a tie hand-painted with the state flower, the bluebonnet, was ambivalent about the Houston private enterprise ethic. "I realize we have a few problems. Houston is known for having an infamous transportation system. It's gonna take a long time to get mass transit accepted around here. People are real macho about their cars; everybody's got to have a pickup. I'd have one if my wife would let me. But with all its problems, at least this city doesn't have a giveaway approach like they've got up in New York." He leaned over his desk. "See, people in Houston understand you don't get it by sittin' on your fanny." He made a fist. "You go out and get it."

Most surveys show that Texas is a jock society. Everybody's into some kind of recreation. Houston has five private auto racetracks, some of them right next to the freeway, where people can drive out their frustrations. The city now has its own twenty-four-hour country-western disco. Gilley's Bar in Houston became famous when it installed a spine-cracking mechanical bull, but a saloon in Fort Worth went Gilley's one better, installing a real bull in the bar for the customers to ride. All of this is, of course, in the private sector. Public-financed recreation is an entirely different matter. In 1980, Houston was one-hundred-and-second on the list of American cities in the amount of parkland per capita. But things are looking up. A year later Houston was ninety-sixth. The city accomplished this by putting its private enterprise ethic to work, netting more than 2000 acres donated by private corporations. Mayor McConn pointed to this "Give a Park" campaign as one example of Houston's can-do, private enterprise ethic. Critics of the project point out that a lot of donated land is unusable as park space.

"Horseshit!" snorted McConn. "And you can quote me on that. It's as pretty a land as you can find in this part of the world."

He paused, with a wry smile.

"Admittedly, the land here isn't very pretty."

Kathy Whitmire, who was still controller when I interviewed her in her modest little office, believes that the city can have more services without increasing taxes, by "cutting the fat" out of the city's budget (a safe theory), and that the city should be run "like a business." As for zoning, "I don't think you'll ever see Houston going to zoning. It's a little late," she said. "What we can do is to make reasonable provisions for traffic arteries."

In some areas of the city, though, it's too late to stop Houston's arteriosclerosis. Sitting in on the interview was Whitmire's chief aide, Jerry Wood, a studious young man with thick glasses, reputed to be one of the savviest political minds in the city. Wood said, "We've got no idea what to do about the arteriosclerosis. Triage might be the best way to deal with it—let part of the city die. It's going to cost millions and millions to widen freeways." Woodway Allied Chemical, for instance, built a huge cluster of buildings, including high-rise condos, right up to the freeway, making the roadway impossible to widen. Wood's hobby, as he calls it, is driving out to new housing developments on the expanding fringe of the city, populated by people moving as far from the city as they can. "There are so many new ones, I can't keep up," he sighed, pushing his glasses up his nose. "There's a real trend toward large developments built by corporations that provide the services, well . . . the services people don't seem to want to accept from government."

SERVICES FOR THOSE WHO CAN AFFORD THEM

The typical Houstonian's response to crime and urban chaos is more Darwinian than civic. The approach is indicative of one of the tenets of the laissez-faire lifestyle: market equity is favored over the notion of equality of opportunity or equality of result. The *Houston Post* columnist Lynn Ashby describes his city favorably as "a better-mousetrap sort of town . . . where all men are created equal if they can afford it." The emergence of this kind of thinking in America II makes sense when seen as part of the overall deconcentration of America at the regional and the local level.

America I cities, based on the old centralized industrial model, also developed at a time when the laissez-faire; ethic prevailed; but over time their essential structure and nature changed. The industrial model had most of the workers centralized within the city. Not only were the workers centralized, and therefore more visible and powerful, but, as political scientist Peter A. Lupsha and professor of planning William J. Siemieda write:

> The very nature of industrial work and urbanization means that any semblance of self-sufficiency must be achieved through cooperative activities, organizational activities. . . . The worker relies on someone else to provide food, clothing, shelter, water, sanitation facilities, and security. . . . The essential needs of this kind of community demand public action, public cooperation, and public services. . . . Thus the very nature of the habitat in the industrial city requires an advanced level of public services.

However, in the America II city, the political structures have been designed with a minimalist conception of government responsibility. The favored values are privatism, individualism, fiscal conservatism, laissez-faire, and the view of good government as good business. In Phoenix, the land has passed relatively quickly from the hands of farmers to the hands of big developers, and Houston has also been built almost entirely by developer decisions, not public decisions. The elite business interests have created what amount to private government networks: in Dallas, the Citizen's Charter Association; in Phoenix, the "Phoenix 40"; in San Antonio, the "Good Government League"; and in Albuquerque, Memphis, Miami, Tucson, and New Orleans, similar groups. A good argument can be made, in fact, that the "nonpartisan" elections—in which the issues are diffuse, generalized—so often seen in America II cities are a reflection of the business culture. Instead of visible voting and potent blocks, as seen in Chicago's 1983 mayoral election, in which blacks could vote en masse for their own candidate, the America II city government is vague and without much power. The real power is held by developers and various forms of small, often private government.

This alternative form of self-government is evident in the degree of privatization. Instead of raising taxes and increasing public services, Houston's residents (at least the ones who can afford to) buy their own services. For crime protection, just about everybody owns a gun. (This is, of course, as much a Texas tradition as it is a form of new privatism. As a hefty assistant manager of a country-western saloon explained to me one evening, "I'm one of the few real honest-to-God native Texans you'll meet in Houston. But I ain't complainin'. All these people comin' down here are real good for the economy. Only thing I don't like is I'm runnin' outta places to shoot my gun.") Crime protection is, however, becoming a big business. Says pollster Richard Ryan: "There's been a phenomenal increase in guard dog services, burglar alarm companies, private paramedics, and private cops. The biggest market for these services is the residential enclaves."

The enclaves—corporate urban villages—are increasingly self-sufficient, with their own office buildings, shopping areas, and recreation centers, and they are cut off from the rest of the city so that residents (even more than in Phoenix) can live, work, and play without venturing onto the freeway. One of the oldest is River Oaks, described by novelist Thomas Thompson as a place in which a "magnolia did not fall from a branch but a gardener was there to carry it away." The River Oaks Patrol Company, a privately operated and financed police force with strong but unofficial ties to the Houston Police Department, is funded by a special property fee, a private tax. The patrol is allowed to use Houston's police radio and dispatch system, and is listed in the telephone book as a police department. Some River Oaks security guards are certified Harris County deputy constables, even though they are not on the county payroll. In fact, Houston has trouble keeping police on the force, because private outfits pay so much better. Why be a (public) patrolman when you can be a (private) chief?

Houston also boasts the world's largest private garbage collection company, Browning-Ferris Industries. The company was started by Houstonian Tom J. Fatjo in the late 1960s. Fatjo's condominium association, disgruntled over poor city services, jokingly assigned Fatjo, an accountant, to the task of solving the problem, and jokingly suggested that he buy a truck and pick up the trash himself. He accepted the challenge, and targeted the private enclaves as his first customers. Today he dumps not only much of Houston's garbage, but also that of a few foreign countries. Fatjo has also established the Houstonian, a private "inspiration and perspiration" resort for wealthy entrepreneurs who fly in from around the nation, seclude themselves for a few days, then fly out, refreshed.

Hundreds of Houstonians are flying right over the anticity's most visible problem, the crumbling freeway system, referred to by traffic reporters as "that parkin' lot." In 1981, one out of every twenty commercial helicopters sold in North America by Bell Helicopter was shipped to Houston. Every day, 200 passengers take two new "helishuttles" from the city's two airports and several business centers. The number of Houston's licensed landing pads nearly tripled between 1978 and 1982, with 50 permanent pads and over 100 helipads operating under temporary permits. So why worry about such public issues as drivable highways? If life gets tough, rise above it—if you can afford to.

The laissez-faire lifestyle does not, however, mean the end of government. On the contrary, it means even more government —private governments. These private, small-scale governments can be seen in many forms in suburban neighborhoods and planned communities, which buy their own services instead of relying on city, state, or even federal government. One example of this new level of government is the system of private "zoning" that has arisen in the absence of government zoning; another, and related, example is the growth of private enclaves.

There are two major aspects of private zoning. The first is shaped by the free-market system itself, from which a natural zoning does seem to arise. As Dick Bjornseth, a former Houston city planner (now a private land-use consultant) points out: "Contrary to popular impression, the marketplace is not chaotic." People worried about gas stations moving in next door should, he contends, remember that gas stations have quite specific locational requirements; they must be on major thoroughfares, preferably at an intersection. "Even if you were to *give* them property in the middle of a residential area, they wouldn't locate there." The disadvantage of this kind of private sector zoning is a fluidity that boggles any sense of community stability (unless one lives in a private enclave); the benefit is that what it produces is a staggeringly diverse, and stimulating, variety of land uses and architectural styles. The second type of private zoning is the more varied and formalized private land use control that comes in the form of deed restrictions: stipulations, commonly referred to as restrictive covenants, that are put into the deed by private property owners at the neighborhood level. "Houston probably has the most extensive use of these covenants in the nation—there are between 7000 and 8000 subdivisions in Houston covered by them," many of them planned enclaves, set back in the woods in their own little worlds, governed by their own little private governments.

One gets the sense that there are really two Houstons: one governable, albeit privately; the other one not so governable, a wild and woolly environment. The private Houston is idyllic, a collection of wagon trains pulled into circles, a place of interior environments. This Houston is the one of what urban expert O. Jack Mitchell calls "air-conditioned magnets"—enclosed shopping centers such as the Galleria, a huge mall with high-rise office buildings and an ice-skating rink comparable to Rockefeller Center's, where skaters make figure eights beneath a gigantic chandelier. Even Houston's relatively small original central business district has become an interior environment: the shiny new office buildings are linked by an underground tunnel system.

These two Houstons—the protected and privately governed, and the wild and woolly—live side by side.

"The theory behind privatization," Richard Ryan told me, "is this: if an urban system is broken down into smaller units, people will care for their own nodules. We could take this further; why should I have to pay taxes for Houston's downtown? Face it, people don't occupy the downtown area, corporations do. If corporations want lower taxes and a safe working environment, they can make sure their employees do volunteer work downtown."

As for the poor, well, "they get screwed," said Ryan. "But the poor get screwed in Philadelphia and New York, too. No matter what kind of urban system we come up with, the poor still only end up with partial services. The results in Houston aren't much different than in New York, but the costs are a lot lower."

THE BLOB MOVES ON

When urban analysts write about new cities such as Phoenix, Houston, Denver, Albuquerque, and the rest, they often place these cities in the context of the "convergence" theory. This theory, as Lupsha and Siembieda write, "has been built up through many years of comparative analysis in the fields of sociology, economics, and geography." It is one of the most widely held theories of urbanization, and states that, given enough time, "all [cities] will exhibit similar patterns of growth, stability, service provision, and decline."

Lately, that theory has been under attack from some urban experts, since there is little expectation that the America II cities will repeat the patterns of the older, America I cities; that is, that they will eventually have higher density, large central cities, a political culture that defines public services as a legitimate obligation of government, and the shared view of equity as a common goal. The current trends point in exactly the opposite direction. Not only are anticities spreading ever further into new shapes independent of downtown, but public services all over the nation are being decimated by budget cuts and replaced by privatized services for those who can afford them. This is even true in the older cities. There, massive public payrolls and government social services operated smoothly until corporate America no longer needed the central cities and completed the move out to the spreading, evolving suburbs. When the national economy began to transform, public services at the municipal level became even less potent.

So, in a sense, the old and new cities are converging, but in the new form, not the old. There is something quite peculiar about deconcentration (or "counterurbanization," as some demographers are calling it). The process contributes to three distinct physical changes in the urban environment: decreased density, decreased size, and decreased heterogeneity. Social change inevitably follows. Deconcentration means that the farther apart we move from one another, the more we are inclined to: replace public services with private services; shift our allegiance from large governments to little private governments; and live, work, and shop in interior environments, cut off from people unlike ourselves.

Houston, in other words, is catching.

So the process continues. Houstonians, like so many other people in America II, head ever farther out of town to escape their own excesses. But because of a Texas law called extraterritorial jurisdiction, no community within ten miles of a municipal boundary may incorporate. Thus Houston sends out long tentacles into the countryside, annexing the private enclaves, grasping what taxes it can. "Extraterritorial jurisdiction is Houston's foreign policy," Kathy Whitmire's aide had told me. "Next we'll be annexing Poland." Such an annexation policy is an important distinction between the old urban form and the new, because it helps cities such as Houston and Phoenix avoid becoming encircled with suburbs. The city, in effect, becomes an endless suburb; but as the anticity spreads, one wonders how far it can go before the sense of city is lost completely.

I followed one of those tendrils beyond the fringe. On the road out was a dead armadillo, legs up in the air like four stilled pistons. Some of the region's original black population live in run-down communities such as Tamina, twenty miles outside Houston, not far from The Woodlands, where Ryan lives. Some of the shacks of Tamina have no running water, but The Woodlands is a private enclave guarded by its own cable television security system, with its own private educational television programming, its own private shuttle buses to whisk people around Houston, its own high-tech industrial and office park. The people in poor Tamina, like most people in Houston and within its reach, are ambivalent about the laissez-faire lifestyle.

One woman, twenty-five, who grew up in Tamina and lives with her children in a hundred-year-old shack, felt that Houston's boom had completely passed her by. "I been lookin' for a job as a housekeeper for months, and I ain't found nothin.''

Carl Atkins, a young man with a gold star implanted in a front tooth, is also black, and he was visiting his brother in Tamina: "I'm an artist, live in the center of Houston, and I'm doin' fine. But I miss the peace and quiet of Tamina. Places like this are going to be eaten up by all the growth in a few years, and all these people will have to move on.''

He kicked at some ants.

"But I'm going to save my money and buy me a little place way outside of town in the woods. That's what a lot of people are doing, heading out to the country. Everybody has this dream.''

At the farthest reaches of the anticity, seventy miles from the middle of Houston, at that wavering point where it becomes anticountry, I met an affluent and attractive couple, Dick and Kim. Dick, who had made a killing in the oil business, was in his fifties, and Kim, carefully coiffed, was much younger. They had become so disenchanted with Houston and its apparently self-destructive frontier values that, four days a week, they live on a thirty-acre private lake with a private phone system. In town they live in a private enclave with its own tennis courts and golf course. When they moved there a few years ago, the community only had 10,000 residents; now it has 25,000. It "used to be outside town, now it's a city within the city,'' said Dick.

"People didn't understand why we came out here, but I've been in Houston since the early 1960s. You used to be able to yell at somebody and do this [raises his middle finger] in traffic. You don't dare do that now.'' So they bought a plush A-frame cabin deep in the woods, and, to ensure privacy, they even bought the cabin next door, which Dick uses as a "sort of office.''

As he talked, he sat on the railing of a deck overlooking the lake. In the twilight, turtles surfaced and dived, making ripples in the smooth water. "This is where I come to get away from the Sun Belt.''

Every night an eight-foot alligator swims up beneath the deck. Dick and Kim heat up food in their microwave oven to feed the alligator.

"Pretty soon people are going to be moving in all around us, destroying everything, and then we'll have to move again,'' he said. "Until then, everything's fine. I just like to sit out here in the quiet and shoot the legs off the turtles."

"Oh, Dick," sighed Kim, disapprovingly.

Dick grinned. No apologies.

PART THREE

THE SHELTER REVOLUTION

Something there is that doesn't love a wall,
That sends the frozen-ground-swell under it
And spills the upper boulders in the sun,
And makes gaps even two can pass abreast.
                    —*Robert Frost, "Mending Wall"*

The one thing I learned from Disneyland was to control the environment.
                                        —*Walt Disney*

The landscaping of this building is a decor item subject to change without notice.
   —*sign next to a shrub in a singles-only condo project, Aurora, Colorado*

THE COMING OF THE
SHELTER REVOLUTION

Sometime during this decade, the shelter revolution will be complete. It will have happened quietly. No shot will have been fired, but the American notions of private property, privacy, local government—and that part of the American dream symbolized by the single-family suburban home—will have been permanently altered. The nature of shelter in America is changing so rapidly that within a decade or two only a minority of new home buyers will be able to buy the kinds of homes in which they grew up.

From the beginning, Americans desired to own their own homes on their own property. Because of the sheer breadth of the American landscape, they naturally believed they held a manifest right to land. The whole notion of Jeffersonian democracy and personal independence was tied to that assumption. However, for a good portion of the twentieth century, the dream did not match the reality. For example, census figures show that the 1890–1930 period was an age of renters; this was due in part to the influx of so many immigrants, who rented first and hoped one day to own. In the 1940s, the dream began to become reality. The wartime housing needs and advances in electronics unleashed a number of developments in construction technology—improvements in lighting, heating, plumbing, and prefabrication. Resin-bonded plywood, lightweight metallic girders, and gluing methods developed for the wartime aircraft industry became available to the general public. Just as important were the government subsidies: FHA- and VHA-loans, public housing contracts, and government contracts for housing in war production areas, all of which pumped money into the housing industry. And so the freestanding, single-family suburban home came to dominate the shelter of America I. By 1955, 56 percent of American families owned their own homes, the vast majority freestanding, single-family structures. The children of the postwar baby boom were born into the era of the dream's greatest fruition, and they have carried with them the expectation that spacious housing and land ownership would continue to be available—even if the single-family home did symbolize conformity and materialism to many baby boomers coming of age in the 1960s. By 1968, single-family detached homes accounted for 78 percent of the housing market.

Then the market share for single-family detached homes began to drop. In the early 1970s, starts of the single-family detached house fell to below 50 percent of all housing starts for the first time in the reported history of the industry. Home ownership, however, continued to rise to about 59 percent by the early 1980s, due primarily to condominiums.

Fifteen years ago, few Americans had ever heard of condominiums or other kinds of common-interest communities, but today they dominate the market. Their arrival on the housing scene has allowed more people to own their own homes, albeit in an entirely new way. Condominiums began in the late 1960s and early '70s primarily as a suburban phenomenon, and have stayed there, despite the popular image of high-rise condos in New York City or Chicago.

The U.S. Census Bureau actually has a better fix on how many bathrooms are in the nation than on how many condos exist. It is known, though, that condominiums dominate new housing starts. In 1979, for the first time, construction began on more condominiums than rental units; in 1981, more than 130,000 rental units were converted to condominiums. In Dallas, single-family homes, lumbering along like dinosaurs not yet aware of their extinction, were still selling faster than condos. But with the construction slump of 1982, the single-family home stopped dead in its tracks while condos leaped ahead. By 1981, in Florida, the most heavily condoized state, one-fourth of the population lived in condos or planned communities. Today, condominiums claim about 25 percent of the national market of newly constructed homes, according to the U.S. League of Savings Associations, and by 1990, probably more new homes in America will be condominiums than single-family dwellings. This is already true in such places as the San Fernando Valley, Southern California's first sprawling community of suburban single-family homes; there, condominiums are outselling new detached houses by two to one. Condos account for 70 percent of the building permits in the Los Angeles area. Even small towns have caught the fever. The Urban Land Institute reports a barrage of calls from remote small-town residents wanting to know how to set up condominium associations.

The rise of condominiums is not the only ingredient in the shelter revolution. Condos are one version of a proliferation of instant small towns that now can be seen all over the country. The new shelter comes in many sizes, from small clusters of attached townhouses to condominium communities that offer an amazing variety of recreational activities and social amenities. These communities bring built-in social structure and private minigovernments. As their promotional literature usually suggests, the buyer is purchasing not just a home, but a lifestyle. Some of the largest are self-contained communities, with homes, shops, offices, industries, private recreation centers, and security forces. Some even include nursing homes, in a gradated housing system designed to carry residents from the swimming pool to the grave.

Until quite recently, just what to call these new varieties of shelter has been a problem. The *Los Angeles Times* has called them "walled communities," the building industry calls the high-security types "gated communities" (since, as one housing expert put it, "walls have a distasteful connotation"). *New York Post* columnist Max Lerner and San Diego State University recreation professor Mary Duncan call them "new walled cities," because the large ones, especially, resemble nothing so much as the walled cities of medieval Europe. In the early 1980s, the building industry adopted the term "common-interest community" to describe the various forms of this new kind of shelter, and that term is being used by the Commission on Uniform State Laws. The term describes a community in which residents own or control common areas or shared amenities: ownership in a common-interest community carries with it, in the title to the property, reciprocal rights and obligations enforced by a private governing body.

It is important to realize that the shelter revolution is not, primarily, the product of flashy new technology. In terms of basic construction, homes (whether detached or attached) are built with the same methods developed in the post–World War II technological surge. However, today's technology does offer an amazing array of security systems and amenities. A few developments now offer "entertainment" rooms with built-in computers and giant-screen televisions, and futurists are agape at the possibilities of the "electronic cottage," a place to live and work, plugged into a worldwide electronic grid. There is talk among high-tech visionaries of "robutlers" who will do the dishes, sympathetic computers that will respond to the homeowner's mood and adjust lighting and music accordingly, "holostages" that will offer television in the round, and computer-controlled window views that will open onto imaginary scenes—for example, the Taj Mahal or Yosemite Valley. All of this is possible, some of it probable, but none of it is as immediately important as the revolution that has already crossed the threshold.

THE MAKING OF A REVOLUTION

In the 1970s, because of rising energy prices, inflated land prices, and skyrocketing interest rates, the detached single-family home was priced beyond the economic reach of most Americans entering the housing market. In the 1960s, when 4 to 6 percent mortgage loans were the rule, a mortgage payment typically consumed about 25 percent of a family's income. It was difficult to meet the mortgage payment then, but today it takes well over a third of the family's income—in some states, more than half.

This meant constrictions not only on the family's budget, but on that of the builder as well. Faced with inflated land costs, builders began to squeeze clusters of attached homes onto the half- or quarter-acre that was once the standard lot for a single-family home. To make these attached dwellings more palatable to a generation born and bred in more spacious surroundings, the developers built into the new shelter a number of shared amenities. Attached homes make economic sense in other ways as well. They conserve energy costs for the homeowner: recent studies have shown that structures of five or more units consume 60 percent less energy for heating and air-conditioning than detached housing. Also, condominium ownership can be economically adapted to refurbished warehouses and large, old homes by dividing them into smaller units. The new shelter fits the economics of the era of limits.

In America I, shelter was geared toward the traditional nuclear family: Mom, Dad, and 2.5 kids. Numerically, if not emotionally, the nuclear family thrived during the years following World War II. But the nuclear family no longer dominates the American scene. In 1980, nearly 20 percent of American families with children were one-parent families, an increase of 12 percent from 1970. Between 1970 and 1977, the number of single-person households of people under thirty-five nearly tripled. Today, 23 percent of all households are made up of people who live alone. The number of nonfamily households, persons living alone or with nonrelatives only, grew by a whopping 71 percent.

Smaller households mean more homes, not fewer. According to Ralph F. Timm, publisher of *House & Garden* magazine, the number of new households in 1980 amounted to 37 percent more than in 1960. In the 1970s, the amount of housing grew nearly twice as fast as the population; a Census Bureau demographer called this trend "a phenomenon we never saw before in this century."

The changing household, reflecting a desire for separateness on one hand and for community on the other, has created an unprecedented demand for a new size and type of housing. Timm declares the 1980s the "decade of the home." Logically, what is needed is a smaller and cheaper unit for a smaller family. Even for the traditional nuclear family, the new compact housing makes sense; with more working wives, more preschool children cared for outside the home, and a growing number of meals eaten away from home, the size of the home is of less importance than before. There is less time to mow a lawn or paint the eaves. The lower birth rate, higher divorce rate, longer life expectancy —all of these trends point to a vastly different style of shelter. One of the approaches is that builders are gearing more of their efforts toward what they call the new "mingles market" by designing condos and homes with two master bedrooms and baths to be shared by single adults who have become mortgage partners. Ten years ago, mingles accounted for only one-quarter of one percent of the housing market. By 1981, that share had grown to 21 percent, and experts forecast it will reach 55 percent of all housing by 1985.

In addition to economic pressures and the changes in the family, shelter is being shaped by a third trend: the new zoning rules of America II. The structure of America I shelter was determined partly by the way cities and suburbs were zoned. This zoning was determined in the late 1920s by a U.S. Supreme Court decision that upheld the right of public jurisdictions to place certain restrictions on how private land could be used. The zoning that came out of this decision (involving Euclid, Ohio) is now known as Euclidian zoning, the basic principle of which is "separation of uses." Euclidian zoning created the now-familiar urban and suburban environment, with large, homogenized sections reserved for residential, commercial, and industrial use. Within the residential sections, certain neighborhoods could contain one single-family home per acre, while other neighborhoods were reserved for three units per acre, and so on. Euclidian zoning resulted not only in the divorce of the workplace from the neighborhood, but eventually in an environment segregated by race and economics.

By the 1960s, a second strain of zoning theory was beginning to gain favor. In 1963, the National Association of Homebuilders and the Urban Land Institute conducted a study of planned communities dating as far back as 1740. The widely circulated results of that study, and the work of such urban thinkers as William H. Whyte and Lewis Mumford, helped stimulate new interest in organizing urban and suburban growth by clustering housing together, preserving open space by establishing strict covenants and architectural controls. Gradually, Euclidian zoning began to give way, especially in the fresh new cities of the South and West, to the "new" approach, a combination of mixed-use zoning, urban villages, and clustered housing. Actually, this method was not new at all, but was steeped in utopian thinking, predating Euclidian zoning by centuries.

In the 1960s, a handful of fashionable planned communities were helping some Americans adjust their preconceptions about density. Traditionally, high density was associated with crime and social problems, but the planned community, as it began to be packaged, offered a kind of high density that provided more security, not less. This was true particularly if the planned community was built beyond the city, on open land—an instant small town in a wide-open environment.

The great majority of Americans still prefer the freestanding single-family home, but if this choice is no longer economically practical, the planned community offers safety, which seems a good replacement for space.

THE UNFORESEEN IMPLICATIONS

The legal, social, and political implications of the shelter revolution are only beginning to be understood. America I shelter was simple enough: there were, essentially, apartments and houses, including farm houses, "ranch" houses (with not a cow in sight), split-levels, and a few other architectural styles. In America I, you either rented or you owned your own house. If you owned your home, you did so "fee simple," that is, you shared the ownership of the house and the land it was on with no one. In an America I home, if oil suddenly started spouting from beneath your rec room, the oil belonged to you. Zoning, police protection, parks, street repair—all these were taken care of by public government. Though there might be a homeowners' association in your neighborhood, membership was voluntary and it held relatively little power. In the traditional America I neighborhood, the distinction between public and private space was, for the most part, taken for granted. But with the new shelter, non of these assumptions is necessarily true.

Home ownership in America II is defined in part by a confusing and overlapping matrix of legal definitions that blur the distinctions between renting and owning, and between public and private space. Should oil spout from beneath your rec room in a condo, the oil is most likely owned not only by you but by all the other residents of the complex. Conceptually, the America I home was a house and a yard within a larger community; the America II home is a dwelling (often without a yard) attached, legally and physically, to a small private community. Residents share communal responsibility for commonly held grounds, recreation areas, and security. Perhaps the most distinctive characteristic of these communities is that they are controlled by private, democratic governments (community associations) that wield the kind of control over people's personal lives and tastes that, heretofore, most Americans would never have accepted from any government.

Many of the legal definitions of the different kinds of planned communities in America are barely a decade or two old, and are still in great flux. Basically, common-interest communities come in three types: condominiums, planned-unit developments, and cooperative apartments. In a condominium, a resident holds a legal title to a specific unit that includes a proportionate share of the common area. In a planned-unit development, a resident does actually own the inside and the outside of his own home; in addition, he or she owns an "easement of use and enjoyment" in common areas and amenities. In a co-op, the resident owns no property, but rather owns shares of stock in the building, with the right to occupy a designated unit. In actual operation, the legal differences between the three types of common-interest communities blur considerably. Some planned communities, for instance, contain all three kinds of ownership, operating under an umbrella minigovernment and set of covenants, conditions, and restrictions. Indeed, there are even "co-opiminiums" (co-ops operating legally as condos). Not surprisingly, a huge new industry of lawyers and consultants has emerged to make legal sense of the new shelter.

What is important, though, is that in little over a decade, the American definition of home ownership and design has undergone a complete redefinition, reflecting deep change in the society. Something similar happened in the fading days of the Roman Empire, giving rise to what were probably the first condos. Out of a desire for security, Romans built walls around their towns, and when land became scarce within the walls, they began to stack their housing. Ownership was layered, like a cake. Condominiums were originally contrary to Roman law, which for centuries had assured people that they owned their property from the center of the earth to the heavens above. So it is today that the forces of practicality contradict the American dream of owning a single-family detached home and land beneath it.

David Wolfe is one of the few people in the nation to focus on the societal implications of the new shelter. Wolfe is president of Community Management Corporation, headquartered in the planned community of Reston, Virginia. His company was among the first to help manage common-interest communities, and he set in motion the nonprofit Community Associations Institute in Washington, D.C., which keeps track of the growth and power of community associations. Wolfe sees the shelter revolution this way: "Not since the advent of the industrial revolution and its major society-impacting product, the automobile, has any event arisen with so much potential for changing the American way of life." Wolfe believes that the coming predominance of common-interest communities "in many ways portends a return to past ways and values of civilized day-to-day life," an antidote to urban complexities.

He continues: "Behavioral science has shown that it's not necessarily population density that causes people to become violent, to exhibit behavioral problems, but the lack of meaningful role opportunities. An organism has to have some sense of product to his existence, and when he's deprived of that he goes to pieces. These new communities have the potential of giving us our roles back, allowing people to live and work in a way reminiscent of the small towns of a century or more ago," with parents forming babysitting co-ops, men working together on weekends to design and build play areas and equipment for the community's children, neighbors bartering, trading skills and talents, arts and crafts, and vegetables grown in community gardens. With the self-containment and self-servicing nature of many common-interest communities—their own shops, their own recreation facilities, their own democratic subsocieties—residents will have fewer reasons for leaving their little clusters of America II.

Lewis Mumford (who spent part of his life in an early planned community on Long Island) once said that "the greatest defect of the United States Constitution was its original failure, despite the example of the New England township and the town meeting, to make this democratic local unit the basic cell of our whole system of government. For democracy, in any active sense, begins and ends in communities small enough for their members to meet face to face." That defect may be redressed, Wolfe believes, by the minigovernments that govern these postindustrial villages, these capitalistic communes. But, adds Wolfe, "the reality is different from the utopian dream." And he suggests we take a very close look at that reality, because in the near future, many of us aren't going to have much economic choice about whether or not we live in one of these America II communities.

THE RISE OF CAPITALIST COMMUNES

Richard Thorson wheeled his Mercedes down a long hill toward Rancho Bernardo, a cultured red pearl held in the rugged palm of arid mountains. "This may not be utopia," Thorson said to me, gazing with admiration at the ordered homes, uniform red-tiled roofs and spotless streets, "but it's close."

Seventy-one years ago, on this same site, then a place of sage and grassland, vigilantes from San Diego taught radical Dr. Ben Reitman a lesson. Reitman had accompanied Emma Goldman, a famous organizer for the International Workers of the World, to nearby San Diego. The vigilantes kidnapped Reitman, brought him here by train, stripped him, beat him unconscious, branded "IWW" onto his buttocks, and, not the kind of men to forgo tradition, they tarred and (because of a momentary shortage of feathers) sagebrushed him. Today, Rancho Bernardo is the kind of place that the leaders of the International Workers of the World might have had trouble imagining in 1912: a capitalist collective.

With its mix of condominiums, townhouses, and single-family homes, and its self-governing subsocieties, Rancho Bernardo is one of the birthplaces of the common-interest community. Its physical design as well as its form of private government is being emulated all over the country, mainly in smaller developments. At the beginning of the 1970s, a report on worldwide "Management and Development of New Towns," published jointly by the governments of the United States and the Soviet Union, described Rancho Bernardo as one of the finest examples of large-scale land development in the world. Homes here sell four times faster than in the rest of north San Diego County, which is itself one of the fastest-growing areas in the nation.

As director of sales, Thorson, an immaculately dressed, amiable man (the kind of man you would trust when reaching to sign a deed) is understandably enthusiastic about this planned community of 20,000 residents. Divided into six "villages," each with its own recreation center and shopping area, Rancho Bernardo is a community of pristine beauty: 5800 acres of red-tiled roofs, buried utility lines, programmed architecture. But Rancho Bernardo's perfection is a result not so much of the genius of the community's physical design as of the amount of communally owned grounds, the architectural regimentation (written into the community's covenants), and the enforcement of taste by consensus.

In 1977, Rancho Bernardo's developer, Avco Community Developers, turned the job of enforcing the community's strict architectural guidelines over to a handful of community associations (minigovernments), which added a few rules of their own.

"For instance, you can't move a boulder more than three feet wide without submitting a plan for approval from one of the neighborhood architectural committees," explained Thorson.

Even vegetable gardens are frowned upon—though some people do grow tiny ones out of their neighbors' view. Fences, hedges, or walls require approval, and may not be more than three feet tall. Signs, other than for-sale signs, are prohibited. Trees must be kept trimmed and may not grow above the level of the roof, which must be covered with red tiles. Residents are not allowed to park recreational vehicles or boats in their driveways; a special communal parking area is set aside for them. One village, designed for seniors, prohibits grandchildren from using the recreation center, and home visitation by grandchildren is strictly limited. The owners of patio homes (semidetached houses that share common grounds, except for patio areas) must gain their neighbors' approval before altering the patio, planting a rosebush, or raising a canopy.

Rancho Bernardo does have one village set aside for individualists. Those residents who desire a wider degree of freedom in home design and landscaping can move into a village called The

Trails. Driving through it, Thorson pointed to a cluster of huge, uniquely designed homes overlooking a lake.

"The average house in The Trails costs $475,000, and some run up to $700,000," he said. "People get a chance to express their own individuality. But it costs a lot more to go individual. The Trails has its own special quality. Lots of kids here. Wrought iron fences, that kind of thing."

He paused and smiled.

"And it's more interesting."

Even in The Trails, architectural or landscaping changes must be approved.

"Doesn't anyone ever rebel?"

"We have our mavericks, you bet. Some of these people are against what everyone else is for. They get in all kinds of arguments about architectural control."

A Rancho Bernardo resident and manager of one of the recreation centers, had told me earlier that week of the power some community associations are flexing here: "Legally, the courts look at community associations as minicities—with essentially the same authority as a town government. I'm on the board of a community association, and the problem I see is people aren't used to this when they first move in. So we need to educate them.

"Take parking, for instance. Each community association sets its own rules. Ours decided on a twenty-dollar fine for illegal parking. We had one couple who didn't believe their neighbors could do it; they thought only the police could enforce such a thing. The couple ran up $160 in parking fines. So we slapped a lien on their house. And then charged them for the legal fees."

What residents do inside their homes is their own business, with a few exceptions. "In Westwood, the section of Rancho Bernardo where I live, the color of curtains is controlled," she said. "If the curtains are visible from outside the home, they must be white or beige."

To outsiders, these rules are remarkable, but for many people who live here, the rules are invisible. Rules set up to enforce a lifestyle magically disappear when everyone agrees that the lifestyle is *the* way to live. Consider Earl Engle. Engle, seventy-seven, has lived in Seven Oaks, a Rancho Bernardo village, for eighteen years. "I can plant anything I want to," he explained. "Sure, they have some rules, like the one that regulates campers. But the community associations are here to protect our interests, not let the community deteriorate. That's not regulation; it's common sense. I don't know why anyone would look at it differently than I do, do you?" He was incredulous that anyone would find all of this a bit strange.

All the rules are just fine with Larry and Kathryn Reischman, who, with their two children, recently moved to a Rancho Bernardo village that allows children. "We're not really involved. Both of us work," said Larry, sitting beside a pool in a village called Eastview. "But I don't think there's any lack of freedom. We don't have to worry about yard work. That's a real relief. And we like the security. We have a block watch—everybody reports suspicious vehicles. Every forty-five minutes Rancho Bernardo's security patrol drives by. I'd say security was the most important reason we moved here; it's more psychological than anything."

In San Diego, as in other cities that attract retirees, relocation assistance companies report that when people move from the big industrial cities of the northeast and upper Midwest, they usually prefer places like Rancho Bernardo precisely because there are so few variables, so little risk. In 1980, according to the San Diego Police Department, San Diego as a whole suffered eighty-seven crimes per thousand residents. But Rancho Bernardo had only thirty-four per thousand. Not only is its crime rate lower, but some studies have indicated that the residents' cholesterol level is lower than the national average—possibly due to lower stress, higher income, and more education.

Though the retreat into these private, walled communities was pioneered by seniors, the movement now includes more and more younger Americans. Rancho Bernardo, for instance, isn't just a concentration of wealthy seniors spending their last years wandering around in golf carts. Although it began as a retirement settlement, only about half of Rancho Bernardo's current residents are retired or semiretired. When Rancho Bernardo is completed, sometime in the next decade, it will have a population of 48,000.

These new migrants, overwhelmingly Republican, are bringing a lot of money with them; the average resident of Rancho Bernardo earns three times that of the average San Diegan. Rancho Bernardo claims the title of "Wall Street West" because of its concentration of financial institutions: a block-long row of thirteen banks and savings and loans, with several more on the way. On a hill, out of sight of the homes, is Rancho Bernardo's high-tech industrial park, which includes the first Sony plant in the United States, as well as Hughes, Burroughs, Hewlett Packard, and Oak Industries. Many of the executives live in Rancho Bernardo. The plants provide 7000 jobs, mainly to electronics assemblers of modest income from outside Rancho Bernardo. But despite the number of minority workers employed in the industrial park, Rancho Bernardo remains a monochromatic community. Only 2 or 3 percent of the population is made up of minority group members. No low-income housing exists in Rancho Bernardo.

Thorson stepped out of his car and walked up to one of Rancho Bernardo's plush, private, high security recreation centers; this one served a village called Oaks North. He passed through an open security gate. Inside were rooms for art classes and crafts. Matronly jazzercise students wearing leotards were kicking in unison.

"Wonderful services here," Thorson was saying. "The residents run these centers themselves. A feeling of community, self-rule." He was standing next to the swimming pool, explaining all this, when a uniformed red-bearded man, an employee of the recreation facility, walked up, with a look of moral authority in his eyes, and demanded to see his visitor's pass.

Thorson explained that he was Rancho Bernardo's director of sales. The bearded man stared at him suspiciously.

"I've been here since '72 and I never met you."

The director of sales was becoming a bit nonplussed. "Look," he said, "I own two houses in Oaks North. I rent them out."

"That doesn't give you the right to use this facility."

Though Thorson finally convinced the security guard that he was, indeed, director of sales, he remained slightly embarrassed.

Later, he was asked if Rancho Bernardo wasn't . . . well, socialistic, one big commune for those who can afford to buy into it.

"To a degree, yeah, but . . . different," he said. "You could call it socialism. Highly democratic socialism. Where do you draw the line?"

SEEDS OF REVOLT

Everything in Rancho Bernardo is under control. This kind of community, now spreading throughout the United States, represents a strain of development that has been around for a long time; it is, in fact, a strain running parallel to the rise of the typically zoned neighborhood consisting of rows of suburban single-family homes. For most of the nation's history, planned communities were an interesting but relatively unimportant form of housing, reserved primarily for religious zealots and collective idealists. But now this second strain is gaining momentum and surpassing the single-family tract home.

The idea that a community could be planned from its architectural design to its social fabric is, of course, an old idea. Thomas More imagined a *Utopia,* an island with fifty-four city-states, each with a maximum population of 40,000. Albrecht Dürer's "City of Tomorrow," conceived in the sixteenth century, was designed as a guild city, with each trade having its own separate section or district, all of it protected by heavily fortified walls. Indeed, in colonial America, many cities and towns were planned communities, including the Spanish settlements of the Southwest. Much of the seeming confusion of Boston's streets was actually due to ecological planning; the colonial designers carefully followed the local topography when they drew up the first plan, and then stuck to it. From the beginning of colonization, the British Crown encouraged its subjects to plan and settle towns; yet these towns, as they grew and prospered, eventually became the agencies of rebellion.

Particularly after the American Revolution, the large American towns, which had often begun under principles of tight social and religious control, became more cosmopolitan and tolerant. The utopians moved on: during the nineteenth century, more than 200 utopian communities were established in the United States, places such as Harmony, Pennsylvania; New Harmony, Indiana; and Oneida, New York. Religious and sexual-freedom groups established new towns separate from the perceived evils and restrictions of urban life.

But another strain of planned community, not based on the attractions of religion or sex, was beginning to emerge: elaborate company towns. The most famous of these was constructed in 1880 by the railroad car innovator George M. Pullman, who built a factory and the company town of Pullman south of Chicago. The town had impressive sewerage and water systems, terraced front yards, rows of neat houses, a shopping center, a library, a theater, a church (no saloons or brothels). *Harper's New Monthly Magazine* described it as "the only city in existence built from the foundation on scientific and sanitary principles. . . . Its public buildings are fine, and the groupings of them about the open, flower-planted spaces is very effective. It is a handsome city with the single drawback of slight monotony." Others were not so generous. The well-known economist, Richard Ely, described it at the time as representing ideas alien to democracy: "It is not the American ideal. It is benevolent, well-wishing feudalism, which desires the happiness of the people, but in such a way as to please the authorities." After the violent Pullman strike in 1894, the town of Pullman was absorbed into Chicago.

Meanwhile, the theories of the most influential utopian urbanologist, Ebenezer Howard, were catching on. In the late 1800s, Howard, a Britisher attempting to relieve England's disastrously congested metropolitan cities, developed the concept of "garden cities": planned communities lying within a twenty-five- to thirty-mile radius of a central city, surrounded by an inviolable greenbelt. The new towns should, he said, be limited to 30,000 people and contain an industrial base to ensure self-sufficiency. Most importantly, all leases would include detailed building codes and rules protecting the green areas, and the profits from future growth would go to the community, not the speculator. Over the following decades, the idea spread that new towns based on scientific principles could be built out beyond the edge of a city, and that they could be more than bedroom communities, that they could be places where life was under control.

In the 1920s, the new town of Radburn, New Jersey, was developed with a few of the radical garden city features, including an autonomous form of private government. Several more were built with U.S. government financial help in a bailout of the housing industry, which suffered disastrous years in 1919 and 1920. Social reformers saw an opportunity to push legislation that would, in helping the housing industry, also open up the early suburbs to the masses. Wilson's Secretary of the Interior, Franklin K. Lane, urged resettlement legislation that would create "a new rural life with all the urban advantages"—in effect, new towns in suburbia. The legislation amounted to little, however, because the housing slump suddenly ended. Developers quickly forgot the more radical ideas connected to new towns, concerning shared ownerships and profits, but they retained the goals of carefully planned garden villages and garden homes designed to preserve the natural setting. As a promotional device, this became quite fashionable.

Outside Cleveland, on the site of what had once been a Shaker religious community, two promoters built Shaker Heights, a tightly controlled suburb divided into separate sections of homes in different price ranges, so that the cheaper houses would not depress the prices of the expensive ones.

The federal government was not yet out of the picture. During the Great Depression, hundreds of thousands of poor farmers and their families were being shoved out of rural areas and into the cities by foreclosures, dust storms, and mechanization. To house these people, the Roosevelt Administration proposed that 3000 self-contained garden cities be built, primarily around metropolitan areas. But once again the role of government fell far short of the intention. The economy improved, and only thirty-three were built, including Greenbelt, Maryland outside Washington, D.C., and Greendale near Milwaukee. They were not self-contained, nor did they house poor families pushed off the farm. The communities became, instead, attractive suburban villages catering to middle-income commuters. But government remained committed to the idea of new towns. In the 1960s, faced with the urban breakdown and the failure of urban renewal, the federal government again jumped into the act of planning communities with its Model Cities and New Towns programs. Again most of these projects failed financially, but this foray into utopian planning did pass the torch of planned communities with community associations and restrictive deeds to the private sector, to a generation of architects, developers, and speculators.

What is different today is that no one is talking anymore about direct federal involvement in planning new towns. Three times during our history, twice during difficult economic times and once during an affluent period, government had promoted the idea of new towns as a way to help lower-income people escape economic privation and the ills of urban life. In contrast, during the most recent and severe recession, the building of new communities was never discussed as a national approach to growing poverty and decay. Instead, planned communities are now seen as a way for the relatively affluent to escape the results of economic privation and the ills of urban life.

The capitalist commune, as an inheritor of utopian thinking, is the leading edge of the shelter revolution. About seventy of these call themselves "new towns," but the vast majority of planned communities do not. Today, the number of large planned communities (defined as those with more than 1000 units) totals more than 7000, according to Community Associations Institute. The largest concentrations are in Florida and California, followed by the metropolitan areas of Chicago, Washington, and New York City.

If success is defined financially, the degree of success of almost all new towns and planned communities was in retrospect dependent on the extent of corporate involvement. The more corporate support, the more successful the community; the more direct support from the federal government, the less successful the community. Rancho Bernardo was accomplished with relatively little government financing and The Woodlands in Texas was pumped up and pushed out into the world by an oil company.

Indeed, though some developers are saying the day of large planned communities is over (though the rise of smaller ones is definitely not), Doug Klein, director of the Community Management Institute Research Foundation foresees a move by large corporations into the construction of planned communities. "There's a shift," says Klein, "from the personal ego trip of the stick builder or subdivision guy who just wanted to do something bigger and better, to the corporate ego." Corporate egos are, indeed, diversifying and moving into building planned communities: corporations such as Ford Motor Company (which named its eighty-three-acre new town in Chicago Fairlane, after a car), American Cyanamide, Philip-Morris, General Electric, Avco, Ralston Purina, U.S. Gypsum (which has proposed a two-tiered town, one for pedestrians, one for vehicles), Westinghouse Electric, Sears Roebuck, Marshal Field, Aetna Insurance, Goodyear Tire & Rubber, Mobil Oil, McCulloch Oil Corporation, the Mitchell Energy & Development Company. (McCulloch Oil actually purchased the London Bridge in 1968 and reassembled it in its own planned community, Lake Havasu City, Arizona.)

The corporate ego may be surprised, though. Like King George III, the corporate ego may discover that the seeding of semiautonomous towns can breed a new kind of separatism, the dissolution of colonies, the revolt of the Postindustrials.

COMING HOME TO AMERICA II

George Mitchell, the guiding force behind Houston's The Woodlands, is perhaps the most idealistic of the entrepreneurial Utopians. Mitchell, a balding futurist and friend to Vice President George Bush, is also one of the richest men in America. *Houston* magazine pointed out that he is probably worth more than the combined gross national products of the world's five poorest countries. His share of Mitchell Energy & Development is worth at least a billion dollars.

His common-interest community, roughly the size of New York's Manhattan Island, is tucked away in the woods fifteen miles north of Houston International Airport. The Woodlands is a paradise of lakes, streams, and forests of ancient magnolias. It has its own equestrian center, offering 2500 acres of wooded trails and the only facility in the Southwest for "event jumping, dressage, cross-country, speed, and endurance" training. Two helipads are located in the Village of Grogan's Mill, for those who want to skip the traffic. The place is studded with lakes. Among other amenities, The Woodlands boasts an athletic center with a fifty-meter Olympic-sized swimming pool, racquetball courts, and one of the largest golf complexes (eighty-one holes) in the nation. This is a town that bugged itself, with its own two-way interactive cable television network and computerized central command post.

The Woodlands illustrates three aspects of the shelter revolution: the feeling among many affluent Americans that the best way to deal with urban problems is simply to secede from urban life; the growing technological sophistication of the capitalist communes (technologically, The Woodlands makes Rancho Bernardo look like a western Kansas farm town); and the new packaging of the common-interest community, a packaging that appeals to the deepest longings for home and control.

Every two years, Mitchell sponsors the Growth Conference, a gathering of distinguished scholars who discuss alternative urban scenarios, and offers a $100,000 prize for innovative urban problem solving. He sees The Woodlands as the wave of the future, an alternative to untrammeled growth, the kind of "cluster city" that will ring large metropolitan areas, especially in fast-growing urban regions of the South and West.

"American cities are in deep trouble," he told me. He spoke softly and quickly, sitting in his bright, open office. One of his aides says that Mitchell talks so fast that his staff tape-records him during meetings. "The middle class has fled, the brain base is gone. It will take sixty years, three generations, to stop the deterioration of cities, break the poverty cycle. But we have to do something in the meantime, don't we? What's destroying all of the cities in the northeast is the tremendous encirclement of cities by suburbs that could not care less about the cities. Irvine, Laguna Niguel—they won't be part of Los Angeles. But The Woodlands will be part of Houston because of extraterritorial jurisdiction [recently challenged by another enclave]. We can help the urban process. This nodule will be a complete industrial node, self-contained.

"Look, why should people drive an hour a day to go to work? My wife quit going downtown to shop fifteen years ago. Eighty percent of trips don't have to be taken. How do you dispense education without brick and mortar? Through closed circuit television. Community colleges do a great job, but this is the next step. It's cheaper. My daughter took one three-hour course on *The Ascent of Man* on TV—finest course she ever took. It's a way to get community college to the disadvantaged. We have to start thinking creatively. The urban crisis today is much more crucial than energy. In fifteen years we'll be fine in terms of energy, if the Saudis last that long. But what about the cities; where will they be? If we succeed with The Woodlands, other companies will want to do it. We've tried for twenty years to restore the inner cities, and it didn't work. But there are solutions. The no-zoning in Houston is very successful; let the subdivisions do it for you! Opens up a diversity of housing. We've got to be part of the community, though; part of the political whole."

His fellow oil barons said Mitchell was crazy to sink $450 million into this fanciful Oz. But the city that Mitchell built took only seven years to reach a population of 12,000. By the year 2010 the population is expected to reach 170,000. The residents, who live in condos, detached homes, and apartments, are mostly new migrants, members of the technical and professional class lured south by the scent of Texas bucks.

Twelve percent of The Woodlands residents live in low- or moderate-income housing. The Woodlands was built, in part, with $50 million in federal loan guarantees linked to HUD requirements that the racial mix reflect that of Houston. In 1981, 28 percent of Houston's population was nonwhite, but only 5 percent of The Woodlands was nonwhite—barely better than Rancho Bernardo. Progress toward the original goal has been slow. (Among the privately financed new towns, Columbia, Maryland, is a notable racial exception, with 20 percent of its population black. Other developers, such as Rancho Bernardo's Barry McComic, president of Avco, suggest that "it's not so important to bring the poor into these communities; what we need to do is build Rancho Bernardos for them." There is, however, no stampede of exuberant developers in that direction.) A few miles away from The Woodlands is a black rural shantytown. Some of the shacks, crowded with children and full of a kind of befuddled anger, have no plumbing.

In contrast, The Woodlands is a technological marvel. It represents the first attempt to equip an entire city with a twenty-four-hour, computerized cable television security system. "At The Woodlands," says the town's promotional literature, "you can not only watch 'Emergency' on your television, your television can help you watch out for emergencies." All new homes come with such standard features as cable TV outlets and a manual alarm system (hooked up to the TV cable) that features wall buttons for fire, police, and medical emergencies. Sensors are planted in hallways, rooms, doorways, and windows in more than 70 percent of the homes. These sensors are connected, through the cable, to a central computer command post located in The Woodlands fire station. When residents leave their homes, they switch on the system. The central computer scans the sensors in all homes every ten seconds.

If the silent alarm is activated, automatically or manually, a twenty-four-hour dispatcher is alerted. But this is no simple alarm. At the dispatcher's elbow an automatic typewriter starts whirring away, spewing forth a print out that tells where a break-in or fire is occurring, which floor, which room. If the emergency is medical, the print out whips out the family's medical history: blood types, for instance, and special health conditions such as diabetes. In minutes, help arrives: officers of a special Montgomery County Sheriff's Department unit, firemen, or paramedics privately contracted by The Woodlands Community Association. At The Woodlands an average of six minutes transpires from the first appearance of flames to the arrival of fire trucks. In downtown Houston, the police average twenty-five minutes to get to the scene of a robbery. But at The Woodlands, the response time of a specially assigned unit of the sheriff's department is almost instantaneous.

The television cable has uses beyond security: scores of viewing channels, including twenty-four-hour news, a children's channel, and a business channel. The Woodlands' two-way cable system is equipped to televise meetings for schools, churches, and community associations. The system soon will be used to shop or bank from home. Gas and electric meter readings will be collected over the television cables. And a video-based community college is on the way. More than ever before, it helps to live in the right neighborhood.

So far, this brave new world is a stunning success. A mix of single-family homes, condominiums, and town houses, priced between $40,000 and $500,000, are selling twice as fast as in Houston, Boomtown, USA. Sales are up 125 percent over last year.

Visitors to The Woodlands are asked to sit in a darkened auditorium and watch a rather hypnotic multimedia show, a masterpiece in subliminal sales strategy. In front of the screen, a real railroad crossing gate lifts, and the image of a train rumbles past. A mellifluous, masculine, assuring voice talks of the "train we feel inside that carries our life along . . . a crazy runaway train, toward some station whose name we can't quite read. We pass through communities of identical houses like boxes to hold identical lives. Past pastures of trucks and traffic grazing on concrete and noise. And through vast, vaguely frightening countryside where everyone is a stranger one from another. We look out at the strange and troubling countryside our lives pass through and we wonder . . . when will this old train we're on bring us home again? Now, at this moment, you are at a station that lies somewhere between where you've been and where you wish to be. You may not pass this way again. So get off that train you're on . . . and come home."

The train's raucous clattering is replaced by soothing music and photos of life in The Woodlands, of homes arranged in six "villages" with names like Grogan's Mill and Panther Creek, separated by belts of woods and meadow.

Indeed, everything from the community association "town meetings" to the physical design evokes the ghost of Main Street America. Here's how The Woodlands' slide presentation describes the community: "A new hometown. All the best of the traditional hometowns that bloomed across America when this century first began. Those towns where the barber and the banker were on a first-name basis with everyone in town. Where the most abrasive sound to be heard was a screen door slamming. When living in harmony with nature was instinctive rather than fashionable. . . . The Woodlands is not a subdivision. It is a self-supporting, true hometown. You can sink roots deep into the forest soil. Your children can be grandparents there."

A University of Houston campus and a medical research facility are planned for The Woodlands, along with a 100-bed hospital. The community even has its own private social services with more than 100 volunteers to serve their neighbors.

If the residents do have to venture outside onto the anarchic Houston freeway system, they can catch one of the forty air-conditioned vans operated by The Woodlands Commuter Service, which calls itself "a secret weapon for the car wars." Then there's the private heliport.

All of this is so energy efficient, according to Mitchell, that normal suburban driving time has been cut by 80 percent.

The criticism that The Woodlands has somehow cut itself off from reality bothers him: "I see planned communities taking pressure off the urban core and contributing to the tax base of deteriorating cities, unlike northeastern suburbs that have drained the urban tax bases. The Woodlands is unincorporated so far, but I've made it clear from the beginning that we were going to eventually be part of the city of Houston, contributing to it."

Having had a taste of autonomy, though, many (perhaps most) of the residents do not share Mitchell's idealism.

I visited for a while with two Woodlands couples, and they talked of how they felt the need to separate themselves from large cities in order to claim some sense of control. This group of residents, sitting in a meeting room at The Woodlands' community center, included Jean Marshall, a housewife, and her husband, Ken, who described himself as "considerably more liberal than conservative." Marshall read about The Woodlands before it was opened, in, as he recalled, a "little squib in the paper. But Mitchell wasn't going to show it until it was finished. I drove down to take a look and was summarily turned away by a couple of guards." Howard and Karen Smith, clear-eyed, young, beautiful, and coiffed, moved here recently from Washington, D.C. As Howard said, "We were part of the problem [by being in government]; here, there's a can-do attitude. Make money, you can help others."

All four resent Houston and its threat of taxation without much representation.

"This used to be called a land grab," said Ken. "I'm in total agreement with Mitchell's goal, but what worries me is that Houston is behaving historically, annexing the tax base but not giving good services."

"They take care of the inner city people more than they take care of people out here," added Howard.

The four agreed that should the day come when the tentacles reach for the gates, there would be, as Howard said, "a hell of a fight." In America II, the underlying ethic is "separate but better."

The conversation drifted to the nature of The Woodlands as a community.

"Out here it's like a small town," said Howard.

Jean spoke for the first time: "Just look at the street names: Crinkle Route, Timber Jack. . . ."

"Wishbone Bush . . . ," said Howard.

"Huntsman's Road . . . Sky Flower. The local post office said it was going to take away our rural post boxes, the kind that sit out in front of your house, all bunched up together kind of on fence posts, you know."

"Blazing Star," said Howard.

Ken added: "Back to the old RFD—latest thing in postal efficiency."

"Anyhow," said Jean, "they wanted us to go to a glorified zip code, instead of boxes with our names on them, using the street addresses, the street names. You should have heard the hue and cry. We wanted our names on them. Organized a campaign and won."

"When people can feel they can impact the post office then they've really done something," said Ken.

Karen sighed. "I remember driving down here to look around, to see if we should buy here. And I thought, 'I'm home! Somebody has gone to such trouble.'"

"Through the community associations we have control over our own neighborhoods," explained Ken. "They sell a lifestyle here, and throw the house in! Why do we need to pay taxes to Houston?" He leaned forward a bit, and his voice grew urgent.

"The Woodlands harkens back to the old values of small town America: the idea of local control, of knowing your neighbors. We're afraid of giving that up. As for minorities, historically, nobody in this region cared about them. Well, most of the residents of The Woodlands are newcomers, and we care. We've started some private services out in the poor districts." He paused. "You see, we didn't come here to get away from blacks or Hispanics. We came here because we simply wanted our kids to grow up like we did. In a real world."

THE DESIGN AND SELLING
OF CONDO AMERICA

Large planned communities such as Rancho Bernardo and The Woodlands set the stage for the design and marketing of tens of thousands of smaller common-interest communities. Newspaper real estate sections are filled with advertisements offering the essential ingredients pioneered in the new towns: nostalgic packaging, separation from the larger community, segregation by lifestyle, private recreation facilities, ersatz nature, and high-tech security systems. The sophistication of these amenities—from plastic gazebos to laser beam security systems—is accelerating, and the nature of this packaging has implications beyond the walls and security gates of these places.

The use of illusion and psychological packaging is, of course, not new to the housing industry; but never before has illusion, and the confusion between what is real and what is myth, so permeated housing. In the past, houses were designed primarily as places of production. Even the suburban single-family home, which came to symbolize conformity and consumerism, was essentially designed as a place to produce and raise a family. But at some point in the past two decades, consumption in the home became more important than production. With falling birthrates, more divorces, and more retirees, the 2.5 children were replaced in many suburban culs-de-sac by the Winnebego in the driveway, and slowly our houses became shelters not just from the elements, but from society. We have begun to define ourselves, as never before, by where we live. Indeed, many of us no longer live in neighborhoods, but in something akin to theme parks.

ENGINEERS OF THE IMAGINATION

If the designers and marketers of the new shelter have a patron saint, it is Walt Disney. Disneyland, along with its companion communities Disney World and Epcot, is the ultimate interior environment, the premier corporate utopia. Disneyland's Main Street, U.S.A., for instance, is a molded version of America's fondest image of itself. Disney copied this Main Street from what he remembered of his boyhood in pre–World War I Marceline, Missouri. Ironically, the real Marceline, at that time, had a grim main street of dust or mud, depending on the season, crowded with electrical wires and poles, not Disneyland's immaculate Main Street. Disney admitted the contrast; this Main Street, he said, is "the way the real Main Street *should* have been." Richard V. Francaviglia describes the effect of this on the popular consciousness:

> Safely within the realm of Main Street, U.S.A., the park visitor is forced to relocate in time as well as space. The small town atmosphere is enhanced by the time frame chosen; namely, the halcyon days of the small town; what has been called the "McKinley Era," or simply the turn of the century. It is this period, a rather lengthy but misty time frame suspended between the Civil War and World War I, that Disney recreated. Historians and social critics are divided as to just how idyllic these days actually were . . . but Disney has effectively instigated a deep collective longing for preurban Anglo-America.

Anthropologist Barbara Myerhoff points out that this street creates a sense of relief, "a sense of coming home. . . . In Disney's parks and products, we experience and reexperience a childhood we never had." So the yearning for Victorian small towns may have been instilled by Disney more than by reality. The crux of the matter is the compartmentalization of visions. Social scientists have pointed out the correspondence of this compartmentalization to the stages in the life cycle: childhood (Fantasyland), adolescence (Frontierland), adulthood (Adventureland and Tomorrowland). Myerhoff indicates "the importance of the visual, auditory, and psychological barriers between each of these realms." She continues:

> Gates, walls, and various boundaries make it impossible easily to
> see from one alternative reality to another. This clear separation
> between imaginative and contrasting zones is essential, lest one
> 'see through' the fantasy being inhabited. . . . All forms of escapism
> other than those provided by the park are illicit and not sanc-
> tioned. Security forces, always dressed in character so as not to
> remind anyone of the need for regulation or the possibility of
> disorder, are found throughout the park. . . . All is well, we need
> not worry, though the world outside seems in shambles—incom-
> prehensible, out of control, indifferent, and in decay.

Disney's worlds, says Myerhoff, represent a form of "hyperculture," an "overdone, inflated version of a value or myth, aggran-
dized even to the point of parody." This, she says, is "an instance
of the tamed and colonized imagination" designed by what Disney called "Imagineers," engineers of the imagination.

In large part, the shelter revolution is being designed by imagineers who face a number of packaging problems that call for the
use of illusion. Consider, for instance, the problem of size (which
is, perhaps, the easiest of the packaging problems). Many Americans who grew up in detached single-family homes have yet to
fully understand just how small many condominiums are, with
only 400 or 600 square feet of floor space. Designers are using
such illusionary techniques as concentrating on the diagonal,
using hanging mirrors, varying furniture heights, using wall
sconces, and floating furniture from the ceiling so the eye can
travel farther along the floor. The solidly predictable, detached
single-family home is being replaced by a house of mirrors.

Packaging Community

A much more difficult problem is the packaging of community.
The imagineers understand, as Disney did, our ambivalence
about real community. Condominiums are frequently organized
around courts, squares, or swimming pools, with people encouraged by the design to face one another. Part of the selling of
condos, therefore, is the suggestion that making friends is easier
in a common-interest community than in a typical tract neighborhood. But marketers approach this carefully; they sell community, in effect, with mirrors.

Marketing surveys conducted by Community Management

Corporation found that Americans are naturally resistant to neighboring, at least consciously. If a marketer or real estate agent promotes common-interest communities directly, saying, in effect, "Move in here and you'll have fun; you'll meet your neighbors," that's a turnoff. People generally respond, "I just want to be me, left alone." So Community Management suggests the use of a subliminal sales strategy. The company introduces into the promotional literature trigger words, subtle pictures conjuring up images of box suppers, bandstands, Sunday afternoon picnics, the Gay Nineties—all the notions that suggest traditional and safe small-town values. And these same totems are built into the physical design of the communities: Victorian gazebos at the entrances, community centers preweathered and arranged like country stores.

Nature and Community

The packaging of nature is important, not just for the esthetic values of trees and water, but because nature helps sell community. Wayne Williams is one of the shelter revolution's foremost Imagineers, an expert at combining a feel for the natural environment with the yearning for community. A fellow of the American Institute of Architects, he designs condominium communities and new towns, with an emphasis on recreational design. Williams, who has done the conceptual design for Watergate at Landmark, the Rotunda and Montebello communities near Washington, D.C., wishes Disney had had more impact, not less. "He really knew how to create character and mood and a sense of place, but you have to go to these phony places [Disneyland and Disney World] to get the feeling of what communities should be doing on their own. His Main Street is so easy to copy! But Disney feeds on the mundaneness of everybody's life—'Come to my park and be whirled, in a teacup, away from your troubles.' You go home with nothing; you were held at arm's length from yourself.

"I started my career doing public recreation design for cities, but I got out of that because I came to hate the whole idea that people had to escape to parks. Their lives are mundane, and so society makes it up to them by giving them a few parks. That's the real Disney message. But the point is not to have to go find a park, but to live in a park. This is especially true these days, with parkland bond issues being voted down 200 to one."

Williams's prescription: introduce nature and nostalgia into a planned community, make a development more parklike, and manufacture what he calls a story line into the design, creating an instant folklore that may or may not have something to do with the real history of the particular land or region. For instance, when Williams designed the land use at the Watergate at Landmark condominium community, he sculpted the landscaping to follow the original lines of the land, and shaped a central pool to fit the original waterline of what had once been a lake in Civil War days. "A hill rises out of the lake just like it used to," he says. "We even had a story written about it, telling new residents that they were going to get to live in an historic area, next to an historic lake." If a salvageable story line does not exist, then Williams manufactures one: if the new development is designed in the old Victorian style, he feels, "people will think, oh, this has been a resort hotel on the Potomac for a long, long time."

In terms of manufacturing a parklike feeling, the smaller condominium developments are much less sophisticated. But still, the effort is there, evidenced by the frequent use of little groves of trees and imported boulders, sometimes with an electrically pumped and plastic-lined stream running through them. The imagineer's theory is that a little fantasy is better than none at all. The residents of these places seem pleased enough with their surroundings; and yet the packaging evokes a feeling of disjointed déjà vu. The packaging suggests: you were here a long time ago in a former lifetime that never was.

THE EMERGENCE OF THEME HOUSING

From the purchaser's point of view, buying a prepackaged lifestyle, not just a house, makes some practical sense. Doing so can give a highly mobile person with little chance to set down roots an enhanced sense of personal identity, and an ability to change identities, from tennis addict to swinging single to parent in the space of a few years. Housing-as-lifestyle, the emergence of placeless theme communities, is a logical outcome in a society in such a state of constant, visible change.

"Most Americans in the housing market are not looking for an ancestral home," says Bernard Jacob, architecture writer for the *Minneapolis Star-Tribune.* "They are looking for a place to live during the next few years. Perhaps there are just more stages, and they come more quickly. . . . This may mean that the number of family heirlooms will be reduced and that furniture will become lighter and easier to move."

If the symbols of nature and community can be packaged, so can personalities and personal fantasies. Because the nuclear family with 2.5 children is no longer dominant, designers and marketers approach the market in the same way that magazine publishers did in the 1960s, when the general interest magazine could no longer command its traditional share. Big general interest magazines gave way to a proliferation of special interest publications targeted on narrower shares of the market; the same process is occurring with radio and cable television. Hence, part of the selling of condo America involves the establishment of theme housing: common-interest communities set up to fit the fantasies of people with particular interests or of a particular age. An essential difference between magazines and housing, though, is that specialized magazine promotion categorizes people only by interest; the new shelter separates them physically.

Theme Villages Within Larger Developments

One approach is prevalent in the larger communities: people are segmented into special villages or neighborhoods much like the division of attractions at Disneyland, with walls, gates, and boundaries blocking differences from view.

Irvine, California, is one of the first large common-interest communities. Even more than Rancho Bernardo, Irvine is a study in compartmentalization. The very affluent live on Harbor Ridge; the more modestly affluent live in Big Canyon, with a private club, golf course, and a guarded gate; sailors cluster in Bayside, in homes with private docks; academics live in University Park; families with more than one child live in Woodbridge; and those with no children live in the adults-only node, San Joaquin. Even play, which does not conform to community standards of neatness, has its own node, an "adventure playground" surrounded by a tall earthen berm, where children can, under supervision, build forts and mudslides.

All of this has been planned and packaged by Irvine, which conducts the most extensive demographic and marketing studies in the building industry. Irvine's consumer-research specialists describe houses and condominiums as products, more like disposable cars than permanent homes, to be matched with the needs of a twenty-segment market categorized by age, marital status, income, lifestyle, and size of family. This kind of segmentation is increasingly popular in the larger communities.

The Single-interest Neighborhood

Usually, the smaller common-interest communities are devoted to special interest groups—for example, golfers, tennis players, singles, or adults (though the California courts have declared it illegal to ban children from condo communities). What's new is how specialized the interest group can be. Techies can move into condo communities that include, as standard equipment, computers with electronic mailboxes. Available, too, are vacation time-share units reserved exclusively for nonsmokers. There are nudist condos (residents, including doctors, lawyers, teachers, and clergymen, can enjoy clothing-optional condo living, surrounded by a twelve-foot concrete wall). Gary London, a condominium specialist with Sanford Goodkin, Inc., describes country condos: "For those with a rural bent, the tightly knit rural village atmosphere is promoted, without the responsibility of farming, gardening, or the upkeep of large lawns. We're getting close to the Kibbutz." Well, maybe. In a rural area outside Boston a condominium development offers (as advertised in the *Boston Globe*) "the delights of country living . . . all year long. . . . Act now and you could spend your summer in a scenic country setting with trees, rolling hills, meadows, and lots of fresh, clean air." Indeed, a basic principle in the packaging of condo America is the rationalization of opposites: city life is country life; country life is city life. Hence, despite the fact that these communities have a high density of population, one sees names such as Diamond Farms and Pinewood Meadows. The latter is a a high density project where any meadows have been covered by parking lots and buildings. Perhaps the most appropos name yet is one that a developer gave a condominium community in Virginia: Lifestyle.

A good case can be made for this kind of segmentation, according to community designer Wayne Williams, who calls it "positive ghettoism. I think it's fantastic. It doesn't have to separate people at all; it can bring them together. Think of a community where all the people interested in the performing arts live with other people like themselves, or people who are interested in horticulture live with other horticulture hobbyists. Or fine arts, or culinary interest. We've been working on a project just like that. The fun and vitality of this is that, instead of a neighbor interacting with another neighbor by borrowing a cup of sugar, he or she can go over to an area of the community where people are actually experts on something. Positive ghettoism gives a reason for the cross-pollination of people. Instead of people living in their ticky-tacky houses or ticky-tacky condos with everyone inside with their own private hobbies, we're creating something like the guild towns of the Middle Ages. You can create a sense of competition between the villages; it's the us-against-them idea."

Golden-age Ghettos

The most important and pervasive type of segmentation is seen in the restrictions on age. Wayne Williams, so enthused about positive ghettoism, is not so enthusiastic about the golden ghettos, as they are called in the industry, through he helps design them.

While most seniors-only housing is in small clusters, the package was perfected in the big senior settlements like the Sun Citys, near Los Angeles and Phoenix, and the Leisure World developments in Orange County, California. The two Leisure Worlds (which are called, by local wags, Seizure World, Cardiac Corner, Wrinkle City), house about 30,000 seniors who have virtually cut themselves off from the demands of all those youth-seekers beyond the walls. Leisure World residents are proud of living, as they told *Los Angeles Times* reporter Doris A. Byron, "behind the wall." Wrote Byron: "There is a smugness to the phrase, a satisfaction that stems from finding safety in a time when octogenarians are kicked to death on city streets and widows are raped behind the bolted doors of their homes." While the courts have, in some states, ruled against adults-only rental housing, common-interest communities can have it their way. About 10 percent of co-ops, condominiums, and planned unit developments in the country now have age restrictions, according to the Community Associations Institute, the national trade association for common-interest communities. These are minimum, not maximum, age requirements set as low as thirty-five or as high as fifty-five—but in none of these communities are children welcome. Some cities have actually encouraged this by making a deal with developers: the cities, eager to tap the senior citizen tax base without having to provide expensive municipal services, have allowed developers to build higher-density complexes in exchange for the no-children restrictions. Senior zoning, as it is called, can be a minor windfall for cities in need of revenue.

David Wolfe, who specializes in the management of common-interest communities, worries about the social effects of the golden ghettos. "The day is coming when the nation will be dominated by mature adults, and if the housing trends continue we may have a nation dominated by people who have, in significant numbers, walled themselves off from the rest of the country." Wolfe's organization conducted a study of the Rossmoor Leisure World, a seniors-only planned community in Silver Springs, Maryland, and found that "basically, once seniors moved in, they didn't leave. About 90 percent of them have voluntarily withdrawn from the outside world. They don't leave Leisure World, except for shopping. They don't go out for theater, movies, vacations. The community is so self-contained that the only thing lacking that would force them to go outside the community, other than shopping, is a cemetery."

Broward County, Florida, heavily condoized, may well mirror the kind of separation of young from old that may be seen nationally sometime after the year 2000, when a third of America will be over sixty. This point is not lost on demographer James E. Smith. Smith is the research manager for the *Ft. Lauderdale News and Sun Sentinel,* a newspaper that recognized early on that, in order to remain solvent, it would have to understand the aging of Florida and the rise of condo America. For at least a portion of the elderly condominium dwellers, Smith disputes the notion that people move into these communities and then draw the bridge up behind them and never come out. Many seniors live in condominium developments precisely because they want freedom, not constriction, says Smith. "Freedom is important for the condo lifestyle. It's hard to maintain and secure a detached private home if you're gone for a long time. A condo takes care of all that. Joining is important, too. With older people, joining is a way of life, a way of passing time, getting involved with their environment, and maintaining some sense of control. That's important for older retired people, who are out of power. They need a sense of personal efficacy, which can be found in a ceramics class or campaigning for a congressman. The seniors in these condos are very much like those who live in the trailer parks in Arizona. They have a frenetic need to join, but it's a strange kind of joining—there's a great camaraderie and wide networks, but people often aren't really intimate. The expectation is that a significant percentage of those people won't be around next year, so why get close?"

Because of the aging process, these communities are, in fact, beginning to suffer their own internal generation gap. The developers of many of these communities provided golf courses but no long-term health-care facilities, so many of the elderly are being forced, because of their health, to move out. In some instances, the ambulatory elderly have come to the rescue of the nonambulatory. Volunteer organizations have begun to appear within the seniors-only communities. And planned developments for the elderly are becoming increasingly sophisticated. Just as the residents of Irvine are segmented on the basis of income and recreational preferences, the elderly residents of some of the newer planned communities are segmented on the basis of health. These "life-care" communities are now in vogue in aging Florida and in other states.

In Virginia, a corporation is planning Williamsburg Landing, a self-contained city for seniors. The project will include luxury condos, nursing home, bank, grocery store, cafeteria, tavern, ice cream parlor, hair salon, post office, library, chapel, tennis courts, and swimming pools. One can buy a "life right" to live in the community; the monthly maintenance fee (for the maintaining of body and home) is $600 to $1300. The project will be finished in 1984. Developers of these communities will enter into a joint agreement with a nursing home, which will agree to locate on the premises; that way, if a resident has a stroke, the spouse can walk over and visit in the nursing home. At one development in Miami, you can move in when you're sixty-five, and take your meals in your own apartment; if you cease being ambulatory, you can eat in a common area. Other developments include graduated housing styles, so people can maintain the same social networks as their health deteriorates and they move from independent housing to semiindependent housing, and, finally, to the nursing home.

The result of all of this, for the elderly, is a sense of independence from what they sense is a deteriorating society. But a resentment that flows both ways is built into the structure. In

Florida, the movement of seniors behind the walls may preview an economic war between the old and the young.

"The problem with the O.P.'s [common term for "old people" in Broward County] is not how to take care of them; it's how to keep them from killing the rest of us," a policeman's wife told Pacific News Service editor Rasa Gustaitis. Gustaitis's research, partially financed by the Fund for Investigative Journalism, found that "the aged . . . have bought the American promise of work followed by earned leisure. So now they shy away from social concerns with the catchphrase, 'We've paid our dues.' Thus, when Dade County proposed a drastic budget cut (in the summer of 1980), hoping thereby to avert a tax cut initiative of disastrous proportions, the biggest slice came out of Headstart, a preschool program." Spending for schools plummeted beginning in the late 1970s; in 1978, Florida, one of the richest states, spent the smallest percentage of its wealth on education. (In 1982, California, another wealthy condoized state, won that distinction.)

"Ocean County, New Jersey, is one of the places that encouraged senior zoning," says David Wolfe, common-interest community management specialist. "The politicians said, hey, now we can enjoy a tax base of social security recipients without the burdens of having to build schools, and so today you can't get a bond issue passed."

With the spread of adults-only planned communities, and the conversion of countless apartments into adults-only condominiums, people with children find it harder and harder to find a place to live. And within the age-restricted common-interest communities, this kind of reverse ageism (ironic in a time when many senior activists insist that people not be fired or retired because of age) has some tragic consequences. There have been cases in which residents who take in children because of a divorce or death in the family are forced from their homes by their community association.

BUNKER SWEET BUNKER

An important underlying motivation for the withdrawal of seniors behind the walls is fear, and the packagers of the new shelter are sensitive to that motivation. Security is one of the easiest marketing devices to insert into the design of a common-interest community; it is far easier to create the illusion, or even the reality, of security than the illusion or reality of community or nature. In the early 1960s, security and health-enhancement were important in marketing the first retirement communities. But with the passage of Medicare in 1966, the marketing emphasis moved almost entirely to security. A 1976 buyer survey conducted for Rossmoor Corporation found that 92 percent of the new and resale home buyers at Rossmoor's California Leisure World rated security as "extremely important." Six-foot block walls topped with two-foot-high bands of barbed wire rim the Leisure World communities, and private security forces with more than 300 officers patrol the grounds.

The provision of security also gives the elderly a sense of control and identity. Sun City, near Phoenix, has its own volunteer posse—average age sixty-eight. The oldest volunteer, in 1981, was eighty-four years old. Volunteers dress up in regulation brown-and-beige uniforms, Stetsons, and pistols and patrol their retirement community. They have cut petty theft by 32 percent since 1971. Insurance companies, noting this, have charged Sun City homeowners lower premiums. The patrol is supported by the 5000 residents of the retirement community, who contribute $50,000 annually. Says demographer James Smith: "On the east coast of Florida, security is by far the most important attraction. There are always guards at the high-rises, a lot of TV equipment, in some cases passkeys and electronic locks. Very often the guards are posted at the gates of the developments. They'll have spikes to blow tires. You need to be known to get in and out. We have a lot of trouble delivering newspapers at these places. We've had to have some of our carriers bonded, their references checked by the bonding company, which is liable for any losses. A lot of our newspaper distribution is by racks in a central location. Some condo developments won't let the paper carriers in even when the kids are bonded. That's a little disconcerting to us, but you have to realize that condos do afford the elderly a sense of security and a fairly large parameter of travel. Without condos, they'd be locked in their rooms without the social networking."

The use of security in design and marketing spread quickly to all sizes of common-interest communities. In fact, as the size of homes has been shrinking, the value of security has replaced the value of land ownership. The phenomenon described by Smith in the Florida senior condos is true of the new shelter in general.

In America II, elbowroom is not just defined by the perimeters of one's land, but by how far one can walk safely. This has been accomplished by two techniques. One is the general design of the developments, which allows "defensible space." This is the equivalent of circling the wagons: designing a community so that residences face a courtyard or other visible, and therefore defensible, landscape. The second method is the use of private police and high-tech security systems, as seen at The Woodlands. (To add to the wagon train metaphor, it should be pointed out that in his later years, John Wayne moved out of his own fortified ranch and into a Newport Beach condominium.) Almost every new condominium project now includes some form of high-tech security. A luxury condominium high-rise in La Jolla, California, has its own exclusive bomb shelter. Survive Tomorrow, Inc., an organization that believes social order is coming apart and atomic holocaust is near, is building completely self-sufficient underground condominiums in La Verkin, Utah.

There is some question as to the effectiveness of all this high-tech security. As of 1981, there has never been a rape or a murder in Leisure World. Some residents even leave their cars and homes unlocked at night. But how much of this is due to the defensible space design, and how much to electronic security systems, is not known. Studies have shown that the concept of defensible space does work, but the high-tech security systems have not proved entirely worth the cost. Says community designer Wayne Williams: "The members of the building industry don't even talk about this themselves. The assumption would be that electronic surveillance systems and the rest work, but they may not. What we do know is happening is that residents, by submitting themselves to these systems, are actually giving a lot of control of their life patterns to criminals. A dog knows when you're afraid of it, and I'm not so sure people aren't the same."

More and more money is going into electronics that could be going into better design, or into social functions that encourage residents to know and watch out for each other. Community Associations Institute reports no studies that reliably prove the effectiveness of the security systems, but, says director David Kleine, "We've been getting a lot of reports of crime inside these communities; they've figured out how to keep people out, but they haven't figured out how to protect themselves from each other." Meanwhile, the race toward high-tech security continues, with implications that extend far beyond the immediate design and selling of condo America.

LASER BEAMS AND JANE FONDA: THE SELLING OF THE ULTIMATE BUNKER-CONDO

I stood in the computerized central command post, surrounded by a battery of computers and TV monitors that keep track of the well-to-do residents of the Towers of Quayside, a condo community that illustrates where the technological and psychological packaging could, for many Americans, lead. The command post looked like a smaller version of NASA's mission control. Standing next to me was Jeremiah Mullane, a large ex–New York burglary detective who, in the bicentennial year of 1976, was chief of security for the Freedom Train, a steam-powered exhibition that went chugging from Washington, D.C., to California to promote patriotism and to celebrate 200 years of freedom. Mullane was saying, in his New York–Irish brogue, "This is a wonderful security system. Nothing happens here without our knowing about it. Nothing. This system is the state of the art; why, we had some Peruvian generals come up and check this thing out."

Around Mullane, a cadre of efficient young men and women, in natty gray-and-white uniforms with American flag patches on their sleeves, were hustling about with a sense of purpose, bending over the television monitors. On two of the monitors, side by side, Quayside's own community television station was airing an exercise program. There she was, the Queen of the Left, on her side stretching her legs, staring seductively into the camera, surrounded by all those high-tech security monitors—Jane Fonda, if you could only see yourself now.

The new Towers of Quayside, like several other large, high-security condominium projects in Florida (one of them is built on its own island), have unleashed all the marketing weapons of the new shelter: nostalgia, community, leisure, lifestyle, and especially security. "Sometimes," Quayside's director of publicity had told me on the phone before my visit, "I have to go across the street to the K-Mart to get back to reality." Quayside's cluster of high- and low-rise condominiums is on the site of what once was a boys' military school. Its sales techniques are targeted specifically at affluent people between the ages of thirty-five and forty-five. The man who envisioned all of this, Ronald K. Lavin, wanted, like Disney, to recreate his own childhood in the 1920s in Providence, Rhode Island. And so Quayside's effusive literature describes "the throbbing soul of Quayside . . . the spirit of the Great Houses of the roaring '20s of the Great Gatsby years. In the Hamptons. Oyster Bay. West Egg. Where colorful frocks still swirl, men are still dapper. Day-to-day proof that all the joy of those happy times in a carefree America can be recreated. . . . The Towers of Quayside is for everyone who has earned a right to appreciate it!" A trolley scoots through the grounds. To avoid the traffic, residents can commute to Miami, across the bay, in a private water taxi—a sleek craft, futuristic on the outside, but all teak and mahogany and nostalgia on the inside. If the residents do not want to venture outside the development, they can turn to Quayside's television channel for a bout of electronic window-shopping. Quayside staff trundle their minicams into exclusive Bal Harbour, interview the shop owners, review new products that the residents can order from their rooms or from poolside. The development is oriented toward the needs of the body; walking through it one is impressed by the number of young men in white tennis shorts sipping oversized drinks, by the grass tennis court, by the daily diet buffet, and by the spa offering mineral baths, herbal wraps, loofah scrubs, and salt glows.

However, as the rate of violent crime in Miami increased 405 percent in the 1970s, compared with 62 percent for the entire United States, security became by far the most important marketing tool. So Quayside developed the most marketable residential security system around. Mullane and his uniformed young administrative assistant, Robert Huseman, are intensely proud of the system. "This is the heart of the whole place," said Mullane, smiling. He motioned to Jane Fonda. "We'll get to her in just a minute. I know she's more interesting than a computer, but . . ." Huseman began to tick off all the wondrous effects of this security system: "Each tower has its own separate computer system; we're decentralized so we're not vulnerable to being knocked out at a central location. Our computer program is called SIRS, which means Security Information Retrieval System. It automatically assimilates all information pertinent to an alarm. We have sixty-five emergency phones located throughout the property. The computer identifies if an emergency phone has been taken off the hook, notifies us where it's at, and it's investigated. You don't even have to say a word. The computer system controls property entry and cross-references this information through an alphanumeric filing system. We call it View."

Huseman requested that a young woman punch a few buttons on a terminal.

"There: Mullane, Jeremiah, 9140. You automatically have all the information and code numbers for Mr. Mullane. If he's at the gate, you can now challenge him or admit him." When a visitor arrives and asks to see a Quayside resident, the guards at the security gate call the resident, who turns on the television, switches to a certain channel, and sees whoever is at the gate before approving the entry. Rudimentary versions of this viewing system are increasingly popular in condo communities.

An alarm, a flashing light, went off across the room.

"This is a normal alarm coming in—a perimeter alarm."

Quayside's perimeter is protected by laser beams. A network of these zipping laser beams scoot along the walls around the community, turn at a radical right angle, head out to sea, turn again, and, above the waves, create an invisible wall surrounding the private marina; then the beams connect again with the real wall, embracing the Towers of Quayside.

I asked Huseman if the laser beams were dangerous.

"Nope. There's laws about how intensified they can be. Should anybody attempt an intrusion, the computer automatically records the point of entry. Response time is seconds! You measure between sixty and ninety seconds on an average. If a burglar alarm goes off or somebody pushes an emergency button inside their condo, we phone the unit. We allow three telephone rings. If the resident answers and provides the proper code number, we accept that as a false alarm. Should they fail to furnish the proper code number, or their phone be busy or the phone not be answered at all, then we automatically dispatch an officer. When the officer arrives we require the resident to step outside the unit and physically show that he is under no duress in order to clear the alarm."

He pointed to the rows of television monitors: "We also monitor the spa, tennis courts and swimming areas, racquetball courts. We get at least one picture a second from every camera on property, and we store that on a videocassette for at least a ten-day period, including license plates as they come on the property, or faces, if we desire. We have a filmed record of who comes on the property, and should anything happen, we're free to check back.

The computer automatically does our time scheduling for us; if anybody tells us that they're going to have guests here for, say, thirty days, we know when they're supposed to be gone. We keep a history, a hard copy of everything that's gone on, for three years. Every night, the events of the day are automatically printed out."

The surveillance system even monitors Quayside's food storage areas and employees. Mullane added, "We keep track of these things because we may have a break in internal security, an employee who is stealing, so we can step right in and correct it."

"We're also in constant communication with the water taxi," said Huseman. "And, in the event of a hurricane, this becomes the hurricane tracking center for the property. We track every hurricane or storm as it starts to take shape, via satellite, via NOAH. In an emergency, we have the ability to plug into channel 11 Quayside and communicate directly to the residents through the TV. They can't communicate to us. We can communicate to them. If the resident is asleep," elaborated Huseman, "we have a manual audible alarm, and we can also address them on the public address system. It has a 90-decibel signal, which I guarantee will wake up anyone, anytime, from a state of unconsciousness."

I asked Mullane how easy it would be to adapt such a system to a town or a city. No problem, he said, not if you imagined a city as just being a lot of condos spread out over a large area. "It would be a good idea if it was economically feasible, and I think you're going to see this with the advent of cable TV. After all, most people in this country are looking for a good night's sleep, and this is the system that affords them a very good night's sleep without the fear of intrusion or what have you." (In fact, Miami Beach recently installed anticrime television monitors on strategic rooftops.)

Mullane, who said he cannot afford to live at Quayside, lives in a house, protected by what he described as "the best alarm that you can have," a large dog. I asked him if Quayside allowed dogs. "They do," he answered, "under a certain size and under a certain poundage."

The psychological effect of such security systems is as important as the physical deterrence. Earlier in the day, I had interviewed a member of the Quayside staff. "It's not just people around here who worry about security," she said. "I have friends in Coconut Grove who get out of their cars with a can of mace and a gun. I can't afford to live here, but I do live in a condo—I'd never live in a house, because of the crime. I get out of my car in a building where there's cameras and a security guy. You don't really have any privacy until you're inside your condo. You have a friend stay over, they know it." She paused. "Everyone here is happy. Most of them are just now moving in, and they're talking about decorating their condos. There's everything here you could want. The three restaurants, the spa. Eventually we'll have the convenience store and a beauty salon. And they all stay here—they pay so much in their maintenance fee to maintain all the restaurants and everything that they do everything here. Some of them really can't afford to be here, so they're really trapped. Some people sit in their condo all day and just watch the security channel, just sit there and watch who's coming in the front gate. I like to get out of a place . . . and I like some privacy. Some of the condos . . . I've heard they have units in there so the security guys can listen in. That stuff's supposed to be used for emergencies, but they can turn it on at any time, if they think there's a good party going on and they're bored."

I asked Mullane if his security officers could listen in on the lives within the condos.

"Absolutely not. There's laws that prohibit that kind of thing. Of course not." People who think that's true, he said, are just believing rumors, imagining things.

At some point, though, in a community where life is so packaged, the illusion and the reality are particularly difficult to separate. The illusion begins to grow beyond its intended perimeters.

That night I slept, or tried to sleep, in a Quayside luxury condo set aside for visitors. It had its own glass elevator, Gatsby-era art deco furniture, mirrors everywhere. The unit's alarm system was not working properly and kept going off. Four times during the night, security guards came to the door, calling back to the command post over their walkie-talkies. Nearby was a life-size mahogany statute of a nude woman, surrounded on three sides by mirrors. I paced. I switched on the television to see if Jane Fonda was still stretching. She wasn't. I switched again. There was the front gate. The cars rolled silently in and people looked at me through the camera, irritated. As the night wore on, the spaces between the cars grew longer.

The next morning I was driven away from Quayside by a cabdriver from Haiti. "Am I glad to get out of there," I said. He laughed. He told me he had come to the United States two years ago. He had friends in the Haitian refugee camps across town, and he said he wanted to go home. "I came here because I thought I could go to college. I was wrong. I end up driving a cab. Three years, maybe things get better back there, then I go home."

I asked him what he thought of the Towers of Quayside.

"I did not know places like that were in America."

CONTROL THY NEIGHBOR

One of the myths of the 1980s is that Americans want less governmental control over their lives. Big government may be out of fashion, but not little government—especially private government. In a single decade, a whole new level of democratic self-rule has arisen: tens of thousands of private minigovernments, called community associations, controlling common-interest communities. For the first time, local government faces a private government competitor in the delivery of public services, and what may become a formidable challenge to its political status. This new level of private self-government is less dramatic than laser beam security systems, but it may well have a more lasting effect on the culture, raising serious questions about the promises and excesses of democracy and about individuality and social conformity in America II. To those who do not live in condominiums or other types of planned communities, community associations might not seem particularly important. But soon, over half of all the new housing available will be in these communities. Indeed, the Eleventh Commandment of the shelter revolution may be "Control thy neighbor."

These private governments proliferate at a time when local government faces serious challenges: budget cutbacks, the weakening effects of population deconcentration, the difficulty of responding quickly to citizens' needs in a complex age. In a sense, city halls and statehouses are becoming as distant from people's lives as Washington, and a new minor league of politics has entered the scene. According to Wendell E. Hucher, former mayor of Ann Arbor, Michigan, local governments are so busy keeping track of paper and computer work that they no longer have much time for the everyday concerns of people. As a result, writes Hucher: "Evidence is accumulating that homeowners desire even more local government of their own choosing, in the form of community associations through which they can express their needs and desires." Community associations have been recognized by various courts as minigovernments within democratic subsocieties. Community associations are similar to other groups, such as tenant organizations and voluntary homeowners' associations. But in most condominium complexes and other planned communities, membership in a community association is, as part of the founding covenants, mandatory.

These associations are established under the guidelines of covenants, conditions, and restrictions (CC&Rs) drawn up originally by the developer. The developer initially appoints the board of directors and the officers, but as title to the property is turned over to the residents, they take control of the minigovernment, electing a board of directors and officers. Community associations operate within the general guidelines of the CC&Rs and bylaws, but these and any other regulations can eventually be changed, through voting, by the residents. Also, the board can act in a semijudicial way, arbitrating disputes between the owners or between the owners and the association.

Community associations assess fees and levy fines, contract with maintenance and security firms, and perform many of the duties normally associated with more traditional forms of government. Community associations often control the color of the units or houses, who can use the pool, what kind of trees can be planted, what boulders can be moved, or even the color of the curtain liners. The associations in many condos fine residents for taking their trash out during daylight hours. In Florida, a woman was fined by her community association for hanging an American flag on her balcony—no hanging objects were allowed on balconies. Indeed, the control often reaches into the intimate details of residents' lives in ways that may be infringing on constitutional rights. This is happening even as community associations offer, to many Americans, their first opportunity for a real community role. To some residents, of course, participation in one of these private minigovernments is a burden and a bore; but to others, such intimate self-governance is part of the package, a way to get a sense of personal efficacy and power.

PRIVATE POWER

Statistically, the phenomenon is amazing. In 1980, the number of community associations surpassed the national total of small-town governments, as well as every other formally recognized elected local government. At last count, according to the League of Cities, there were approximately 38,500 units of elected local government in the nation (townships, boroughs, cities, and counties) compared with nearly 50,000 community associations, governing populations of a few dozen to tens of thousands. Almost all of this growth has occurred since 1971, when there were only 2000 community associations. In 1982, nearly 10 million Americans were members. In Florida, active community associations have grown to more than 6000, compared with only 460 elected local governments. As Community Management Corporation's David Wolfe puts it: "Like a silent fog on a warm spring evening, the community association movement has rolled into modern residential environments barely noticed."

The fog is moving quickly. In 1971, the total annual revenues collected by these entities totaled about $125 million. By 1980, the annual assessments had risen to $8 billion. According to a report by the Department of Housing and Urban Development, community associations will be collecting about $20 billion a year by the end of the decade, placing them among the largest economic centers of activity in the nation. They already collect more revenue than the nation's small towns and may soon come to represent more financial power than all elected local governments in the United States combined.

The range of goods and services bought by these associations is impressive. Fancy electronic surveillance systems, private police, telephone answering services, central utilities, and homeowners' insurance are all purchased with the leverage of group buying power. This communal approach is quite attractive to the service provider; instead of an insurance agent dealing with 300 or 400 individual consumers for property coverage, he or she deals only with the community association. As a result, the cost of such coverage is often reduced by as much as 60 percent. Some community associations are even buying group vacations and communal computers, which could in the future be used for an array of purposes, including shopping from the safe confines of the condominium.

With their ability to raise money and organize, common-interest communities are becoming an important collective political force in the most condoized states: Florida and California, and also New York, Illinois, Virginia, Michigan, Ohio, Pennsylvania, Texas, Arizona, and New Jersey. (In Florida, political activists from the retirement condo communities are called "condo commandos.") Jimmy Carter was the first major politician to recognize this. In the Florida primary of 1975, Carter sent telegrams to all the condominium associations and promised that he would abolish certain unpopular recreation fees (established originally by developers in the form of leases) that were tied to the price of gold, food, or the general cost of living. As it turned out, Carter as President could do nothing about the leases, but in the Florida primary he won the condo vote.

Enormous and, in many instances unrealized, political power is attached to community associations: power in the wider political marketplace, but also power to take on developers, to secede from larger political bodies, and to control the lives of the residents. The revolutionary parallel of this could be the political stages of developing nations: first the colony (the condo) fights for its independence from the mother country; then it does away with the original revolutionary leaders (by suing developers); then, often, it falls into a paroxysm of internal fighting and repression. In some cases, counterrevolution corrects the excesses.

Cutting Loose

The process is set in motion by the developer, who establishes the community association to govern a variety of private services. Traditional local governments no longer have the resources to provide all the streets, sewers, and other amenities required by new development; this is not just because of decreased revenues, but also because of population deconcentration, which, by its nature, works counter to centralized government. Consequently, developers, in order to gain construction permits, are now likely to build these services into a development without relying on local government. For instance, to assure local governments that their developments will not be a burden on the tax base, Shapell Industries, the developer of San Diego's Rancho Carmel, promised that two permanent jobs would be created for each housing unit built, and that the company would privately finance the public facilities—streets and traffic signals, water and sewage lines, library and parks, and even the fire station; all services traditionally provided by cities or counties. This private approach makes economic sense, but in the process the ties and common responsibilities normally assumed by the public are slowly taken under the corporate wing: the public space becomes the private enclave.

Taking on the Developer

Often, once the new planned community is finished and the residents have moved in and begun to take control of their community association, then comes the revolt. Sanford Goodkin, one of the first housing experts to predict in the early 1970s the course that condo power would take, writes: "The builder always knew that in his last development, his buyers were his future enemies on any rezoning. Now the builder organizes an association. The builder is the direct catalyst of his own downfall!" Not only has the builder or developer created a potent and standing unit of citizen action, he has created a physical structure in which people are, logistically, easier to organize. So, when amenities do not live up to the developer's promises, the residents are ready to take up arms—or at least folded copies of the CC&Rs.

One such case occurred at Lake Ridge, a planned community in Prince William County near Washington, D.C. It was sold as a "nature lover's paradise," with brochures depicting three young people sitting on a green riverbank, fishing in placid, pollution-free water. Homeowners were told when they bought into Lake Ridge that fifteen wooded acres in the midst of the development would remain parkland forever, and some buyers paid thousands of dollars extra to live close to the woods. When another development was planned for the woods, the angry and frustrated middle- and upper middle–income homeowners, many of them in the military, formed the Citizens for the Protection of the Lake Ridge Environment. They collected signatures, picketed, and appealed, unsuccessfully, to local government. Some owners claimed that they would chain themselves to the trees in the woods, where, as the Lake Ridge brochure says, "quiet hours can be spent reflecting, relaxing, enjoying the wonders of nature." The dispute was destined for the courts.

Among the first acts of a community association, once the control is turned over to the residents, is quite often the firing of any community managers or community management companies originally hired by the developer. Another likelihood is that the association, eventually, will sue the developer.

The Power of Secession

Conflict with local government arises chiefly from the increasingly blurred distinction between public and private space. For example, are the streets of a condo community public streets or private streets? Some complex legal arrangements are emerging from such questions.

Outside Chicago, the village of Schaumburg, Illinois, where more than half of the residents belong to community associations, has made an arrangement whereby the municipal government fixes the streets, billing the associations 25 percent of the cost. Common-interest communities are following the example of shopping malls, entities that lobbied successfully in the 1960s for the expenditure of public funds to pay for the enforcement of traffic laws in private parking lots. Many common-interest associations, though, are wondering if they really want government involved in their tiny kingdoms; they resent the "double tax" (private fees on one hand, public taxes on the other). Given a choice, most residents seem to prefer private services to those provided publicly.

At least one condominium complex has legally seceded from the municipality it was in. In the mid-1970s, the residents of the planned community of Pennsbury Village, Pennsylvania, were outraged when Robinson Township ordered them to hook into the township's sewer system. The residents of Pennsbury Village, which had its own private system that worked better than Robinson's, were to be required to tap into an inferior public system, and then be assessed for the use of their own lines. So they raised $20,000 to finance the successful secession. As Don Speakman, twenty-eight, the development's fundraiser (and now its private tax collector) said, "We have come out on top financially, but that wasn't really the point. The point was we want our money's worth. We don't mind paying for services but we want to get what we pay for." Outside the condo complex's front gate is an inscription by Abraham Lincoln (who had a lot more to say about secession than sewers), advising all who enter that no man is so wise as to govern another man without his consent.

Taking on Each Other

It is important to understand how different this new level of democracy is from traditional American local government. Planned communities and condominiums were born of covenant law, derived from English common law, which is restrictive: it tells you what you *cannot* do. The federal constitution of the United States, by contrast, is enabling: it tells you your rights, what you *can* do, and what the government cannot. Ralph C. Meyer, associate professor of political science at Fordham University, is one of the few political scientists who has studied community associations. Meyer suggests that America may be witnessing the birth of a strange governmental hybrid, for which he can find no other corollary.

One departure from traditional American government is the use of "weighted" voting. Community associations, Meyer says, are closer to the classical liberalism of Locke and Burke (one-man, one-vote, as long as you were a property owner) than it is to our current form of government, in which anyone, regardless of whether they own property, can vote. In many community associations, the weight of a resident's vote depends on how many units he or she owns, or how expensive the unit was. In other words, a resident who spent several thousand dollars more for a unit with a view may have more voting power than a neighbor who owns a similar unit without a view. Community association law (which today is fluid, but beginning to be tested in the courts) is based on common law, not on traditional American constitutional law. One result is that the minigovernments are more like the British parliamentary system, with condominium boards electing the association president, who serves as a sort of prime minister.

Another departure is that residents own the grounds and amenities in common. This is different from the public ownership of parks and streets, in that the parks and streets are open to everyone, regardless of residency or property ownership. Community associations have been perceived by some as socialistic.

This is not, of course, true socialism: no money or property is transferred from the rich to the poor; nor do residents control the means of production. Rather, community associations could be considered a form of democratic socialism based on property rights, or even a form of communalism (defined by *Webster's New World Dictionary* as a "theory or system of government in which local communes or local communities, sometimes on an ethnic or religious basis, have virtual autonomy within a federated state," and also "the conflicting allegiance resulting from this").

Libertarian ideology suggests that, given a laissez-faire environment, "protective associations," groups of people united in the pursuit of mutual goals, will naturally arise within geographic boundaries. But the kind of rules that often come with life in a condo, at least within the community, have more to do with restriction than with liberty.

Meyer describes what he calls the dictatorial tendencies of some community association boards. "Some of them do all sorts of things to control people: they overthrow committees they don't like, keep the press out of their meetings, prevent residents from talking or even attending board meetings, engage in nuisance lawsuits, verbally harass members. Some sort of power is, of course necessary, but not abusive power. I know of one board of directors who turned a car over when a resident parked in the wrong parking space. I definitely think some people are having their constitutional rights abridged." Meyer's analysis is shared by most condominium management specialists, a whole industry springing up around the nation to take over the books when condo residents become frustrated with self-rule.

The legal messiness and political power of the shelter revolution is slowly becoming more clear, especially to those who have moved in. Fred Blecksmith, a San Diego architect, sued his condominium association because it voted to economize by turning off the central air-conditioning in the development: "My unit was rendered virtually unusable, since it has more exposure to the afternoon sun than any of the others. Why should they dictate to me the temperature of my home? When I put up some blinds outside to cut down the sun, the association threatened to put a lien on my property." Blecksmith, who was vice president of the association during its initial year, adds: "They can sell your place out from under you. That's the scary part. The only way to fight an association which blatantly deprives some of the owners of their rights, the only thing you can do is go to court. There's no method of appeal with an association. Several others and I filed suit at considerable expense to get what was ours in the first place. To top it off, we pay homeowners' fees and they're using our fees to pay their attorney! So we're paying for lawyers on both sides of the dispute. About a fourth of the units are for sale because of all the rules. And it's certainly brought down our property values."

Just as with more familiar forms of government, community association boards have considerable room for monetary abuse and cronyism. According to a Southern California condo management company, the president of one condominium development hired a friend to redo an entranceway; the work cost the residents $25,000, when it should only have cost $2000. A treasurer of a small condominium development in Miami absconded with $45,000. At a large planned community near Washington, D.C., the treasurer stole $125,000 from his friends and neighbors. The degree of condo corruption is slowly becoming more widely apparent. In some areas of the country, "sunshine laws" are being passed to require that condominium boards meet in public. Courts are more likely today than a decade ago to treat associations as true legislative bodies. And the boards are more vulnerable, given this kind of scrutiny, than they might realize. Community associations operate under a dual system of law: they are held accountable under both government law and business law. When community associations legislate equity rights, for instance, they are operating under government law and must, therefore, assure due process. But when a community association distributes assets, it is held accountable under business law. Says Community Management Corporation's Wolfe: "There has been a big question in the legal community as to how much the corporate shield protects a member of the board of directors of a community association. The area is still hazy, but community associations are theoretically putting their entire estates on the line. They're quite vulnerable." Nonetheless, many boards continue to operate without much scrutiny from the residents or from the press.

Why does all this conflict take place? Baird & Warner Mortgage and Realty Investors contends that an apartment renter who becomes a condo owner may undergo personality changes: a tenant who is docile and mild-mannered as an apartment dweller often becomes ill-tempered and aggressive in asserting his or her rights as an owner. In preparing his preliminary study of condo power, political scientist Meyer wondered why the dictator syndrome was so prevalent in community associations. Was it, he asked, that condominiums attracted a certain kind of person more likely to try to control his or her neighbor? He studied the personality types of a number of low-rise and high-rise condo communities, and ultimately concluded that the answer was not to be found in personality types—the personalities of the residents were no more authoritarian than the general population. Future research, he suggests, should look in other directions: perhaps there is something inherent in the design of condominiums, or in the way a particular common-interest community is born. Wolfe agrees: "In the beginning, if a developer is cynical both in the design of the community and in the promises he makes and doesn't keep, the community is immediately off on the wrong foot; the die is cast."

Also inherent in the shelter revolution is a certain discord over ownership, a conflict between traditional American ideals and economic realities. Ownership is an increasingly elusive ideal. After all, the Pan American building in New York is on leased land; so is Park Avenue and a good deal of Palm Springs. But the idea of owning one's own home is different; it is one of the most basic components of the American Dream. In America II, our homes are our castles, plus .28657 percent of the common area, which, as novelist Florence King points out, "is not big enough for a grave." Americans, she writes, "are psychologically unfit to own condos. The whole concept clashes with the 'all mine' exclusivity that lurks beneath our democratic veneer. The feeling that everybody owns everything while nobody owns anything produces a shade of gray that not even the Architectural Deviation Committee can cope with. Where land ownership is concerned, every American is an only child."

THE COMING COUNTERREVOLUTION

Regardless of the strains on our expectations, the new shelter is here to stay. This does not, however, mean that the conflict and the regimentation of architecture, landscaping, and human behavior are unavoidable. If common-interest communities represent the American future, we need to define our choices. Indeed, a kind of counterrevolution is already brewing.

David Wolfe, for one, holds to the original dream that these communities can bring people together rather than segment and restrict them. He moves from association to association teaching "first of all, a consciousness of tolerance. This even comes down to simple things like the names of committees. We've found that when an association has a rules committee or a pet defecation committee, which you'll find in most communities, the leadership tends to be negative; so we suggest resolutions committee or pet committee, which are more positive and enabling phrases."

However, something deeper than better committee names is needed. The design and selling of these communities are inseparable from the eventual tone of their minigovernments. In Finland, a planned community called Tapiola illustrates the difference between a restrictive and an enabling community in its design and government. Instead of grouping people of the same age into clusters, Tapiola provides housing for the elderly adjacent to the school yard; the elderly volunteer as teachers' aides. Tapiola also established a foundation as part of its community association, which awards grants to residents, seed money to start community projects.

What it comes down to is the intent behind the controls. The design of a community and its government are intimately interwoven. Ultimately, the form determines the function.

The Village Homes Alternative

Village Homes in Davis, California, serves as an alternative to the dominant trends in shelter. Unlike most other common-interest communities, the emphasis here is on production, not consumption.

This emphasis appears to have a profound effect on the way the residents govern themselves. The exterior looks no different from other new communities, with beige townhouses clustered together in little culs-de-sac. But the first difference one notices is that the development, which includes about 300 homes, is surrounded by a ring of orchards rather than a wall. A second difference is that Village Homes is an intricate maze; the houses all point inward onto pedestrian walkways, bike paths, gardens, swatches of green. All cars, garages, and parking places are hidden away from the common areas and walkways.

The developer, or "master builder," as he prefers, is Michael Corbett, a lanky, soft-spoken man, disdainful of most architects and developers, "who think they can sit a hundred miles or a thousand miles away, and plan how people will live." Early on, Village Homes was designed by Corbett and future residents who walked across the tomato field, suggesting a community garden go here, a cluster of houses there.

Village Homes was probably the first totally solar neighborhood in the nation. The residents, mostly middle-class professionals, heat and cool their homes exclusively with solar energy and wood stoves. Almost every yard in Village Homes has an attractively arranged vegetable garden. On the roofs of some homes are clusters of grapevines that thicken in the summer, providing shade, and thin in the winter, letting the sun's rays through.

As in most planned communities or condo developments, the residents are required to pay a homeowner's fee. At Village Homes, the fee is fifty dollars a month, unless one chooses to help take care of the common areas; in that case, the fee is dropped to thirty dollars. Ninety-five percent of the residents pay the thirty-dollar fee.

"The grapes are a cash crop," Corbett said as we approached a small vineyard set off to one side of the community in a common area. "We've got 15,000 pounds of grapes eventually coming out of here. We have twelve acres of large-scale projects like vineyards and orchards. . . . This is a little cherry orchard here, and a pistachio nut orchard, and this is buckwheat cover. We have a head agriculturist, a head ornamentalist—he deals with ornamental plants—and two staff members, hired by the community association, just like park maintenance people. The food production is all organic. There's no rule that says you can't use pesticides, but there's a general consensus that we don't use any, or at least keep the spraying to a minimum." He pointed down a path: "Just beyond there, in the latest houses we've built, almost every house has a greenhouse. Over here is a community composting area; everybody composts their gardens in their own yards, but this is for the bigger stuff."

We walked on farther, to the edge of Village Homes. "This

section up here is the beginning of our major agricultural strip. Eventually our hope is that one person could farm this intensively and sell the produce to the other residents of Village Homes and to a community restaurant, which we're hoping to build next to our community office building over there. We're also hoping to build an eight-room inn. We already grow so much food in our own yards that we don't really need to buy that much."

One of the most remarkable facts about Village Homes is that on this small plot, once a tomato field, the land still produces crops. The residents of Village Homes, in fact, are raising almost as much food on this land as when it was in full farm production and owned by agribusiness. This productivity is possible because gardening is more labor intensive than agribusiness, uses much less of the expensive petroleum-based fertilizers and pesticides, produces a wider variety of food, and wastes less. When people buy a house and move into Village Homes, they are also buying into an agricultural reserve capable of providing 40 to 50 percent of a family's food needs.

Food production is not the only means of self-reliance. Volunteers built the community swimming pool and the playground. Residents also own shares in common land held back for future sales or development, shares of profit from rental property in Village Homes, shares of profits from future community businesses like the inn and restaurant. "For now, no one's making any money on this," Corbett explained. "It'll be about fifteen years and then people won't have to pay the thirty-dollar homeowner fees; in forty years people who live here will have some additional income from the jointly owned land. This takes a long time, but it's putting ownership of the country in the hands of the people rather than a corporation."

Unlike most other common-interest communities, Village Homes not only has a built-in social structure for adults, but a social structure for children, as well. Corbett's teenage daughter, Lisa, described this structure: "We've got a group of kids called 'the harvesters.' The orchards are set aside for the kids of Village Homes; we can go out and pick the nuts and make money. It's to give the kids a source of income; we can sell them at a farmer's market at the gazebo in the center of the village. The adults, too, can sell their produce at 50 percent off the market prices. And kids can make money through the baby-sitting co-op. We're starting a Village Homes wine; my dad's trying to get me to design the label."

She continued: "There's a co-op school for kids in kindergarten through third grade. Over half the kids are from outside Village Homes. The nice thing is you know everyone here. I just started teaching dance class at the community center. I know all the parents. I feel safe here; outside, I never did."

Corbett preaches self-reliance not just because it pays off in produce, but because it contributes to the sense of community. "There's got to be a reason to get together, a real reason, otherwise it's too embarrassing for people to go down to the community center and announce, 'Hey, I'm here; let's get together.' So many of the other planned communities assume that recreation brings people together. That may be true, but somehow there's a lack of substance in that kind of interaction. At least half of our community activities revolve around survival—around food and income."

Village Homes is ruled by a democratic community association, but the rules are quite different in tone from those of most other planned communities. Homeowners' votes are all of equal value, regardless of size, value, or amount of property owned, and may be passed to renters. The emphasis of the association rules is not on architectural cosmetics. Rather, the emphasis is on function. While other planned communities worry about the color of drapery liners, Village Homes sets up guidelines for new home construction or landscaping that guarantee all residents unobstructed access to the sun. Other guidelines are designed to protect privacy and encourage community: home designs must not have second-story windows looking into adjacent courtyards; homes must be accessible to the common area. The "social design," says Corbett, should include chances for people to get together and chances for people to get away.

The taboo of Village Homes is fences.

Could somebody build, I asked Corbett, a tree house in his or her own yard?

"Sure."

Would they have to ask permission from the community association?

"Yes. You can't build or grow anything that's going to hide somebody's south glass or solar collector between the hours of ten in the morning and two in the afternoon."

What if they wanted to move a boulder in their yard?

"No, they wouldn't have to ask permission. Anything on the ground that's not in the common areas, landscaping, trellises, decks, anything that's low, they don't have to ask."

If a resident wanted to become a street vendor in Village Homes (taboo in most cities; unheard of in most planned communities) could he or she do that?

"Yup. You have to have a license anyplace in the city, but the city of Davis probably wouldn't bother you here. They don't pay much attention to us; they don't even send the police out unless there's a call. We have the lowest crime rate of probably any place in town.

"What's really interesting about Village Homes is that it was considered, in the beginning, to be a left-wing socialist experiment, yet there's more libertarian behavior here than there is in any of the other planned communities. If people don't like the rules, they break them, and then they gradually work to get them changed. A lot of problems are reconciled at the personal level. The community association here has to meet between two and four times a month to keep the flexibility. It takes more democracy, not less, to preserve freedoms, to keep from becoming too overbearing.

"My estimate is that half of the people moved here because it was a unique community or it was energy conserving. The other 50 percent came because they needed a house and it was a good deal, so they bought in. One very conservative Republican couple moved here because it was a good deal. This couple was definitely not into condominium life. They were a little appalled about the community association having so much control. They got upset at the first meeting when we talked about homeowners owning commercial property in common; they thought that sounded very socialistic. But after a year of being here, the woman got on the design review committee, and then she was on the community association's board of directors. When her husband was transferred to Missouri they had to move, and they wrote a letter back saying how difficult it was to find a house because there was no place like this to live.

"We've had people here, of course, who didn't like it. We did a resident attitude survey recently. Two residents bitched and bitched. They wanted the community association to stay out of their lives; they didn't like the dues; they didn't like having to submit plans to the design review committee. At the bottom of the questionnaire residents were asked if there should be any additional rules. Both residents who had called our rules overbearing suggested that there ought to be a rule against having chickens."

Corbett, with a bemused smile, stopped for a moment and wiped some perspiration from his face. He pointed to a house, its shutters closed: "The fellow who lived in that house was a fireman and his wife was a nurse. He was a real redneck. Village Homes just smacked of communism to him. He moved out. And another guy moved out because there were just too many controls . . . a real left-wing type of guy, real environmentalist. Didn't like the fact that there was a design review board. So here are these two families at opposite ends of the political spectrum who moved out. But were they really? Like a lot of Americans who consider themselves right-wing or left-wing, both these families were actually both centralists; they wanted everything decided someplace else, not by some local person or local democracy. That's a very easy position to take. What Village Homes represents is self-reliant decentralism, something that's really found in the American tradition, something that's beginning to emerge again—a new politics."

One resident, Barry King, a professor of medicine at UC Davis, is vocal in his distrust of Corbett's idealism. "The common areas are a joke," he told me after my visit at Village Homes. "You've got eight households clustered around a common area and trying to agree on what to do with it. You just can't get any agreement. And the community association is a joke, too. It wouldn't be needed if everyone owned their own property." Still, he likes the general design of Village Homes. "I've lived in a typical suburban neighborhood, and I guess I'd rather live here. Actually, the best kind of neighborhood would include the more traditional private ownership, and this kind of physical design."

One of Village Homes' most enthusiastic residents is Janet Friedman, a tax attorney and daughter of conservative economist Milton Friedman (who also lives, part of the time, in a common-interest community near San Francisco). She classifies herself as a libertarian, "like my father." When I asked her later if there wasn't some inconsistency with believing in personal freedom and living in a common-interest community, she said, "The rules are really loose here, and anyway, you have a choice whether you live here or not. If there's a lot of people out there who want to live like we do instead of like they do in someplace like Rancho Bernardo, then more communities like Village Homes will show up. The condo movement is among the most libertarian things happening today; it's certainly an example of free market choices at work."

Corbett's biggest disappointment was his failed effort to establish low-income housing. Davis requires a certain percentage of low-income housing in all new developments, but, since it is a college town, this housing is usually filled up with students receiving money from their parents. Corbett thought he had a better idea: Village Homes would hire migrant agricultural workers, train them in construction, and after a year's labor they would be entitled to use this "sweat equity" as a downpayment on a house. In the process they would also have gained a trade that would allow them to step out of the migrant stream. Corbett financed the first four homes, in part with his own money, and moved the low-income families in. The state's low-income housing program, though, did not recognize sweat equity, and refused to advance loans because the workers had only been employed a year. "I said, damn, you just financed a house for a teacher over there who'd only been working nine months. The state will only fool around with low-income rental, not ownership. I was devastated by that. It was the best part of Village Homes. It could have been a national model, showing how you can get people off welfare, into a trade, and have their children grow up in a stronger kind of community."

Corbett's mood darkened in the bright sun.

"One of the big issues is whether we're going to shut the doors to any more development at all here. I happen to be one of those people saying yes, we should shut the doors. The minute any community gets to a certain size, things start falling apart. There's no reason we can't go eight miles north to some poor agricultural land, where we would be closer to the Sacramento River, where we would be able to get runoff water instead of further depleting the underground water table, and start a new village.

"I'd like to see these villages all over the country, instead of the kind of crap that's being built. But you just can't sell it today. Developers are only building one kind of condo community. They're not really interested in community; and everybody envisions space-age rocket cars, and cars that get 150 miles to the gallon, and commuter trains and high-tech computerized living, and having the air-conditioned tractors running on biofuels so farming somehow becomes a form of leisure. The technological fix. I see things differently. I think we need each other. People don't understand about freedom. They don't know how much freedom has been taken away. How they live is determined by developers. What infringes upon freedom is not so much law as structure. It's already dictated to most Americans what kind of streets they have, what kind of sanitary systems, what kind of community, or lack of community. They don't know they have options."

He had been walking at a fast clip, and now stopped again, shielding his eyes in the sun. We were at the far edge of Village Homes. He pointed beyond the almond trees, across a street, to a condominium development that was not part of Village Homes. It was all white, glaring in the sun. A small child was pumping his tricycle slowly across the white cement parking lot.

"Look at that kid over there. He's kind of limited where he can go, isn't he? Where's he gonna go?"

Beyond the Shelter Revolution

One person's democratic rule is another person's tyranny of the majority. Even Michael Corbett's community, which is based more on enabling principles than most communities, has a certain claustrophobic feel about it. Only a minority of Americans would consciously choose to live in Village Homes, or Rancho Bernardo, or the fortified towers of Quayside. Yet, because of economics and social change, the number of common-interest communities is growing far faster than conventional housing. As political scientist Ralph Meyer says, "It's easy enough to assume that people can move out of these places if their rights are abridged, but economics are making it so that a lot of people don't have much choice. We need to start asking some serious questions about how this new level of government affects democracy and freedom." If housing reflects a culture, what does the new shelter say about us? In 1967, Lewis Mumford predicted that a new kind of housing was on the way, produced by a mythical corporation, "General Space-Housing, Inc.," which would "solve our housing problems, swiftly and efficiently, though not

painlessly . . . by enforcing conformity and destroying choice."
Sooner or later, however, people rebel against conformity, regimentation, and authoritarian behavior, against any kind of packaging that goes too far.

Not long ago, I returned to my childhood neighborhood, a
once-fresh suburb of ticky-tacky boxes in Raytown, Missouri. I
remembered as a child looking up the street and comparing the
'56 Fords and '57 Chevys, the new young trees (two to a lot), the
uniform shape of the houses and the color of the lawns. When
one neighbor put in chain-link fences, everyone (it seemed) put
in chain-link fences. It was so important to fit in then, to control
and be controlled by thy neighbor. But now, in that neighborhood, everything is different.

Standing in front of my childhood home I looked up the street.
The trees and shrubs, insignificant in their smallness and sameness then, are huge and different now. And the houses were
different: a porch added here, peeling paint there. An overweight
woman in her fifties came out of the house, suspicious, walking
past a broken-down truck straddling the ditch in which my
brother and I had once made dams. "You can look around but
you can't come in," she said, though I had not asked to. I walked
down to the backyard. A trace of a hole that my brother and I had
dug was still there. The basement wall was chipped, the paint
peeling. The little cedars my father had planted (in an odd arrangement) were towering, waving in the Missouri summer
breeze. I looked up at them and turned around and around. The
assumption that suburbia would stifle individuality was wrong;
the uniqueness of all the families who had ever owned these
homes had won. Time had accomplished this. Will that be true
of condos twenty years from now? Will human individuality win
out over the dictatorship of the condo proletariat?

I asked several of the experts on the new shelter this question.
They all hesitated, and then said, no, probably not—not with the
new definitions of home ownership, not with all those rules
woven into the design. But I wonder. Perhaps individuality is
already beginning to flourish, epitomized by the social and legal
conflicts within common-interest communities. In the spring of
1983, the board of directors of Mission Viejo, one of California's
largest walled communities, fined one of the community's shop
owners for displaying an American flag (considered by the board
to be a form of advertising). One by one, the other shop owners

rebelled, each of them displaying their own American flags, until the street was filled with flags. The board made a counteroffer of a communal flag pole; the rebellion persisted.

And there is still another option in America II—of moving to some part of the new nation where a freestanding single-family home can still be bought at a reasonable price. When I visited The Towers of Quayside, an employee, wearing the Quayside female uniform, hot pants, told me how she could not wait to leave the place behind. "I hate to move. I've lived in Miami most of my life. I love Miami; I've made it home, as bad as it is, but I can't take this place—I'd never live in a condo. Next summer, along with my kids and my boyfriend I'm heading for the Midwest, a small town. We're going to buy a house, maybe an old farmhouse, turn the bottom into a restaurant, live upstairs. We're going to escape this. We've got it planned."

PART FOUR
THE NEW EDEN

*The towns lay ahead. Small towns. Small enough to be run by men
instead of running them.*

—Ray Bradbury

*Endurance caught the American eye again and 'sense of place' began
to mean something to a nation of itinerants. . . . In the sage-strewn,
rocky country . . . dams rise across the river valleys and oil pumps
dip like mosquitoes into the bare shoulder of the earth. Towns brace
like boxers against the arrival of the hard, haughty, displaced people.
. . . Cattle go to market and cattlemen go to trailer parks and
retirement condominiums. . . . Yearning has always been elemental
out in the provinces, and perhaps nothing is finally more universally
American than that wide-eyed kind of wishing, reaching back for
what you thought was fine and free, reaching out for something calm
and steady now amid the whirl.*

—Russell Martin, *"Writers of the Purple Sage,"* New York
Times Magazine, *December 27, 1981*

I painted the way I'd like life to be.

—Norman Rockwell

EDEN REDUX

From the beginning, Americans have thought of the great open stretches of the countryside as the makings of Eden. Appropriately, there are sixty-one Edens in America; in naming our towns we have always been a hopeful people. There is, fortunately, only one Truth or Consequences.

The association of rural and small-town living with the American ideal is woven deeply into our national culture, though the reality of rural America was often something else. Writers from Sherwood Anderson to William Faulkner described small towns as the scene of repressive stability. Western mining towns were often company-owned, barricaded, and surrounded by barbed wire, with guards at every entrance. During the 1960s, small towns, especially in the South, became associated (not always accurately) with racism and anticounterculture sentiment. Yet it was during the same decade that so many of the young headed for New Hampshire and Colorado with their tepees, I Ching coins and transcendental expectations. They were drawn to a different image of rural America, a pure one experienced by Native Americans and articulated by Thomas Jefferson, who believed that those who worked the earth were the chosen people of God, and that the "mobs of great cities add just so much to the support of pure government as sores do to the strength of the human body."

Now, a new and different vision of Eden has emerged. Transcendentalist philosopher Ralph Waldo Emerson wrote: "I wish to have rural strength and religion for my children, and I wish city facility and polish. I find with chagrin that I cannot have both." The new ruralites are trying to have both, and sometimes they are succeeding. They are creating—beyond the suburbs that failed to fulfill the dream, even beyond the more sophisticated anticities —a transformed countryside, not really rural, not quite urban, something altogether new.

RESETTLING AMERICA

For years, rural and small-town America were in eclipse. People from rural regions, from a thousand little towns all over America, poured into the large cities, pushed and pulled off the farms and out of the towns by the attraction of better-paying jobs in the larger cities, by new capital-intensive machinery, and eventually by the Great Depression. The enervation of rural small-town America continued for decades. As people fled the small towns, they took with them the tax dollars that supported the communities that were barely surviving. The children grew up and left, driven out by boredom and joblessness. Those people that were left behind, the old and the poor who could not move, watched as their communities began to decay. Houses weathered, barns collapsed, and fences went unmended. Farmers, farm workers, and small-town shop clerks whose businesses could no longer function moved up from the South, the whites from Tennessee and Arkansas traveled to Chicago and Indianapolis, and the blacks from Alabama and Louisiana and all the southern states moved north, fleeing slavery first and joblessness second. Thousands of square miles in New Hampshire, Vermont, and Maine that once were cropland became woodland, the old stone farm fences snaking through the overgrowth of firs and maples.

Jay Davis headed for Maine in 1971, in search of a new life. He began as a counterculture homesteader, got a divorce, was elected a small-town selectman, and is now the young editor of the *Republican Journal,* housed upstairs in a 130-year-old building in Belfast, Maine. In the one-hundred-fiftieth anniversary issue of the *Republican Journal,* Davis published a painstaking account of the history of Waldo County, Maine—a study in how great economic shifts can, in a few years, turn a region inside out. In New England, not only the small farms disappeared but a whole generation of industry. Electricity replaced waterpower, and the mills of Waldo County were abandoned. Farming became concentrated in the West and Midwest, and the small farms of rural Maine faded. Between 1850 and 1950, the people just left. "With the people went most of the early industries. Not just the water-powered mills and the shipyards, but the canning plants and cheese factories, granite and lime quarries, sarsaparilla plants and fancy clothes shops, spool mills and furniture makers. . . . America's destiny seemed to be in the West."

For a century, as Davis puts it, Waldo County, like much of rural America, was a Sleeping Beauty. The Civil War "cut through the ranks of young men in the same way that they had cut through the standing timber of New England." Few new young men came to replace them. Driving through small-town and rural New England today, one is struck by the war monuments, a sad and perverse testimony to rural depopulation. The lists of war casualties for each successive war are shorter, the monuments diminish in size. What made Waldo County and much of New England special "in its sleeping century is what didn't happen next. No developers came, no speculators. No large industry capitalized on the captive work force. No new roads rent the land, few new buildings rose from it. The ubiquitous urban ooze moved north, but it bumped up against the walls of the turnpike corridor and stopped. The county was left remarkably as it was a century earlier." Little changed in Waldo County between the Civil War and Vietnam. Writes Davis, "As the fences of Waldo County knelt and fell and the trees stepped out to reclaim what had been theirs, and the mills decayed into the streams and the ridges were deserted, as people left and the survivors worked hard for a living, what emerged was, at least relatively, a twentieth-century wilderness."

The rural outmovement in America was especially heavy in the 1940s and '50s, beginning with World War II, when the worker-short cities welcomed rural manpower. On the average, more than a million people left the farms each year between 1940 and 1960. In the South, the most rural of regions, farm population dropped by 40 percent in the 1950s. Poet and farmer Wendell Berry writes of the effect of this, in *The Unsettling of America.* He remembers, during the 1950s, "the outrage with which our political leaders spoke of the forced removal of the populations of villages in Communist countries." But he also remembers that at the same time, "in Washington, the word on farming was 'Get big or get out'—a policy which is still in effect and which has taken an enormous toll. The only difference is that of method: the force used by the Communists was military; with us, it has been economic." Here, writes Berry, was "surely a cause for mourning: a forced migration of people greater than any in history, the foretelling of riots in the cities and the failure of human community in the country."

Even as the rural people were heading for the cities, another great shift was forming, barely visible, like the high thin clouds that signal rain after a long dry spell. The Department of Agriculture, concerned about the high level of rural poverty and the flight to the cities (which it had encouraged by favoring big farms over small ones), began to advocate general rural development and the creation of nonagricultural rural jobs. New rural roads were built. The same federal highway system that firmly linked the South and the West to the northeast also helped link isolated rural areas to the rest of the nation. Federal and state governments constructed numerous reservoirs, which attracted recreation and retirement communities to rural areas. By the close of the 1950s, according to Calvin Beale, widely recognized as the leading expert on the turnaround in rural migration, there were "the beginnings of revival in the Colorado slope; the start of recreation and retirement communities in the Ozarks; oil-related development in south Louisiana; and the sprawling influence of Atlanta, Kansas City, or Minneapolis–St. Paul on nearby rural counties." The new country was in its infancy.

In the mid-1960s, the flow of people out of much of rural America began to slow considerably. Though the growth of cities was still twice that of nonmetropolitan counties, nonmetropolitan counties lost only 2.2 million people—60 percent less than during the previous decade. Opinion polls were showing a peculiar disparity between where the vast number of Americans lived and where they would have preferred to live: millions of people who had been content in their big-city and suburban homes were now showing a preference for living in a rural area or small town. Two large areas of the South even began to gain people. One stretched over a vast oval shape from Dallas to St. Louis, encompassing northeast Texas, the Ouachita Mountains, the lower Arkansas Valley, and the Ozarks. The other area was bounded by Memphis, Louisville, Atlanta, and Birmingham. Industry and business were moving into these formerly poor, rural regions. The economic growth of these two large rural areas clearly illustrated the potential rural future once the local economy shifted away from total reliance on agriculture. Even so, most demographers and social scientists believed that the future was with big cities, the ones over a million in population, and that the rural eclipse was total, the urban rise ongoing.

But new and deep structural and societal changes were loose in the land, some of the same forces that were beginning to open up the cities of the South and West to the national and world economy: the development of knowledge-intensive/high-technology industries that are not raw-material or large-assembly based, such as computer manufacturing and optics. At the same time, dramatic improvements were occurring in rural education, social welfare, and public services. Rural social and economic isolation were ending. Better airline connections and electronic communication further reduced the sense of isolation. Rural areas adopted cable television long before it gained popularity in cities; throughout the 1960s and '70s, government regulation greatly restricted cable television in urban areas, so the cable companies turned to nonmetro areas, where electronic reception was poor and legal reception was high. As a consequence, many rural areas had (and still have) higher quality television reception, and more choices, than some la e cities.

In the 1970s, industries, businesses, services, and educational institutions found it increasingly profitable, because of tax benefits, land prices, and new technologies, to move to remote rural counties. The Arab oil embargo created a demand for coal and other extractive energy sources in rural counties. These technological and social shifts came at a time of steady economic growth and unanticipated disposable income. Spending patterns shifted; only so many refrigerators and other necessary consumer items could be bought. Leisure and status became the new focus of consumption—outdoor recreation fit the bill.

Suddenly, to the surprise of most demographers, the slowdown in rural outmigration became an absolute turnaround. In the mid-1970s, for the first time since 1820, rural areas began to grow faster than cities. According to the 1980 census, between 1970 and 1980, when the nation's metropolitan areas grew by only 9.1 percent, nonmetropolitan areas were up 15.4 percent— a rate almost 5 percent higher than the nation's total population growth. In the 1970s, a net of at least 4 million people moved into rural areas, compared to the 2.8 million people who had left small towns and rural counties in the 1960s.

In the Midwest, nonmetropolitan areas grew by 7.8 percent.

In the West, nonmetropolitan population increased by almost a third.

In the vast area embracing western Wyoming, western Colorado, northern Arizona, most of Utah, all of Nevada, and the Sierra Nevada section of California, rural and small-town populations grew by more than 50 percent.

In California's rural areas, which had never experienced the dramatic loss of population felt in rural areas throughout the nation, nonmetropolitan counties grew at a rate three times that of metropolitan counties.

Florida's nonmetro growth was 50.8 percent.

In the South, growth was 17.1 percent. The South was the only region where city growth, at 20.1 percent, was greater than rural.

A common first reaction to the data is to assume that rural growth is simply spillover from the metro areas into adjacent nonmetro counties. Adjacent counties are indeed growing the fastest, acquiring about five-eighths of the total growth of all nonmetro counties. But the more significant point, according to Beale, "is that nonadjacent counties have also increased more rapidly than metro counties. Thus, the . . . trend is not confined to metro sprawl. It affects nonmetro counties well removed from metro influence." The most dramatic reversal in population growth has, in fact, happened in the counties well removed from the influence of cities.

The preference for life beyond cities has been showing up in opinion polls for at least twenty years, and the trend is increasing, with an odd twist. In a 1972 Wisconsin survey of people who wanted to move out of big cities and suburbs, a majority said that the ideal rural or small-town residence would be within thirty miles of a city of at least 50,000 people. A later national study revealed that, for those who would prefer to live in a small town near a city, their second choice, by a wide margin, would be to move to an even more remote town; their third choice would be to stay in the big city. A survey by the Gallup organization revealed that, by 1977, a majority of Americans who wanted to move to the country didn't even want to live in a town, but preferred moving to farms or very unpopulated areas. Clearly, something deeper is going on here than just a desire to live in a semisuburban small town near a big city. Urbanites moving to the country are showing a preference for ever-smaller levels of population density.

THE ASSUMPTION OF A NEW EDEN

Wendell Berry, for one, sees no cause for celebration in the movement of urban people into the country; that, he says, "only *looks* like a balanced equation. The people who move into the city and those who move out into the country are hardly the same people." Even many of the people who once lived in the country and are now returning from a city bring with them new expectations that are as much urban as they are traditionally rural. Nonetheless, the changed economy and shape of rural America are new contexts within which to act out our fundamentally American predisposition for rural or small-town life. Just as the vast regions of the southern and western states had been left relatively untouched by industrial urbanization, and so are perceived as fresh places for development, rural America's new attraction is that it has laid fallow for so many decades. Now come the postindustrial industries and people seeking elbowroom. As the nation's big cities become more unlivable and as land in the more populated regions is paved, air poisoned, and waters fouled, people seek a new wilderness. The people fleeing the cities come slowly at first, then faster, in numbers that rival the waves of early settlers.

Privacy, elbowroom, refuge, safety, a fresh start—it all must be out there, over that next hill. To urbanites considering the rural option, the crime statistics are alluring: in 1979, New York had 1733 murders, enough to obliterate the population of Arlington, Kansas, three times, but Arlington, pop. 503, has never had a murder in its entire history. In North Carolina, a largely rural state with no large cities, the robbery rate is only one-tenth that of New York. Then there is the cost of living. To an urban person thinking about moving to the country, housing is an enormous attraction. Though high mortgage rates make it difficult to sell a house in a big city in order to move to a small town, once the house is sold and the move is made the trade-off is remarkable —especially for a generation that grew up in single-family homes and now finds condominiums to be the only affordable housing available in large cities. Many older Americans are selling their New York and Southern California homes, buying nicer homes in seemingly safer towns in New England or the Midwest, cashing in their huge equity and living on the profit. While many people may not move to the country to maximize their earnings, they may well move to minimize their expenses. Generally, the cost of living in rural areas is much lower; even those costs that are usually higher in rural areas can be offset by other rural advantages—in the case of higher grocery prices, for instance, rural living offers enough space for a vegetable garden. Commuting, too, can be surprisingly less expensive. According to studies by Beale, rural residents travel a shorter median distance to work than do city residents: 4.6 miles for rural commuters compared with 7.6 miles for urban commuters, which can mean less money for gasoline.

Many people moving to small towns and isolated regions are trying to achieve a sense of social control. Sociologist Andrew J. Sofranko, who studied people moving to small towns in the Midwest, is amazed by the attitudes he finds among the new ruralites: "I would have expected that seniors moving to rural areas would move into the small towns so they'd be close to what few services there are. But no, they were moving way out beyond the edge of town. I couldn't believe it. When I asked them why they'd moved to the country, one of the reasons they gave was better services. That logic defies every major gerontological study ever done, all of which point out that the worst place to be if you're old— especially in terms of health care services—is in a rural area. But these people were saying, 'Hey, we don't *want* your Meals on Wheels!' There was a feeling that back in the cities they were paying for services that they didn't get, and that the services just weren't that important. These people were putting much more of a priority on self-sufficiency, quality of life versus length of life. And even more important, they felt that what services were available in rural areas were actually better because people cared on a very human, nonbureaucratic level."

Sofranko detected the same attitude among younger migrants, who believed that municipal services were better in their small town, despite the fact that many of the towns had more frequent service interruptions, because of water shortages and other disruptions, than large cities. "A lot of the young parents said they moved to a small town because the schools were better. Again, that defies all logic—all the studies show that, academically, rural schools are the worst. The bottom line is this: people are looking for something intangible out there, something that has more to do with human caring than with government programs." Sofranko wonders if, by believing so fervently that schools are better in small towns, the new ruralites may eventually fulfill their own prophecy. "They'll pay more attention to education, and it will get better. I've certainly learned one thing about migration," he adds. "Perception counts more than reality."

What binds the various kinds of new pioneers—the corporate vice-presidents, the retirees, the voluntary poor, and all the others—is the belief in Eden, the assumption that it can be found again, and, to the extent that America itself was once considered a new Eden, that America can be found again. The path to the new Eden has been worn smooth by retirees and those who seek mystical release from modern society, who seek not just freedom but identity. They move into ghost towns and take on the affectations of the ghosts; they wear the clothes of Americans long dead; they begin to talk with a twang and walk with a swagger. They are starved for contact with nature, aching to be whole, yearning for family life, for values almost as faded as the lace and the collars of those old clothes salvaged from trunks in the attics. Gradually, the retirees and counterculture have been joined by all sorts of people streaming out of the big cities into small towns and small cities and the open countryside, into the woodlands of New England, into tiny towns in the Rockies, into ghost towns of New Mexico, into strange new high-tech clusters in North Carolina: new ruralites who are white-collar, blue-collar, older, younger, wealthy, and not-so-wealthy; bank executives with pinstriped suits and New York accents, and young professionals bringing their urban ethics and Apple computers to the new Eden.

12

IN SEARCH OF NORMAN ROCKWELL

Among the new ruralites of New England, where much of the migration could be seen first, the issue is less economics than identity. Personal identity. National identity.

Sociologist Thorstein Veblen once wrote that country towns "had a greater part than any other [American institution] in shaping public sentiment and giving character to American culture." Norman Rockwell knew that, and he must be alive and hiding in New England, because so many Americans are looking for him there. Rockwell epitomized, not only in his illustrations, but in his own life, the American nostalgia for country life. In his autobiography he describes his memories of growing up in New York City, of the night when McKinley was assassinated, when "the streets were dark except the yellow pools of light beneath the gas lamps. . . . People were gathering under the gas lamps, reading the news and brushing off their faces the moths and flies which swarmed about the light. There was a kind of horror in the streets." And he remembered drunken brawls between men and women, and of an old man leaning against a window, collapsing and dying and disturbing Rockwell's dinner. "These things happen in the country, but you don't see them. In the city you are constantly confronted by unpleasantness. I find it sordid and unsettling." The country, where Rockwell spent his boyhood summers staying with farm families who took in boarders, infected him with an idealized image of what American life could be, though he admitted that this America existed more in his own dreams than in reality; and he lived part of his adult life in rural Vermont, chasing the dreams in his paintings.

In much of rural America II, the new pilgrims come looking for those dreams. They are searching for a personal and national identity that can best be found, it seems, in the past—or that part of the past that Rockwell's paintings and Disney's Main Street and all those dulcimer-strumming balladeers have impressed upon the national consciousness. The search transcends political sentiment or economic status; what began, primarily, as a migration of hippies dreaming of Thoreau has widened to include straitlaced Republicans, who talk almost mystically of small-town life. Many of them seem to be seeking a kind of healing. In recent years, the pilgrimage has sought different meccas: the little towns of the Rockies, the dancing mirage of New Mexico, and especially New England, perhaps because so much of the nation's history, its childhood, began there.

Lewis A. Ploch, a professor of rural sociology at the University of Maine, Orono, has been tracking the in-migration to New England and throughout rural America for several years. The new pioneers, he says, are "relatively young adults, educated, with small families . . . from the scruffy to the near baronial." He describes a "rural romanticism": a kind of spiritual search for Americanism (which some social scientists consider a type of religion), for some kind of contact with something beyond themselves. A growing number of people moving to small towns, he says, see this move as a practical way of dealing with family disintegration, either the disarray of their own family, or the perceived threat of the mainstream society to family values. Many of these people do not want technology, they want the past—they want what Norman Rockwell painted.

Native New Englanders are, by nature, a reticent people; but sit for awhile with the *new* New Englanders, and the stories come easily—stories of searching and finding, and sometimes not finding. . . .

THE HOMESTEADERS

The homesteaders of the late 1960s and early '70s moved way out beyond the fringes of the small towns, built log cabins, hauled their own water and their own wood and, during the long winters, some of them slowly went crazy. Paul Fackler, now a graduate student in Orono, Maine, with long and thinning hair and small-lensed wire-rim glasses, was one of them. Sitting in a little office in Winslow Hall, an old brick building housing the agriculture department, Fackler, who is a cheerful and optimistic person, told me about those days: "I did it for one winter, used kerosene lights, lived alone in a cabin that was ten feet by eight feet. I had to walk a quarter to a half mile for water, used a shoulder harness that had a couple of buckets on it. It can be a life of drudgery. It was cheap, convenient . . ." except for the winters, when the temperature would dip to forty below, bringing the "terrible isolation. . . . You wouldn't believe the number of hippies who moved up here and turned to drinking, got divorced, committed suicide. In April, the suicide rate is highest because you keep waiting for spring and it doesn't come and doesn't come, and then you hit a freak storm in April with eight inches of snow. You get in a depression, a mental state that says, is this the way things are? This is the way life is? It's a despair—it must be like what it is to be always poor. It is not romantic. Husbands and wives start taking axes to each other."

Most of the early homesteaders, if they did not return to the cities or head to some other mecca, moved back to town after a time. The small town was really what they were after, not all that pain and isolation. They continued their education, or opened up little craft shops. Maureen Babicki, like Fackler, came looking for some kind of solace in the early 1970s. She too found life beyond the fringe of the towns to be much more rugged than she had imagined that it would be, and moved back into town. "But I learned, you know," she said, standing in the doorway to Fackler's office. She was wearing a long, print dress. "The older people here taught you." The early in-migrants who succeeded were the ones who respected the local culture, who, rather than continuing their fetish for self-reliance, asked for help. Many of the Maine locals were resentful of the newcomers at first, but the hostility slowly faded. The older residents of rural Maine became enamored of the eagerness of the newcomers to learn the old ways; many of the young natives of Maine were turning their backs on the old ways, still leaving for the big cities, but these newcomers actually wanted to know how to can pears and cut wood and handle draft horses. One day, just after she arrived from "Suburbia, U.S.A.," Babicki decided to make some maple syrup: "I found myself a maple tree in the backyard (it was really an elm tree but no one would tell me different) and put buckets all around the tree. I never did get much syrup from that tree."

The shopping-center economy has been gradually moving into

this part of upstate Maine, but it is still a relatively poor rural area, and this remains part of its attraction to people like George Ritz, who arrived in 1971 after a Peace Corps stint in Chile and worked his way through college as a woodcutter. He tells of what people will do to hang on to rural or small-town life: "We do whatever we have to to survive here. I became an independent wood contractor. I have some of my own land, but mostly I work on the land of others. Most people work at three or four or five different things. One guy works in the mill, and he builds houses on the side and rototills gardens . . . anything to make enough. Just about everybody in small-town Maine is an entrepreneur of some sort. Nobody does just one thing. Foresters let go by big paper companies have to do something, so they call themselves consultants. And they get by.

"There's two in-migrants in town that started a sawmill; I supply them with all the logs, they mill the logs, sell the lumber. They don't know anything about sawmills, but they learned by talking to the old-timers around here who used to run sawmills and by reading books. We sell largely to people building unconventional houses, refurbishing falling-down old houses, who can't find the cut wood in a conventional lumberyard; so I custom-cut the logs. The wages here in Maine are incredibly low but the work ethic is incredibly strong. People do anything and everything to make a buck. Because of the underground economy, people are doing a lot better than they might appear.

"I think people here look at life totally differently. I've been in California, Seattle, and the first sixteen years of my life I lived in Newark, New Jersey, so I have a feeling of what the rest of the world is like. Here at the university, the people don't go out and buy a lot of expensive food; we grow our own. It's a way of life, where in most other places it's a stigma. You grow your own meat, too, or if you don't, then you shoot your own meat. Some out-of-staters are looked at really strange if they say they don't hunt. People figure if you're making $10,000 per year, then you're doing good."

This yearning for nonmaterialistic values can't be divided along political lines. Take, for instance, John Wilson and his puritanical conservatism. In 1969, Wilson, from the University of Kansas, moved with his Brooklynite wife far out into the Maine countryside. He lives a life, "as much as I can, by the values of Socrates, Christ. . . . I have come theoretically and philosophically to damn materialism. We're in a hedonistic and materialistic age." Wilson is a barrel-chested, bearded man with short red hair, who wears wire-rim glasses and has cautious eyes. His ideology is practical: he owns a color television but he uses draft horses for plowing. He built a rustic tennis court for his kids. We sat out in a patch of tall, cool grass under two trees behind his 120-year-old house, swatting blackflies as we talked. His collie was barking. "The local people have generally come to accept the in-migrants and their values, though: they bring in new ideas, energy, a willingness to work. But most importantly, most of them, at least around here, are pretty conservative, they make few government demands, you know, for street lights or superhighways through every town, make the place look like a suburb. These people are reclaiming old land, rebuilding old houses, providing work for some of these local craftsmen, carpenters, and so forth. The one complaint I've heard that seems legitimate is that property values go up because of all these newcomers; some of the locals can't afford the taxes, so they have to sell out."

Behind him, his two huge draft horses ran a few yards toward the tennis court. The earth shook as they ran. "There's been a blend of values. I use draft horses not for any romantic reason, but because they're practical. They serve the land better. They give me great profit, certainly pleasure, too—but profit. I bought all the equipment to farm this place probably for less than $1000. My main crop is hay. Plus, I raise cattle, hogs, turkeys, and chickens. We're pretty well self-sufficient in meat and dairy products. I made my own tennis court out of local materials: my own clay, my own cedar poles, a net from chicken wire. The whole thing cost me less than $1000. Over the years I'll save that in gas just not going places for recreation; it's a good sport for my kids."

Wilson calls himself a radical redneck, "in the sense that my neck is red from hard work done outdoors," and radical in the sense of his social conservatism: he runs his family on the old patriarchal system—though his wife, who serves on the local school board, is, as he says with a smile, an independent-minded woman.

"This will probably embarrass you, but I believe in a providential order, God at the apex and a hierarchical relationship all the way down. I believe in the distinction between males and females, in their working relationship, and in the authority of the parents over the child, because I see too many students who have never had their asses whipped by anybody and they can't write, they can't spell, they don't think, and they aren't willing to work. I vowed that whatever I gave my kids I would never send them to any teacher undisciplined and not willing to work. So from that point of view, I suppose I'm different from a lot of people around here. There's a tendency among professional people and the hippies in town not to discipline their children. I may be wrong —we'll find out in ten or fifteen years when my kids get older. But I do insist that they work, that they extend themselves mentally and physically as much as they can and that they learn what they can do with themselves. My kids are required to learn to play a musical instrument. Most parents don't insist that the kids practice. Our kids do. Number one and number two sons have taken statewide honors in instruments. It's their choice after they're eighteen whether to continue.

"I think Marx was mistaken in believing there could be a paradise on earth. . . . I accept the fact of evil and I govern myself and my children accordingly. I'm continually aware of the possibility of the Devil." Out here, he said, you begin to see things, to believe in guardian angels, to believe in evil. "I was out haying with my horses one day and the pole broke. We had a heavy load of hay, and they had a full head of steam coming down this hill. All I could do was steer them. We went straight through that barn. It was like a Laurel and Hardy movie. Straight through the barn and we got out the other end of the barn and had to turn. I was aware at that moment that I wasn't steering, that it was something else steering that wagon for me. I knew that if I were to turn over I would have had a broken neck and died. I realized I was going to go. Well, something took that wagon from me and I ended up all right, kept it upright."

He swatted a fly and picked at a piece of grass and was silent for a moment. "There's a lot of fear up here. The fear of nuclear holocaust has driven people to try to gain greater control over their lives. And it's also driving them into self-indulgence and hedonistic pleasure. . . . You get that point of view expressed, too, in those who would come out just to scrape by and have pot parties and change wives and husbands: they're desperate to enjoy themselves. Perhaps they're driven by the same forces that drove me here. . . .

"If we have an economic breakdown, I might be able to survive and feed my family. And it's possible if we have thermonuclear problems we could survive, depending on which way the wind is going and whether enough people can get together and blow up the Piscatiqua Bridge that separates New Hampshire from Maine, so that the city people can't get up here and raid us."

DOCTORS, DIPLOMATS, AND SURROGATE FARMERS

Along with the homesteaders came another economic class: doctors and a surprising number of retired journalists. Every major hospital in Maine has more than doubled its staff in the past decade; towns that had not had a doctor since 1910 now have one. Every newspaper in Maine was sold in the last ten years, always to in-migrants—including one paper that was owned, for a short time, by Walter Cronkite. The quality of the local press has been, by most accounts, greatly improved by the incoming owners.

J. Russell Wiggins was one of them. Wiggins was once the executive editor of the *Washington Post.* When Lyndon Johnson was president, he was the United States ambassador to the United Nations. Now he owns and edits the *Ellsworth American,* and is the very picture of the country editor. "I bought a farm up here in '66, then I picked up this little paper which was on its last legs." The word that comes to mind for him is . . . crusty. He takes a dim view of some of the newcomers. "A lot of the in-migrants are young people with a romantic, nostalgic notion of a rural life that simply is no more. It never was here. And the centralization that they're running away from in the big cities is still taking place in New England. The control of retail business, the recreation business, the banking business, and the automobile business—control is still emigrating out." A strip of franchises outside Ellsworth, said Wiggins, "might as well be in Boston as far as its effect on local enterprise. . . . People may be moving up here, but look at the caliber of the people running these stores. These people are agents, they're not the principals in an enterprise, they're agents. I don't know any chain store that hires anybody locally to run 'em; they hire a lot of clerks locally, but the management is all imported. Particularly in the shopping center. They have no discretion to spend any money without consulting Boston or New York or Connecticut or Rhode Island. They can't spend a dime without consulting their home office. There is no self-generating enterprise in the community collectively. Try to get a charitable donation from them, nine times out of ten the answer is no. Many years ago, if you had a crisis in town, like the dam had busted or a bridge blew out, God, there'd be a meeting of the local business families within twenty-four hours and they'd see how much each of them could put up and they'd fix the thing. But today, up and down this street, you couldn't sell tickets to the Last Supper with the original cast for five bucks a ticket, because they wouldn't have the authority to buy it. Most of them are no more identified with the life of the community than the local survey crew for ESSO in Saudi Arabia. They're just transient visitors."

Up and down Ellsworth's main street, though, is evidence of a whole different story, a growing service sector. Small entre-preneurs and conservative middle-class suburbanites make up the most recent waves of in-migrants, and, along with the ex-homesteaders, they have populated this street with small, locally owned shops: a storefront Down East Dance Arts company, and two travel agencies—for a town of 5000. The Ellsworth Chil-dren's Ballet has moved into an old theater. The standard cloth-ing stores may have moved out to the shopping center, but these little downtown stores are bursting at their hand-stitched seams with crafts. One of these stores, the Grasshopper, dealing in nostalgia, was started by ex-urbanites who are franchising the operation. The Grasshopper is now all over Maine, selling a kind of California/country paraphernalia, from bongs to blueberry flats. This kind of development does two things: it helps the local economy and it feeds the dream—especially the mail-order com-panies that send out the artifacts, like packets of seeds, to the cities and subdivisions and condos all over the country. This pulls new migrants in, who continue the facelift of rural towns. It is a tight, almost seamless circle.

Since farming is, in reality, such a rugged life, many of the new wave of rural entrepreneurs are buying and running what Lewis Ploch, professor of rural sociology at the University of Maine, calls "surrogate farms." In their mind's eye they picture them-selves living a truly rural life, with family pulling together on the land. But the land is too expensive, and they acknowledge that real farm life is brutal, so they buy a small-town general store, a hardware store, even a restaurant, and fix it up with the symbols of what they feel has been lost. Bruce Fearer and his family moved to a tiny village in Maine a few years ago; they bought a general store, restored it to the way it looked a century ago, and now they live upstairs. "We had a new home in Ann Arbor, Michigan," said Fearer. "It was out in a country subdivision with a golf course; it was beautiful. But we'd have been forty years paying for it, and here we've got the place just about paid for. This is the first time in my life that I will have completely owned something—residence or store or whatever. That feels good."

Bob Hall, with his wife and children, moved up to Maine in 1973 and bought a hardware store. Hall had been a corporate mainstreamer, president of Greyhound Van Lines. He and his family had lived in Hinsdale, Illinois, an "up-scale bedroom community near Chicago." Before that, he had been a New York City regional manager for Chrysler, a former Chrysler-Imperial sales manager for the entire East Coast, and a vice president of marketing for North American Van Lines. As he approached his fiftieth birthday, he had in mind semiretirement on a farm. Scouting around before the move, Hall and his wife visited South Dakota, "somewhere around Rapid City, near the Black Hills . . . that looked like the end of the world." He had always fantasized about New England, though. And in Belfast, Maine, he found an old hardware store for sale, with his name already on it. Across the front of the store was an old sign: Hall Hardware. So he bought it and left corporate America.

"Don't misunderstand me. That was pretty easy living, in corporate America," he said. He is a big man, with thick black hair and bushy eyebrows. When we met, he was dressed for work in baggy jeans and a light-blue work shirt, his belt speckled with white paint. He was sitting at his rolltop desk, upstairs above his hardware store. This is his second store, actually; the first one in Belfast had proved too big and expensive, so he moved out to a smaller one on Penobscot Bay, filling it up with used and new "antiques": mail-order items such as lumberman's cant dogs, pulp hooks, Maine woods folding camp cots, one-pound butter molds, ice cream freezers, and round wooden boxes. Surrounded by piles of boxes, he leaned back in a squeaky, rickety chair that threatened, several times, to tip all the way back. "Sixty grand a year at that time was nice. Company cars and flying hither and yon. . . . It was all very nice. But we decided that we would like to do something else before we passed on to whatever else you pass on to. Well, we found out this is just a lot harder work than

I've ever worked in my life. We had grain here for awhile. We had a feed store. I had to give that up because I picked up a 100-pound sack of grain one day and fell right down. Just couldn't do it, couldn't handle it. Course the other thing we had going for us was that all our children wanted to come. My son came right along with us, to help.

"You know, at Greyhound, if you wanted money it was a question of calling the corporate comptroller and saying, 'Charlie, I need $3 million,' and Charlie'd put it in the bank, and you paid the half-a-percent over prime and that was it. Today if I need money, I've got to go to the local bank, and it's all different. Anyway, we started a mail-order operation, which is struggling but it's showing signs of growth. We did that because the local economy is tough. We felt it would be helpful to bring dollars in from wherever. . . . Some of our best customers are in California."

He pushed some boxes aside, pulled open a closet door, and dragged down a wood box, a Bull Dog tool kit from the early 1900s. "See, we're gonna manufacture this, make copies of it. I found this at a flea market, had some new decals made up from it. Gonna put it out as a whole tool kit. We'll make 'em ourselves." He brushed some dust off of it and fondled it as though it were a puppy. He smiled to himself. As Hall sees it, you don't get off the fast track by moving to a small town, you get on a smaller track and run twice as fast.

"The payoff is you can open up this window when the sun is shining in here so brightly and look out across Penobscot Bay at probably as nice and peaceful a sight as you'll see. I've got the most beautiful apple tree I've ever seen in my whole life out in the backyard. You don't have hordes of people streaming in on you like you do in New York City, where I grew up. And the expenses are much less here. Given enough time and a few lucky breaks, I'll be able to have a business set up for the family to continue with when I'm gone: enough business to support a son, two daughters, and their respective husbands and wives. I don't know that I could have done that if I'd stayed with Greyhound. What I think I might have ended up with is a few dollars, but dollars tend to get dissipated very quickly.

"This way my son and I get to work together, going to auctions. I'm a creature that used to move on command: the company would say, 'Hey, Hall, we need you here,' and we'd go. For

a long time when I was with Chrysler we were moving an average
of every nine months. Well, that was the old corporate road to
success. When the corporation said jump, everybody lined up
and said, How high? I used to travel two weeks at a time. I'd leave
on Monday morning and go back two weeks later on a Friday
night, and my wife would meet me at the door with these sweet
kids and we'd go out to dinner that night, maybe someplace else
Sunday, and I'd get ready and leave again. Well, this way we eat,
live, and sleep together twenty-four hours a day, seven days a
week, fifty-two weeks a year. . . . You know . . . if you've got any
problems with your spouse, this is not the thing to do. Everything
comes together . . . much, much closer. And I think there's a lot
of value to that."

I asked him if, over the years, he had built up a reservoir of
anger against the corporate culture. His eyebrows shot up.

"Oh, no, I loved it. I loved it. It's a great way to make a living.
But it's a short road. It's a very short road.

"I can remember the day in Illinois in 1959 or '60. We got
orders from Detroit to cut our force in half by 5:30 that afternoon. We had fifty people working in that Chicago office and we
had to get rid of twenty-five of them. I remember going home
that night and being sick all over the floor. Throwing up. People
who would say that's easy to do are full of shit. Over the years
that gets a little hard to cope with. But you do those things. It's
no . . . personal animosity, but it's not an easy thing to do.
Corporations want to make money and that's really all they hon-
estly care about. The myth of corporate America is this: that these
bastards that run these companies have got the rest of the population thinking they're smart. They're not smart at all. They simply are the ones that are there. You could take the graduating
class of the Harvard Business School and put them in Belfast,
Maine, and 95 percent of them would be starving to death at the
end of the first year. The only way those guys could survive is to
have all these platoons of people to dig out reports and all these
bank accounts that they can go tap to get money. Well, years and
years ago, I read the biographies of the Adams family, John
Quincy and the various Adamses, and at one point, I think it was
John fell flat on his ass—lost a lot of money and had to go back
home and recoup his fortunes. The amazing thing about it was
that he could do it, because the economy in those days was
rural-based. He planted a whole bunch of crops and moved ap-

ples and sold 'em and got himself back on his feet and away he went. Eventually became president. Today, let's take the next fifty people that declare bankruptcy down in Boston—how many of them could do it? Is it available to them to do it? The farm isn't available to them anymore, but stores out in rural areas are available.

"What are you going to do with a guy who lives in Arlington and he comes home and he tells his wife that the plating factory he's worked at in the South Bronx for the last thirty years has just closed? This guy's fifty years old and started to work there when he was thirty. What the hell is he going to do? What can he do? Nothing. He's got to go down to city hall and say, I gotta have some help. And some bureaucrat says, what's the matter, you can't hold a job? There's something out of whack here . . . very, very bad. There has to be some escape for some of these people. And it isn't in any of the *ism*'s—it isn't that. The emphasis has to be brought back down to that which originally existed when this country was in its formative years, and that was very, very small entrepreneurships. . . .

"You ask me if I feel in more control of my life now. I think my life is controlling me. I've got to get out tomorrow and cut the grass because it's Memorial Day and we want to have a nice-looking place for the tourists, who may not stop.

"So," he said cheerfully, "somebody is controlling me now."

On the way back to the car, I heard someone lumbering down the grassy slope from the old hardware store and up behind me. It was Hall, the man who used to run Greyhound Van Lines, holding out a five-inch paring knife.

"Here, take this as a souvenir. See, it's got my name on it. Hall Hardware, right there."

PETERBOROUGH: REPUBLICANS, LESBIANS, AND OTHER SEEKERS

Maine, because it is still somewhat beyond the nation's economic mainstream, has been able, so far, to hold to the past. But Peterborough, New Hampshire, a day's drive from Bangor, is another case. There, people are even more fetishistic about the past, yet bits (or bytes) of the future are arriving each day.

At an artists' colony here, Thornton Wilder wrote parts of *Our Town,* in which he described the fictional town of Grover's Corners as a "very ordinary town, if you ask me. Little better behaved than most. Probably a lot duller . . . on the whole, things don't change much around here." Peterborough is only about two hours from Boston, and so draws a group of ex-urbanites different from those who head for upstate Maine. On the surface, the place is frozen in time. One expects Thornton Wilder—or Rod Serling—to step out from behind one of the colonial homes or the church spire with the clock dial that glows all night. But despite its outward appearance, Peterborough is something new. With a population of 4000, Peterborough swells during the day to over 25,000; the affluent, who live in old, restored farmhouses outside of town, come swooping into town in their Volvos and four-wheel-drive recreational vehicles.

Peterborough has fast become one of the minicapitals of America II, a center for information and small entrepreneurs: publishing and mail-order companies. Its post office is the fourth largest in the state because of the volume of information coming in and out of the village. Peterborough even has an office of the New York Stock Exchange. *Byte,* the nation's largest computer magazine, is published here, and so is *Robotics Age.* Peterborough's computer magazine industry makes up only one side of the town's publishing empire; the other half is pure nostalgia. *Yankee* magazine, a "wish book," as it is called in the trade, is comparable to *Arizona Highways* or *Sunset. Yankee* is filled with nostalgia, with stories on New England crafts, gentle families hovering over turkeys at Thanksgiving, kindly mailmen, picket fences, intact nuclear families. Even the ads, which make up half the magazine, are geared toward the rural–New England fantasy: the magazine will not accept a four-color, two page ad for Thunderbird automobiles, though it will accept spreads for four-wheel-drive vehicles. The magazine enjoys a huge circulation, over 900,000. Up until a few years ago, almost all of *Yankee*'s circulation was in small towns, but now the demand comes mainly from large urban populations; its largest single concentration of readers is in Orange County, California.

Peterborough exports both dreams: the future dream of computers and robots, and the dream of the past. Indeed, the hunger for the past is still more dominant here than the fascination with the future, and the attempt to work out a compromise between the past and the future sometimes takes on comedic tones. One fellow makes a living writing computer programs in his cabin back in the woods; ideologically, he wants a simple life, so his cabin has no electricity. But to write his programs, he needs a computer. To run his computer, he needs electricity. So he has rigged a long extension cord from the home of a friend who lives near the highway.

As in Maine, the dream is this: to slow down, to come home, to plug into a social system that allows people to know each other. Joan Leach, originally from Tulsa, Oklahoma, is now the editor of the local paper. She rejects the notion that moving to a small town insulates children from reality, or decreases tolerance: "Without a doubt, they learn more about human beings. At the age of eight, they're well aware of the guy who lives in the little shack, aware that he's sick and has serious problems, and the whole town keeps an eye on him knowing that he can't take care of himself. They're aware of a level of poverty that exists in New Hampshire, and I don't think people in any of the suburban communities I've lived in had any real contact with poverty. In the suburbs everything is stratified; kids there don't have a sense of what makes the world tick—they don't know the policeman, the plumber, the telephone repairman." Here, they do, though the plumber, as one Peterborough resident told me, is likely to be a "preppy" plumber, recently moved from a big city.

"We've got a lot of drugs here," says Leach, "but whatever my children do I've got a heck of a lot bigger chance of knowing about it. In Tulsa, it was eight and a half miles to the closest city library. It was an ordeal to get there, therefore the kids didn't use the library. But here they can walk to the library, and it has an Apple computer, too. They can go to a park, alone —I'd never have sent them alone to a park in Tulsa."

The nasty side of small towns still exists—the gossip, especially —but the caring more than makes up for it. A year ago Joan's daughter, then five years old, was hit by a car. A few days ago, Joan happened to comment to the fire chief, "Chief, guess what tomorrow is." The chief answered, "Well, it's a year's anniversary of when your daughter was hit."

The tolerance in the new small town is impressive. Gays, for instance, are moving into small towns in New England, and some of them hold on even tighter to the Rockwellian way of life than do the most conventional of families. "I'd rather be blacklisted by people who know me than ignored by people who don't," Bess Foulke told me. Foulke is a handsome woman who, along with her partner Margaret Way, operates Up Country Enterprise, a small woodworking and mail-order company in Jaffrey, a town near Peterborough. On her desk is a Richard Nixon campaign medallion. "There isn't a person around here who doesn't know, if they stop to think about it, that we're gay. But all they're interested in is how hard we work and if what we do is good work." Foulke spent most of her adult life hiding her sexual preference while teaching at private girls' schools. But when she moved up to Jaffrey, "I quit making a secret of it, because I came here to start my own business—because nobody can fire me for it."

She and her partner started out, in 1968, with a window-washing business, graduated to restoring old houses, and then moved on to making custom colonial furniture, eventually moving into a building in a small industrial park out in the woods. The business totters on the edge of bankruptcy, but Foulke is not dismayed; she epitomizes the rural work ethic. "I could lose everything I've got in the next three months, but I'd just start all over again. The market for former company presidents, especially if they're over fifty like me, is not great. But I've been reading the help-wanted ads and I find that there's a variety of things I could do. American Messenger Service wants drivers. . . . God knows, I can drive. I know a great deal about horses, so I could get a job mucking out stalls. But I think I'd like the driving the best, because I wouldn't have anybody looking over my shoulder all day." Not only is it good to be out of the closet, says Bess Foulke, but it's good to be out where people *know* her, and know that she is an individual with her own ideas.

Before moving to Peterborough, Bob Pettigrew and his family had moved around the country at the corporate behest eleven times in twelve years. He was on the road most of the year, working for IBM, the *Wall Street Journal,* and Control Data Corporation. Then one evening a few years ago, one of his few evenings at home, he tried to discipline his three-year-old daughter at the dinner table. "You're not the boss," said his daughter defiantly. "I never even see you." So Pettigrew, as he tells it, "got up right then, went into the living room and picked up a copy of *Yankee* magazine, looked at the masthead, and sat down and wrote the publisher a letter, asking for a job." A few weeks later he moved his family for what he hopes is the last time. Now he exports the dream, as advertising director for *Yankee.* "It just represents the feeling of New England," he says. "It's very wholesome. You'll never see a screaming headline about who Jackie slept with before she married Ari. It's made up of all those basic things that America consisted of a long time ago. I think people want to get back to that. All of the slick sophistication, the fast track, I think it's becoming very, very tiresome to a lot of people." Pettigrew's wife, Hope, a former schoolteacher, has started her own national magazine venture, *Cobblestone,* a history magazine for young people. *Cobblestone,* like *Yankee,* emphasises faith in the American dream and the old-fashioned symbols attached to it. Indeed, these conservative Republicans consider themselves part of a counterculture, a kind of postindustrial counterculture: people who believe that affluence and antimaterialism are not necessarily mutually exclusive, and that the best place to work out this new equation is in a small town.

"A lot of people who come here bring a lot of baggage with them, mainly materialism," said Hope at lunch at the old Peterborough Inn. "You go to some of the suburbs in major cities and you see kids and all they're concerned with is the labels on the other kids' clothing."

"We just gravitated for years toward New England," said Bob, "It's a feeling that we had to get back to the roots, back to where it all started, to where the nation started."

Hope interrupted: "The nation's history didn't really start here. But most of us WASPs think so."

They get downright mystical when they talk about Peterborough.

"There was an emptiness," said Bob. "I think we were directed to come here."

"By another force," added Hope.

Norman Rockwell painted, as he said, not the way life was, but "the way I'd like life to be." Can the dream come true, can these people find what even Rockwell said was an illusion? Peterborough's almost obsessive attachment to the past has resulted in rapidly rising property values. Soon, only the wealthy will be able to live there. "The strict zoning that keeps everything looking colonial means that there's almost no rental property available here," says Joan Leach, whose newspaper office is in a former Baptist church built in 1842 (with horsehair insulation), then owned by Bess Foulke and Margaret Way. "If we keep trying to freeze this town in history, the kids will have to live with their parents or leave. The average age of the voters at a town meeting is over fifty. Where are the younger parents, where's their sense of the future? Most of them don't even know who their selectmen are. If we don't start encouraging housing and more entry-level jobs for our children—not just the high-tech jobs for the professionals—then in twenty years or so we're just going to be a town of old people. Just like before, years ago, when all the children left and went to the city." Other changes are afoot, she says, working against the Rockwellian image. While the population is booming in Monadnock County, the number of children is declining. Divorces are on the rise. Twenty percent of the children in the area come from single-parent families.

There is a certain dynamic at work here: the more people try to hold onto the past, the faster the past seems to slip through their fingers. As the evolution of the small town continues, a curious switch in urban and rural values sometimes appears. Boston is aflurry with indignation over video games (the city's liberal, cosmopolitan mayor is vowing to have the distribution of the sin-machines curtailed), yet in some small New England cities and towns government officials are scrambling to get more of the things as a source of municipal revenue to support the services that the newcomers demand. And in the New Hampshire woods, grown men, many of them urban exiles, skulk through the woods in camouflage suits and face paint, shooting each other with Nel-Spot automatics, which fire paint-filled gelatin balls, as part of the National Survival Game. The tempo of change is quickening, with brand-new forms of neorural life beginning to spread through the woods, across the pastures, into the mountains. Yet the dream of a simple life survives.

Dick and Eleanor Moore, who are older, have seen the new pilgrims come and seen them go and seen them come again. The Moores live out on a plot of land near Peterborough that Dick's ancestors settled on in the seventeenth century. The Moore family has never left the land. Dick Moore, a gentle man who looks like Jimmy Stewart in overalls, is respected in the community. He talks in riddles sometimes, but people listen. He stood on his porch one afternoon and looked out across the misty green fields and unchanging stone fences. "You know, we don't know everything about how places affect us. This is good land, healing land. There are bands of good land and bands of bad land. The Celts knew this. The Indians knew this. Just over that ridge is a band of bad land. Been that way as long as my family's been here. People move in over there and something always goes wrong: divorce, poverty, murder. You have to be careful where you settle, because where you settle can become what you are."

He is bemused by the people who come expecting quiet, but sometimes find the voices inside them amplified. He likes to tell about an ex-urbanite next door, who could not sleep because the apples kept falling. "She was always waiting for that next apple."

Some of the people who have moved here from the cities come to see his wife, Eleanor, a pixyish, bright-eyed woman. Eleanor is a psychic. On her business card it says "consultant." She specializes in people who have moved from the city. While I sat with her, three middle-class women who had moved here recently waited on the porch.

"They begin to have strange night dreams," Eleanor told me. "They find out how afraid they are. Very afraid. It's like they don't realize their fear until they get away from the cities."

She smiled and leaned over toward me.

"Some of them come here to live out their nightmares."

13

THE NEW AMERICAN GOTHIC

The difficulty in discussing rural America II is that it is changing so quickly. The forces that allow people to move backward in time are the same forces that, inevitably, drive them forward into a future that they may or may not desire. Each rural area, small town, or small city approaches the new dynamic in its own way. Some resist "progress," others welcome it. But the forces, like an approaching front, move closer, regardless of what the new and old ruralites think about it. The real question is whether what comes will replenish rural America, like the rain, or become a storm of such fury that nothing will be left intact. The new is as much a process as it is a collection of places.

On the window of Hezzy's General Store in Davis, South Dakota, a village thirty miles from Sioux Falls, is a handwritten sign advertising a high school play. It reads, *Requiem for a Small Town.* But Dean "Hezzy" Lodde thinks a celebration is in order. Davis is experiencing what Hezzy considers a population boom: the number of residents rose from 101 in 1979 to 125 in 1981. "Couple years ago, they all started coming back. The young folks who left a long time ago, but mainly new folks. One couple from New York were lookin' around last week; just wanted to get out of there," says Hezzy, a grizzled man in his fifties who has lived in Davis all his life. He was sitting in the back room of his store, where he maintains one ragged, red vinyl booth and a microwave oven as the town's restaurant/poker parlor. "Thank God they're openin' up the cafe again. Takes the pressure off me." He grinned. "The local people are tickled pink. Fill 'er up, that's what I say!" Davis is becoming a suburb of Sioux Falls, thirty miles away.

To the Census Bureau, Sioux Falls, population 81,343, is a city; but to someone trying to escape New York or Los Angeles or Chicago, Sioux Falls is a small town. It is a town that still epitomizes rural values, yet it is also one with an apparently great economic future. Indeed, the rural rush is a regional phenomenon, not just the rebirth of small towns. Especially in those regions distant from large, older metropolitan areas, small cities such as Sioux Falls are on the rise. In the midst of the worst national economy since the Great Depression, Sioux Falls is enjoying one of the lowest unemployment rates in the country and is growing steadily, having gained almost 20,000 residents since 1960, a growth rate twice the national average. "Invest in a Profit Frontier," exclaims a four-page ad for South Dakota in *USA Today.* In one column, the ad mentions the low crime rate (fiftieth in the nation in murders). Appropriately near this column is a photograph of a row of books—Laura Ingalls Wilder's *Little House on the Prairie* series. Among the reasons for Sioux Falls's prosperity: Citibank recently moved its entire international credit card division to Sioux Falls—one gigantic computerized brain, zipping and zapping the debits of millions of people all over the world. Like many businesses leaving the old industrial cities, Citibank was attracted to South Dakota's favorable business laws and the absence of personal or corporate income taxes. The move brought several dozen New York executives and 3000 promised jobs to Sioux Falls.

Richard G. McCrossen, president of Citibank, South Dakota (which also owns Carte Blanche), sat in his office beneath a stuffed pheasant and talked of his surprise at life in Sioux Falls: "I was born and raised in New York and I've managed Citibank companies all over the country, always relocating for the company. But if they asked me to move again—as they often do with executives, about every five years—I'd have a tough time deciding. Friends in New York think I've gone over the line, gone native. They don't understand. When I was in New York, I'd spend three hours a day commuting by train; I rationalized it as reading time. Here, it takes me about ten minutes to get to work, and I live out on a little ranch." There is something here, he adds, in the people: a set of values that an army of management consultants could not teach. "We spent a *lot* of money in New York trying to change the attitude of tellers. Well, the teller has traveled an hour and a half to get to work; no wonder he or she is difficult. Out here, it's understood that people should be treated humanely. Maybe it's the commute. It's different here. You can get things done. There's a lot of volunteerism. I'm a board member of the South Dakota Symphony. I contracted a $7.5 million building project here on a handshake. It was 80 percent completed before we ever had a written contract, and then it was 12 pages instead of 120. The New York office thought I was crazy, but I insisted that we do things the way they do them in South Dakota." He paused and a pained look came over his face. "I'll tell you another thing," he said softly, "Sioux Falls is the first place I've ever lived that I didn't have to worry about my wife getting her head cut off."

Yet the values and insulation from the rest of the nation's problems are being chipped away by the economic forces he has helped bring to Sioux Falls and its rural surroundings. Sioux Falls and similar towns are assuming a form more like San Diego or Houston than the older cities; they are surrounded by lacy concentric circles and clusters and nodes of new development near or beyond the edge of town: shopping malls, a boom-town strip of new service industries. Condominium developments are now popular in Sioux Falls. The movement is outward, into the most rural areas, into little villages like Davis. Suddenly, strips of mobile homes are showing up along the roads for miles into the country; many of the new arrivals prefer to move out of town, into once-vacant farm homes sold or rented by farmers. The future is moving across these plains.

THE FORCE

The force behind the transformation is the changing rural economy, which has, in many areas of the new country, moved far beyond recreation, tourism, and the kinds of small entrepreneurial enterprises found in upstate Maine. The growing rural prosperity is the product of industrial and business deconcentration, a movement that began at the turn of the century. Companies like Citibank are establishing branch offices and plants in small cities in regions that are primarily rural; and beyond the cities, in small towns; and sometimes even beyond the small towns, far out and physically isolated in the countryside.

Most people think that moving to the country means earning

less money, sacrificing an urban standard of living. That was generally true in the past, and it still is true in many nonmetropolitan areas. In fact, many rural people are still locked into poverty. But a new body of evidence suggests that people with the right postindustrial skills can often increase their income by moving to the country. Several studies show that three-fourths of the people who move to rural areas are of preretirement age. Most of them, therefore, would not necessarily move to a rural area if jobs did not exist. The surveys of sociologist John Wardwell suggest that people who move to rural areas may anticipate one year of income loss; but after that year, income often shoots back up, to a level higher than their previous income in the city. "Realizing that they can have their cake and eat it too," he says, "Americans are a practical people."

The rural economy is now more urban than rural. At the turn of the century, half of all Americans lived and worked on farms; today, just over 3 percent do. The pace of economic transformation has picked up considerably in the late 1970s and early '80s. By 1980, almost two-thirds of all nonmetropolitan workers were employed in the service sector. Rural areas are experiencing a rate of increase in new jobs twice that of metropolitan areas; between 1970 and 1978, while the 225 largest metropolitan areas suffered a net loss of 513,000 manufacturing jobs, nonmetropolitan counties experienced an increase of 619,000 manufacturing jobs. Even this increase in manufacturing jobs is insignificant compared with the rise in service jobs. The yeoman farmer has, for the most part, been replaced by the fast-food service worker. Over three and a half million service-sector jobs emerged in nonmetro counties in the 1970s. By 1980, nearly two-thirds of all nonmetropolitan workers were employed in the expanding service sector, and the trend continues. The new rural economy is especially nurturing to such exportable service industries as printing, direct mailing, data processing, and warehousing.

Jobs are springing up in new office parks and industrial developments along or near interstate highways, and the trend is outward, to smaller communities well beyond the pull of big cities. One Kansas official notes that, of new industries setting up shop in his state, almost 70 percent located in towns of fewer than 50,000 people. The continued dispersal of business and industry to rural areas is encouraged by tax policies that favor new construction over the rehabilitation of old facilities. More importantly, by emphasizing low taxes, minimal union activity, and eager workers steeped in the work ethic, some primarily rural states have aggressively courted industry. The tax benefits work in two ways: first, the rural states generally have fewer taxes; second, the rural localities have become adept at offering special tax breaks for incoming business. By its nature, a place with fewer people means lower taxes: the fewer residents in a town, the less tax revenue required to support municipal services and schools —and that means lower property taxes for the incoming corporation. In some instances, towns make themselves attractive to business by building industrial or office parks, new roads, and airports. Moving a plant to a rural area also has the benefit of much lower relocation costs than if the plant was moved to, say, Los Angeles, or even Houston.

Indeed, the movement of people and industries into expanding southern and western cities may be only the beginning of a long turn. Like a wind deferred, the America II migration heads first to such cities as Houston and San Diego, but then, finding these destinations too high-priced, too overblown, too lonely, bends toward rural areas. Californians who chased the American dream west now find that it cannot always be found on the coast. And so they look elsewhere; they head off to Oregon, or they move to the rural Midwest.

According to a 1981 report issued by the Joint Center for Urban Studies of MIT and Harvard, titled "Regional Diversity, Growth in the United States, 1960–1990," the nation is headed for a resurgence of growth in the west-north-central states, and in northern New England. Futurist think tank Chase Econometrics notes that the farm belt, with low unemployment rates, few large cities, and low wage rates, is beginning to attract inmigrants, after a long hiatus during which the sun belt states drew most migrants. Some regions of the country (one notable one is the Silicon Valley, in and around San Jose, California) are suffering excessive concentrations of one industry, permitting people to job-hop for increasingly higher wages. Similarly, small entrepreneurs are learning that service industries successful in big cities can be exported to fresh rural markets.

So the force of the new rural economics is increasing, moving across the landscape, changing everything. In a few years, rural

America may be only vaguely recognizable; the nostalgic vision that so many people are trying so hard to grasp is turning in their hands, transforming.

One eventually has to ask if the word *rural* has any meaning left to it, at least in the way we have grown accustomed to using it. It is still associated with farming, even though only 3 percent of nonmetropolitan people still live on farms; and the word *urban* is still associated with modernity, even though most nonmetropolitan business and industrial facilities are more modern than city structures. In a sense, what most of us consider rural America has disappeared.

THE URBANIZING COUNTRYSIDE

George Orwell described a nation's culture as "an everlasting animal stretching into the future and the past, and, like all living things, having the power to change out of recognition and yet remain the same." Can the same be said of rural America? Sociologist John Shelton Reed, a North Carolinian, looks at the rural and small-town South and wonders at all the transformations he sees, the new forms rising from the old and yet retaining some essence of what has passed. New technologies and economic evolution, he says, simply provide new ways to do old things: Muslims are summoned to prayer by electronic *muezzins,* and Orthodox Jews ride automated elevators on Shabbat. Likewise, *Southern Living* magazine advertises "Old-South columns" for the homebuilder. (The columns are made of extruded aluminum.) A Burger Queen in Pikeville, Kentucky, attracts the after-church crowd with a salad bar including hominy and fried okra; and a newspaper recipe column reports the return of Southern beaten biscuits, now that they can be made with a food processor instead of a wooden mallet.

One thinks of *American Gothic,* the famous painting of a grim-faced, rock-hard, possibly Presbyterian rural couple. If Grant Wood were to paint it today, he might depict a younger, ex-urban couple: the man might be holding a pitchfork, the woman have one hand on a personal computer. As the new rural economy changes the job patterns, so also it changes the physical landscape and social structure of rural America. We have gone looking for the country, and we have found the city, albeit on a much smaller scale. Rural areas are losing, have already lost, the characteristics that made them different from urban America: the social isolation, the economic homogeneity—dependence on agriculture, and extractive and small-scale manufacturing and processing industries—and now that they are integrated into the national economic system they have lost whatever degree of autonomy they once had. What has been retained is the small size and low settlement density. In return for what they have lost, they have regained population and economic activity.

Nonmetropolitan America can no longer be thought of as the stereotypes we have usually applied to it—the bucolic farm; the sleepy, tree-shaded, and unsophisticated small town; the visions of Rockwell. As Wardwell writes, if one word could capture the nature of contemporary rural society, it is the word *diversity:* "Freed from both the dependence-induced homogeneity of earlier decades and the crushing size and density of large metropolitan systems, growing smaller cities and open countryside have the flexibility to develop in a wider variety of ways than could have been imagined even so short a time as two decades ago." The gaps between urban and rural have been narrowing dramatically in the past few decades, so that now, Wardwell contends, differences between rural *now* and rural *then* are greater than the residual differences between urban and rural.

The new Eden is expressed in three entirely new forms: the far suburbs where the anticity becomes the new country; "buckshot urbanization" that amounts to huge, almost invisible cities; and the growth of sophisticated, complex "micropolitan" small towns. Within these forms, the kind of homes rural people are living in are changing as well.

The Anticity Meets the New Country

The line between the city and the country is growing thin indeed; as are the definitions of the words *rural* and *urban.* The everlasting animal stretches. . . .

Middle-class residents who moved from St. Louis, Missouri, suburbs years ago to rural areas near the city are now moving farther out, building full-time homes on farms or in rural subdivisions. For many, using the interstate highway system, it is quicker to get to work from these areas than from downtown St. Louis.

The Denver, Colorado, metropolitan region now sprawls from Fort Collins through Boulder to Denver, and beyond to Colorado Springs and Englewood. A few years ago, much of this was devoted only to farming and ranching, but today a thinly urbanized countryside extends 150 miles across the eastern edge of the state.

To further understand this postindustrial fuzziness regarding the definitions of rural and urban, one need only take a long drive from San Mateo Canyon, California, 150 miles east past the desolate Salton Sea and into the desert, turn north and drive on 90 miles to Needles and 90 miles beyond, take a left to China Lake, and then drive south another 150 miles to San Mateo Canyon. "Believe it or not, you have never left metropolitan Riverside, California," according to Cheryl Russell, writing in *American Demographics.* The Riverside–San Bernardino–Ontario standard metropolitan statistical area (the Census Bureau's term for a city with a population over 50,000) is the largest in the nation, covering more than 27,000 square miles of urbanity, mountains, sand, and sagebrush. Riverside's population density is only forty-eight people per square mile, lower than the U.S. average of sixty-one. (In contrast, Jersey City has 12,000 people per square mile.)

As this demonstrates, the size and characteristics of what government considers to be a city are quite flexible. Some cities comprise as many as ten counties and thousands of square miles, as Russell points out; others are just a single county and a few hundred square miles. "All are metropolitan by definition, but not all their residents have a metropolitan lifestyle."

What is urban and what is rural, and where does the anticity leave off and the new country begin?

Buckshot Urbanization

At some point, these "urban" formations cut loose from their physical attachment to big cities or even, to some extent, to small towns. A new form of living arrangement, even more difficult to define than the anticity, is then born. This new form is not considered by government agencies to be a city of any sort—and yet it is. The fastest growing nonmetropolitan areas are not specifically the small towns, but the regions of open country around and between them. So the definitions of urban and rural are further weakened when one considers the arrival of a peculiar new form called "buckshot urbanization," which in some areas of the new country can be considered a "countrified city," or "suburbs without cities."

Buckshot urbanization is scattered along country roads and highways. Seen from up close it does not look like much—a house trailer here, a new electronics firm back in the woods there—but if one can imagine it from a great distance, one begins to get a sense of a fairly intricate form. A countrified city, as the Urban Land Institute describes it, is "a loose collection of small towns, crossroads communities, and other development strung along country roads, bound together by common economic, social, and cultural pursuits which are basically urban in nature." New housing is strung along newly paved rural roads; occasionally, culs-de-sac are cut from cornfields; brick ranch homes, many of them financed by the Farmers Home Administration, are replacing the old, swaybacked "shotgun" houses of earlier decades. The new settlement pattern is essentially a semisuburb stretched out over wide regions of landscape, seemingly independent from any large cities. Unlike the metropolitan suburbs, buckshot settlement does not require a central city—it does not even require a major employment center. It just grows slowly across the land, arms and legs stretching out, headless. It just happens. A countrified city, invisible as a whole settlement from close up, can be spread throughout a single county or several counties. In the northern plains, numerous and nameless countrified cities are scattered thinly over sweeping, wide regions. In Appalachia, the countrified cities are scrunched down into long, narrow valleys connected like sausage links, sometimes hundreds of miles long. In parts of New Hampshire, long rows of houses are strung along once-remote roads. In central Illinois, factories have appeared, far from any town or city. The map of Nash County, Tennessee, looks "as if it has the measles," wrote John Herbers of the *New York Times,* so many new subdivisions have been started in the most rural sections of the county, usually by farmers who have sold off a section of land, usually providing no water or sewer systems, just wells and septic tanks.

One example of the countrified city is in Montgomery County, North Carolina. Some 20,000 people live sixty miles east of the city of Charlotte. About 6000 of them live in five small towns, but the rest are scattered in a network (or, more precisely, a web) of open country, farms, crossroads villages, small subdivisions of split-levels on a few acres, and strip communities of mobile homes along the country roads. What is interesting about this invisible "city" is not just where the people live, wrote Herbers, but what they do:

> They work in offices and factories and at service jobs. They send their children to consolidated schools not much different from those in the suburbs of big cities. They shop mainly in suburban-type shopping centers. This means that despite the spread-out nature of development in this country, the residents have a large number of common interests and concerns regarding public services and other matters that are very 'urban.' Yet to the outsider, particularly the outsider from the big city, Montgomery appears 'down-home country' in every aspect, the very model of the rural mid-South.

The existence of this invisible web of new settlements has been barely recognized by planners, politicians, or the public. It's not just the availability of sophisticated satellite television reception discs or better highways that is making this possible, but the mundane technology of septic tanks! Small-but-beautiful waste-water treatment systems potentially could have more effect on the dispersion of people into the countryside than the personal computer. In recent years, in order to protect the environment, federal agencies have begun encouraging alternative small-scale wastewater treatment systems. Some twenty types of these alternative systems exist, including hybrid septic tanks, sand filter systems, mound systems, and evapotranspiration beds, allowing people to build houses in places that would not previously have tolerated a primitive septic tank. New ruralites can now bypass community sewer systems and the local governments that operate them.

Buckshot urbanization is also creating a new kind of urban/rural person, and an inherently antigovernment environment. J. C. Doherty, a former Agriculture Department official, writes, "An urban-in-rural man or woman may work in the next county, shop in several different towns and cities, send the kids to school in two, three, or more different directions (depending on the number of kids), go to a doctor in the growth center fifty miles down the interstate, and to church in a nearby village. To such people, these are all familiar urban neighborhoods." Except, writes Doherty, that they sprawl over a "city" that may be hundreds of square miles in size, without anything that could be considered a center. The countrified city is for those Americans who are basically urban in character, but who have turned their backs on higher density living in big cities, or even in small towns. As an Urban Land Institute report puts it, "This new form of rural settlement is different from both suburbs and city. It is different primarily because it attempts to mesh the freedom and environmental satisfaction of rural life with the convenience and amenities of urban development." Not just the counterculture/libertarians have settled in the invisible webs, but corporations, too. For instance, as California's Silicon Valley fills to overflowing, high tech companies are moving out far beyond the cities to the foothills of the Sierra. Rural North Carolina has attracted scores of big corporate plants, hidden away in the woods; North Carolina may, in fact, be the most dramatic example of dispersed urbanization: the state has no big cities, yet it is the tenth most populated in the nation.

The Small Town Becomes Micropolis

Scattered through the new webs of settlement are small towns that are far from rural or unsophisticated. What distinguishes so many of these new or revived towns is that they do not depend on the traditional sources of rural income, farming and mining. They are, instead, plugged into the postindustrial economy. Social scientist Luther Tweeten has suggested that the word *micropolitan* be used to describe the many small cities and towns whose economies are no longer much different from those of big metropolitan areas. Small towns once dependent on agriculture are now becoming important manufacturing centers: Centerville, Iowa, population 7000, has evolved in a single decade from a trading center for farmers and unemployed coal miners to a "bustling manufacturing center" with six new factories; in the county in which Centerville is located, more people work in manufacturing than in agriculture. Just two decades ago, the ratio was seven agricultural workers to every manufacturing worker. These new manufacturing centers are joined by "information towns": the spread of colleges and rural university extensions has created a network of information repositories, as in Winona, Minnesota, and Peterborough, New Hampshire.

The attraction of high-tech companies to rural America means that small towns often represent the technological leading edge. Consider, for example, The Waitsfield-Fayston Telephone Company, a private concern that has earned the reputation of being one of the most innovative telephone companies in the nation, having wired the Mad River Valley, a rural Vermont resort area, with a network of telephones, cable television, and computer operations. Years before the Bell System began its charge-a-call program, Waitsfield made its public phones payless. And the company plans to introduce an electronic mailbox that would allow callers to leave messages in a central computer for second parties. This was announced in the same year that the last hand-crank phone system in America, in an isolated region of rural Maine, was phased out—and then saved by outraged and nostalgic citizens. Not far away, on Monhegan Island, a tiny lobstering community off the Maine coast (population sixty), islanders who have traditionally used kerosene lamps and candles are installing rooftop photovoltaic solar cells for electricity generation.

The countryside has always been more technologically sophisticated than it was given credit for. (The automobile, for instance, came first to the rural areas, where the need was greatest; in 1920, the states with the greatest car ownership per capita were South Dakota, Iowa, and Nebraska.) What is different now is not just that small towns are using high technology, but that so many small towns have become the producers of it; small towns in Arizona, such as Chandler, Sierra Vista, and Casa Grande, attract over half of the new industries coming into the state: corporations like IBM, Hexcel Corporation (which produces parts of the space shuttle), Motorola, and the Itel Corporation.

HYPERCULTURE COMES TO THE COUNTRY

The transformation of nonmetropolitan America doesn't stop with the three major new forms, the urban/rural fringe, buckshot urbanization, and micropolis. Within the new rural framework is a variety of new forms of rural shelter and planned community. In some ways, new rural shelter is even more creative than the new shelter of older cities and anticities. *Mother Earth News* bulges with plans for energy-efficient country solar homes, "hybrid geo-

tempered envelopes," low-cost earth shelters, solar-heated subterranean guest houses, and what one article calls a "Hobbitat."
New rural shelter ranges from the energy-experimental to the
prefab—prefabricated log cabins. But the new rural shelter doesn't stop there. In several corners of the new rural landscape,
home is where the hangar is. People who would rather fly than
drive live in a new kind of small town: some forty air parks around
the United States, in California and the farm country around
Chicago, in Florida, Arizona, New York, Colorado, and New
Hampshire. The homes in these new communities have driveways out in front and taxiways in back. "When the kids ask for
the keys to go out," says one air park resident, "you don't know
what keys they mean—for the car or for the airplane."

As rural and small-town America becomes less recognizable,
the imagineers (who have designed rural, small-town affectations
in so many condo communities in the cities and suburbs) arrive
with their blueprints, remanufacturing the past. In rural shelter,
the most marketable idea is that you can have it all: a trash
compactor in the kitchen, antlers over the fireplace, a view of a
wild stream, and an entertainment room with a giant-screen view
of the world. This is particularly true of recreation towns, like
Blue Eye, Mountain Home, Eureka Springs, and other villages of
the Ozark Mountains in northwest Arkansas, given new life by the
U.S. Army Corps of Engineers, who built a series of scenic Ozark
lakes in the 1950s and '60s. In the Rocky Mountain states, dying
mining and ranchers' trading towns such as Aspen, Colorado,
have come roaring back with the clatter of skis and arrival of
luxury condos. Even tiny Telluride, Colorado, has, as writer Edward Abbey puts it, an "eighty-seven cell condominium." The
rural planned community, a new "improved" small town, is often
a parody of the past—a kind of frontier chic. These communities
are especially popular in the Rocky Mountains. One of them, in
Jackson Hole, Wyoming, offers "natural moss" fireplaces and
"fully automatic" two-car garages. Marketers focus primarily on
the airline magazines, with full-page color ads for new communities like Caroline Point Estates & Yacht Club in Lakeside, Montana, "a premier waterfront development on Montana's fabulous
Flathead Lake," with "only" eighty-four prestigious townhouses
available, priced from $179,000. The community offers golf
courses within sight of Glacier National Park, dogwoods along

split-rail fences, tennis courts, and a marina—all separated from
the rest of the country, in one of the least populated areas of the
country. At times, these thriving, packaged, neo–small towns can
be seen right next to dying traditional small towns.

The language of ads that sell the frontier chic developments is
revealing. Here is one for Forbes Wagon Creek Ranch in Fort
Garland, Colorado, *Forbes* magazine's private mountain hidea-
way. It describes what amounts to a reservation for Postindustrials:

> Do you love the wide open spaces? Clean air? The beauty of
> nature? Are they part of the legacy you have planned for your
> loved ones?
>   Owning a large piece of land in America is possibly the most
> important decision you will ever make. Not only will you enjoy the
> rare privilege and pleasure of owning sizable ranchland today, it
> can remain a private corner of America in the future history of
> your family. . . . Here in the foothills of the magnificent Rocky
> Mountains, with restricted access to more than 17,000 acres (over
> twenty-six square miles), you can hunt deer, elk, grouse, and all
> kinds of wild game in season. . . . Your ranchland bestows on your
> heirs the privilege of an unspoiled way of life.

The wealthy have always had their mountain cabins and re-
treats, but the separation is taking on some curious characteristics. These places are the "wilderness" equivalent of The Towers
of Quayside and Rancho Bernardo. In the postindustrial age the
gap is widening between those with access to the new economy's
skills and knowledge, and those without; and so there is reason
for the Postindustrials to head for the hills and, once there, band
together in psychic and physical defense of one another.

Such rustic living seems to have some natural limits. In the
mountain towns of Colorado, a lot of relatively affluent people
have set up housekeeping to get away from such urban discom-
forts as air pollution. Now they encounter what one Vail resident described to a reporter for the *Los Angeles Times* as "our
own brown cloud," caused by the burning of wood in frontier
chic fireplaces. Beaver Creek's coping mechanism is the ultimate in frontier chic, the essence of contradictory America II.
Beaver Creek is a luxurious (house lots start at $300,000)

planned community high in the Rocky Mountains offering, well, the finest in rustic living. But state air quality officials noted Beaver Creek's growing air pollution problem, so the state slapped a limit of 1000 fireplaces on 3223 housing units under construction. This was a major blow to the developers, who knew they could ask up to $20,000 more for a house if it had a fireplace. An agreement was struck. Cliff Simonton, "environmental coordinator" for Beaver Creek's developers, Vail Associates, described the imposed wood-burning controls, allowing fireplaces in every home: Beaver Creek will monitor the air. When pollution in the planned community reaches excessive levels, a central computer will turn on a red light placed on every fireplace. The light will direct residents not to start a fire, or to add fuel to a fire already burning. In each chimney, a heat sensing device will tell the Beaver Creek computer whether the family is complying. "The company is going to know when a fire is burning in each home," Simonton said. "Security guards will be dispatched to offending homeowners with buckets of water and a schedule of fines—ranging from a warning the first time to a $500 penalty for the fourth offense."

Mobile Homes and Movable Towns

One factor allowing more people to live where they want to live, despite booms or busts or high interest rates, is advanced technology in mobile homes, which can be bought for 10 to 30 percent less than traditional homes of similar size and design. For many Americans, especially those less affluent, the mobile home is the new log cabin. But here, too, there is growing sophistication. In the Napa Valley, a new resident in 1982 paid $81,000 for a triple-section, colonial-style 2400 square foot mobile home that includes a library with a fireplace, huge bathroom with Jacuzzi, kitchen with a microwave oven and trash compactor, and even a roof of wood shingles. The home could easily have cost twice as much if built conventionally.

One of the ironies of picturesque small towns like Jackson, Wyoming, is that many of the people drawn there, who work in low-paying service jobs, cannot afford to live there. In Mammoth, California, the problem is so severe that some merchants have had to shut down because good help, priced out of the housing market, was so hard to find. As a consequence, outside small towns all over the country are parks of trailer homes, pushed in together. These parks are the antithesis of country living.

Among the most bizarre new forms in nonmetropolitan America is the mobile town, sometimes made up of people who are escaping the effects of urbanization on the small towns from which they come.

A good example can be seen in California's Imperial County. Each fall, as the Chocolate Mountains shimmer violet in the diminishing heat, an unlikely population of migrants arrives in the desert near the Salton Sea, hauling trailers, driving vans and pickup campers with "Senior Power" bumper stickers. These are primarily people from small towns in the north. Many of them say that they can no longer feel at home in their own hometowns, with the growing crime, with all the change. So they have gone off and created their own movable towns. They bring with them their cardiac medicines, crutches, books, bicycles, and dominoes —and a fierce independence learned a long time ago. These "snowbirds," as they are called, winter without electricity or sanitation facilities on a desolate stretch of federal land called "the slabs," where General George S. Patton trained his troops during World War II. These are scores of these movable towns in California and Arizona. Imperial County's Sheriff Oren Fox, who counts snowbirds from the air, estimates that the population of his county's movable town reaches 20,000 in the winter. Nationally, there may be as many as several hundred thousand living in this manner. Economics draws seniors into the migrant stream, but something quite different keeps them coming back: a sense of community that they often don't find in their own home towns. "We make more friends and better friends on the road than we do at home, and we almost always see them every year," one woman told me. "We feel safer here than we do at home."

A few winters ago, an evangelist organization set up the non-denominational Campers' Christian Center in a mobile home out on the slabs (also known as Slab City), where campers are spread out over several square miles. The Christian Center attempted to set up a formal registration system for the incoming snowbirds. But when they erected a sign outside the center that said "Registry Slab," it disappeared quickly. As one resident explained, "We lived with regimentation all our lives, and we just don't want it anymore." Over the years, the snowbirds have agreed, without any formal vote, that rules were fine as long as they remained voluntary and subtle. Phil Shirey, a nurse practitioner who comes out to visit the residents of the movable town, describes it as "a form of anarchy that works." As they arrive each fall, the snowbirds can, if they wish, enter their names and the names of their next-of-kin, to be contacted in case of emergencies, into a voluntary registration system operated by a somewhat humbled Campers' Christian Center. No signs designate its existence.

Since the slabs are in such a desolate location—distant from emergency services, without telephone service—the seniors have established their own radio station, of sorts, on a CB band. At seven each evening a snowbird called Good Sam clicks on the CB station and calls roll. If anyone fails to answer, a search party goes out. "Why, we had some folks from Alaska here a while back. They wandered away from their camper one night and couldn't find their way back and we had to go out and find 'em," says "Tex," a woman with fiery red hair. "Ever since then, we called that family 'the lost Alaskans.' " The CB radio station has become so popular, in fact, that some residents are beginning to complain about all the gossiping that goes on over the airwaves.

During the last few years, a new element has been added to the social fabric of the slabs. Younger people are beginning to arrive, families down on their luck, who are taken in by the seniors. A family from Oklahoma came through: a young mother who owned only one blouse, her two-year-old child, who had no shoes, and the father, who had no job. The snowbirds fed them, clothed them, helped them obtain welfare and work in nearby Brawley. The seniors are not particularly enthusiastic about their Good Samaritan role. Life for the snowbirds goes on much as it has for the last decade. Men and women who have lost their spouses move in together. They ride their bicycles along Highway 111, arrange potluck dinners, throw horseshoes. One fellow from Iowa misses his pastures, and so tried to plant a little lawn out in front of his van. He laughs: "I planted grass and got snakes." Each evening, campfires light the desert, in pinpricks which stretch toward every horizon. The small town never dies, it just moves on.

Resistance

Ultimately, one wonders how much small-town and rural America can change in form before they lose all essence of self outside of those packaged reminders that once upon a time, on this land, was a naturally born American small town—one that disappeared into parody during an era that revered the small town and all that was rural.

Certainly, many people in rural America welcome the new rural economy and the new variety, but the new ruralites most passionate about nature and the past feel only pain when they consider the growing number of people moving to their Eden. They wish to close the door behind them.

In a seemingly lost little New Mexico valley along the Pecos River, settled sparsely with Hispanic farms, I met a family who had gone as far as they could go from big cities and from technology. Sick of an essentially urban life that seemed to them to be empty of meaning, Nick Raven, a teacher at Eastern New Mexico University, and his wife, Isabel, a steno clerk, gave up their jobs and spent their savings, $15,000, on a little plot of land and a decaying old one-room adobe house—no electricity, no plumbing. For three years now, they and their two small children have scraped a living from the land, and from odd jobs in a little town nearby.

One hot afternoon, while dust devils spun along the dirt road and skimmed up the red rock ridges, Nick talked about his life in the valley. As he talked, he mixed adobe—mud, sand, and straw —in a hole in the ground. "We can't go backwards completely. After three years of cultivating with a hoe, cutting hay by hand, digging irrigation ditches with a shovel, you realize why farmers leapt at the tractor and irrigation pumps. But there's a limit. This kind of community is good for the land precisely because it's so underutilized. All the "wasted space" is used by nature: mesquite patches for quail, fence lines for pheasants, apple trees in the fields, forests full of deer. If this valley is tamed, what I love about it will just cease to exist. A fellow just moved here from Albuquerque, rich fellow, a politician, very unhappy about our ditch system and our community water system, which works only 80 percent of the time. Out here we're used to it. Anyway, after a really divisive struggle—some of the residents actually physically prevented the state engineer from installing new pumps and water towers—we now have higher water rates and water more often. But it took the state police to come down and give it to us. Are we happier? Maybe the next advance will be paving the roads, then perhaps a new 7-Eleven with gas—then a retirement community, maybe a trailer park and a couple condos." He stood up straight and leaned on his hoe. "What's left then of the old valley, where everything except bringing in the hay could wait till tomorrow, when Spanish was the language, where everyone was related to everyone else, where it was downright provincial and didn't know the word?" He attacked the mud again with the hoe, angrily. "If this valley goes, I hope it doesn't go quietly."

THE PRICE OF EDEN

Currently, the new Eden is calm, the kind of calm that comes before one of those electrical storms on the plains that fill the skies with a rain of lightning. One survey indicated that of those who have moved to a nonmetropolitan area, 91 percent say life is healthier in the new location, 82 percent say they now feel safer, and 87 percent say the rural area is a better place to raise children. And 78 percent say they're unlikely to move again within the next three years. Yet, one wonders how long the calm can last. The contradictions and forces built into the new country guarantee conflict—between the poor and the arriving migrants who are chiefly affluent; between the new rural economy and agriculture; between those who wish to close the door behind them and those who still want to come, who still yearn for the image of elsewhere. Ultimately, the conflict is between the dream and the reality.

Charles E. Little and W. Wendell Fletcher, authors of a two-year study by the American Land Forum for the Council on Environmental Quality, write: "To those observing the changes that are occurring in rural America, it might appear as if a modern version of the Jeffersonian promise of an enlightened rural society is finally beginning to emerge," a rural society with a revival of small farms and the latest in electronic communication; a rural society with cultural activities ranging from Shakespeare in Ashland, Oregon, to the opera in Santa Fe, to the regional theater in tidewater North Carolina; a rural society with first-run movies and all the other amenities of suburbia, but with clean air and intact natural beauty. "This promise of a rural environment replete with cultural, educational, and social amenities may have never seemed so real. And yet, the chance that this historical ideal will slip away, just as it comes within grasp of the average American family, is almost foreordained unless decisive new policies to direct rural growth and change are instituted almost immediately." The euphoria of rural romanticism can mask several unsavory realities. Here are a few of them.

THE HIDDEN AND NOT-SO-HIDDEN IMPACT ON LOCAL CULTURE

In many ways, what remains of the traditional rural America that so many of us romanticize is like a foreign culture. In the *Small Towns Book,* James and Carolyn Robertson write:

> It is quite correct that change is bound to occur. . . . What concerns us is that as the pressure of urban migrations mounts, rural communities will be forced to abandon the traditional qualities that we most seek in them. At the very moment we most need those who are trained culturally and occupationally to assist us in relearning the skills of self-sufficiency, we are obliterating them by assimilation. . . . But there is no need to feel contrite over the way in which we trample the countryside—providing that as we trample it, we are continuously seeking to understand what is underfoot, and how to tread more lightly.

Secondly, though the movement to the country has been called a "rural renaissance," one wonders who the revival is for. There are at least two rural Americas: one going uphill, one going downhill. Full-time farmers in the early 1980s face the worst economic conditions since the 1930s. Large segments of rural Americans have never tasted affluence; in 1968, President Johnson's National Advisory Commission on Rural Poverty reported that, contrary to popular belief, it was rural America that suffered the highest rates of poverty, infant mortality, malnutrition, illiteracy, and underemployment. That rural America still exists. While rural economic development teams religiously await the coming boom in high-technology manufacturing, many nonmetropolitan counties are tied to the automobile, steel, and other fading industries. Often, the new and prosperous rural America exists right alongside intense poverty. Sugar Loaf Mountain, in Franklin County, Maine, is one of the East Coast's great ski resorts, a scenic refuge offering condominiums at the mountain's edge and a pulsating nightlife for affluent New Yorkers and Bostonians. But, as the *Chicago Tribune* reports, there is "another Franklin County that the ski crowd sipping Irish coffee at Judson's or the Red Stallion Inn never see." This other Franklin County is one of proud down-easters living in cold one-room shacks; of families of six subsisting on $200 a month when their fuel oil alone costs nearly that; of malnutrition and chronic unemployment as the old-style factories and mills lay off long-time workers; of "a new but pervasive sense of despair."

More people moving into a rural area or small town usually does bring more jobs, but it also brings inflated prices, undoing part of the attraction. For example, the residents of Eden, North Carolina, have discovered that the coming of a large employer has brought higher prices in local stores, along with higher incomes for only a select group of people, which means hardship for everyone else, especially the people who lived there to begin with. As rural sociologist John Wardwell puts it, "Poverty in the midst of poverty is one thing. Poverty in the midst of a community transformed by the arrival of more affluent people from the cities may be quite another. Relative deprivation may be increasing, and absolute deprivation may be increasing also, as the poorer residents are bid out of competition for higher-priced goods and services."

The problem here is that the presence of so many relatively affluent new ruralites masks the reality of rural poverty. In past decades, the rural poor could move to the large cities for employment. Now, the very forces that have diminished cities as employment magnets have opened up the rural areas to economic development—but the development of jobs calling for sophisticated skills and education. The rural poor must now compete directly for these new local jobs with generally well-educated and highly skilled in-migrants. Cutbacks in training aid to the rural poor are coming at a time when, because the rural environment is changing so quickly, the poor need economic assistance and training programs more than ever.

The Toll on Agriculture

As the urbanites move into farming and ranching regions, their values often come into direct conflict with the values that sustain the production of food. The farms that seemed so bucolic to the newcomers when they first drove through the valleys soon present a problem. Their dreams of peace and quiet are destroyed by the reality of nearby farm activities: tractors in the early morning, noisy livestock, cows squaring off against joggers on the country roads. The agricultural communities and small towns that once were relatively homogeneous societies are now fragmented by the newcomers and their desires for better roads, better schools, better jogging paths. The new ruralites try to control the nuisances of farm noise, odors, and the potentially dangerous spraying of herbicides and pesticides through regulation and litigation. Theft and vandalism of farm equipment and crops are increasing. Farmers even report harassment of their livestock and personal threats against themselves. Politically, farmers are increasingly disenfranchised. Local governments eagerly attract light industries through tax concessions and the building of industrial parks, while the native industry, farming, languishes.

True, because of the new service industries, small farmers now have the option of keeping their struggling farms going by taking part-time jobs—though the incoming population also increases the value of the land and the taxes, making it more difficult for a farmer to resist the temptation to sell off his farm and open a McDonald's franchise.

In particular, buckshot urbanization encourages the farmer to sell his land and also blocks the farmer's opportunities to acquire additional land at a reasonable price for farming. In New Mexico, for example, the new residents revere the old culture: the traditionally Hispanic valleys with their village economies and self-sufficient, small-scale agriculture, which have remained essentially the same for centuries. But the valleys are filling up with suburban-type developments that are spreading out across the patches of rare irrigated land. A 1975 report released by Santa Fe County showed that 60 percent of the valley's new homesites were built on such land. All over rural America II, real estate speculators are moving across the land, buying up 250-acre tracts for, say, $300 to $500 an acre, and dividing them into a dozen or so parcels for sale at twice the per-acre price. Farm real estate prices have in the last decade outpaced general inflation and outperformed the stock market. Near Medford, Oregon, land prices are rising so high (up to $7000 per acre) that the orchards are disappearing, just as they disappeared decades ago in the California valleys of Santa Clara and San Fernando. This especially works to the detriment of those small, traditional farmers, who were part of the attraction of these areas in the first place. (When *Esquire* ran a cover article announcing Santa Fe as *the* sanctuary of young, disaffected urbanites, a dismayed New Mexican wrote to the editor: "This is the way New Mexico ends, not with a bang, but with a nasal accent.")

There is something enticing about this new freedom to live in the country, something mythically Jeffersonian. But little attention is being paid to potential consequences. As we spread out over the countryside, celebrating the new freedom, an essential truth may be lost to view: rural counties are the nation's working landscape, where most of our food and fiber and energy are produced. Farmland produced, in 1979, one-fifth of all U.S. exports. Between 1967 and 1975, according to the Council on Environmental Quality, 8 million acres of prime U.S. farmland were converted to vacation homes, rural and suburban subdivisions, reservoirs, new roads, and other nonfarm purposes. At the same time, much new cropland was brought under cultivation, but much of this new land is prone to erosion, salinization, compaction, loss of organic matter, and other destructive factors. Certainly, American agriculture is the envy of the world, but the technology-induced increased crop yields since 1940 are beginning to slow down at the very point when the movement of people has shifted from rural-to-urban to urban-to-rural for the first time in two centuries.

In the near future, most of the world's people will be dependent on food grown in another area and transported to them, putting increased pressure on American agriculture. Is it pragmatic to cover productive land with new rural condo complexes and housing developments and "clean" industrial parks? There is also a moral issue lurking here. The figures on disappearing farmland are controversial (another set of figures have been arrived at by the enthusiasts of America II, who put more faith in future technology). This is by no means a simple question. Many rural areas are in a double bind, caught between the need to preserve farmland and the economic needs not just of the new in-migrants, but of the rural poor as well.

The Toll on Nature

Like farmland, the natural landscape is an essential part of the attraction of rural and small-town life. In some corners of the new Eden, the recent newcomers live gently and modestly on the land. But many Americans, in the process of re-creating the countryside, in search of magic and healing, are establishing a landscape in which—subtly, slowly—the magic that they seek dissipates. The new ruralites, though sick of urban water and air pollution, bring their pollutants with them. Some planners point out that rural areas—because people in them are usually so dispersed—have a natural "flushing" system that tends to dissipate air and water pollution. ("In the Ozarks," joked one planner, "everything is flushed to New Orleans.") But natural flushing has its limits. North Carolina, one of the states where the new country is prevalent, is experiencing severe water problems: chemical dumps near streams and sewer and septic runoff are joining the more traditional agricultural sources of water pollution—pesticides and herbicides.

Then there's wood smoke. In 1972, fewer than 250,000 wood-burning stoves were sold nationwide. Less than a decade later, well over 1.2 million were being sold annually. In Missoula, Montana, a university town and logging center, winter wood burning accounts for 39 percent of the carbon monoxide and 68 percent of the most dangerous airborne particles, according to health officials. Some elements of wood smoke are potential causes of cancer. According to Paula R. Machlin, an air pollution technical adviser for the Environmental Protection Agency in Denver, wood burning is a major new source of air pollution, "not just wood-burning for energy but for esthetics—wood chic." Oregon air quality officials call wood smoke the most rapidly growing source of air pollution.

Some of the most pristine natural landscapes are now filling up with luxury getaway condo communities. In Teton County, Wyoming, the scenic valley containing Jackson Hole, more land has been subdivided in the past four years than in all its previous history. In New Mexico, nine recorded subdivisions, waiting to be built, lie within five miles of the Tres Piedras Wildlife Area, where one of the last herds of antelope grazes. Some parts of southern Oregon, once open agricultural valleys, now look a lot like the regions of California from which people are trying to escape. All of this suggests a toll on the landscape more subtle than pollution. It is a toll on our perception of nature, the demystification of nature.

People value nature in basically two ways: one is exploitive, the other participatory. We exploit nature or we nurture it. One way perceives nature as akin to television, behind glass, a nice backdrop; the other views nature as a partner and teacher. "The standard of the exploiter is efficiency," writes farmer/poet Wendell Berry,

> the standard of the nurturer is care. The exploiter's goal is money, profit; the nurturer's goal is health—his land's health, his own, his family's, his community's, his country's. . . . The exploiter typically serves an institution or organization; the nurturer serves land, household, community, place. The exploiter thinks in terms of numbers, quantities, "hard facts"; the nurturer in terms of character, condition, quality, kind.

Large numbers of Americans are moving to towns where nature is a backdrop only, a backdrop for high-tech factory work, a backdrop for luxury condos and cowboy discos. Familiarity with nature without participation in it makes nature a consumer item, a backdrop, and breeds a subtle contempt. What happens to our perception of nature if we're able to look out our picture window any time of the day or night at the Rockies or a farm, field, or forest without participating in it, without nurturing the land and growing much of anything on it—if we move into our planned communities with sensors in the fireplaces, or into our high-tech computerized offices, and view nature only as a backdrop? Perhaps the magic goes out of nature then, and we're left with just another condo in the woods. Most of us, as children, perceived the outdoors as a place of mystery and wonder. Now children go to computer camp ("I swam, I hiked, I ran a computer," reads a testimonial in an ad for Computer Camps International). Atari's computer camp advertisement is illustrative: a young boy is inside, bent over a computer. Beyond the glass is a lake, woods, a sailboat.

The demystification of nature is a toll that may not seem as dramatic as, say, disappearing farmland, but it underlies our ultimate treatment of nature, each other, and ourselves.

The Toll on Our Illusions

The mythology of the small town and the countryside is that they are places of healing, places where people care for each other. But as more and more people move to the new country, the mythology of community often gives way to new conflicts, ones that may seem small compared to big-city life, but ones that contrast sharply with the ex-urbanite's expectations. For example, Santa Fe, which the ancient Indians called "the dancing ground of the sun" and the Spaniards renamed "the city of the holy faith," has been touted as the new mecca for disenchanted urbanites seeking inner peace and higher consciousness. But, as Robert Mayer writes in *Rocky Mountain* magazine, "Santa Fe has always been asked for more than it can deliver." He quotes a counselor who spent years in Santa Fe working with couples whose marriages were falling apart, who says, "It seems like unrealistic expectations. . . . People come here from the big cities thinking they'll leave behind the technology, the bureaucracy, the pollution. They're looking for a more spiritual life. But the place can't do that for you. It's inner work, not outer." Continues Mayer: 'Caution', the signs should say, in soft adobe colors. 'Beware the illusions.' They are as numberless here as the dogs, and far more dangerous." This is a small town, but Santa Fe, like many of the frontier chic towns, contains few emotional support networks. This is not a place of barn raisings or extended family. According to a local van line, for every eleven people who move to Santa Fe, ten move away, a statistic that contradicts the satisfaction most new ruralites express—perhaps because the spiritual expectations are so much greater in New Mexico.

One does not escape from interpersonal conflict by moving to the country. Newcomers must worry not only about conflicts with the locals, but among one another as well. As demographer Calvin Beale points out: "The young, better-educated families, in demanding changes in school policies or more funding to school and related services, may confront retirees whose needs for better health care, transportation, and physical security are paramount. School bond issues in smaller communities are especially difficult to get passed." All of this of course depends on the particular community.

   Unless strong personal ties, networks, institutions come about (and, most of all, stronger values based on caring and the public space rather than on privatism and withdrawal), the contentment the ex-urbanites now feel could dissipate quickly.

   There are other unexpected consequences. Just as the early movement to the suburbs, which was stimulated in part by a fear of urban crime, brought crime with it, rural America, too, is suffering from a rising crime rate. The rate is, in fact, rising proportionately much faster than in even the largest and oldest cities. The ultimate crime, nuclear war, is not escapable either. The federal government's Civil Defense Preparedness Agency has plans to relocate residents of dozens of New England cities to rural New Hampshire in event of nuclear attack—or of a major accident at a nuclear power plant. Indeed, the first lesson of rural life is that there is no real escape. To consider the new Eden a place to hide is to consider trading one set of conditions and problems for another.

COMING TO TERMS WITH THE NEW EDEN

One begins to think about the love of nature and the nature of love, of obsessive love and nurturing love. The attraction that so many Americans feel to nature and rural life often ends up consuming and destroying what it seeks. It is easy enough to blame what is lost in the new country on technology, but the real problem is how individuals use the technology. Rural and small-town America remains, to millions of Americans, the nation's best hope: a fresh, green frontier, a new chance, a wish frontier. The tensions and growing conflicts built into the new rural America guarantee a kind of ambivalence about it, a worry that this frontier will accomplish only a transformation that verges on destruction. And yet there is something so hopeful about it, so intrinsically American in its ability to tolerate (at least for now) so many conflicting visions of its future.

   There is no question that the new country will continue to grow. Recessions have tended to hurt some small cities, small towns, and rural areas more than big cities, but these same areas have a recent history of bouncing back faster than large cities as a recession ends. Migrations, over the long haul, have a way of mathematically validating and extending themselves. Andrew Sofranko's studies show that 75 percent of those who have moved from a big city to the rural Midwest knew someone in the area before moving there. Knowing someone in a rural area increases the likelihood that an urbanite will take the plunge into rurality. The more people who move outward, the wider is the support network. (Any voluntary stream of migration is followed by a reverse stream of return migration; nothing works out for everyone. Indeed, during the European migration to America, at least a third of the immigrants returned to Europe.) Assuming the continued growth of the new country means that eventually some kind of planning will have to occur.

The question will not be to plan or not to plan, but at what level —local, regional, national? The growing tensions and contradictions will demand a public weighing of the demands of various groups for natural preservation, recreation, farmland, and housing with the employment needs of the rural poor.

Yet, there is an antigovernment, antiplanning bias built into the structure of the new Eden. Like the rest of the nation, local small-town and county governments are having difficulty paying their bills. The trend, as in the anticities and condo America, is toward privatizing government services. Some small towns have hired private security firms to provide all local police services, reviving a practice popular in the early years of the nation, when volunteer watchmen, not police, kept order in the community. Further, it is entirely unclear under whose governmental domain falls buckshot urbanization, the most pervasive of new rural forms. As former Agriculture Department official J. C. Doherty writes, this is a little-recognized reality: "There is no polity to match the variety. In other words, [buckshot] urbanization is, inexorably and methodically, rendering local government jurisdictions, functions, and responsibilities awkward at best and obsolete at worst." Who or what, he asks, is to govern such a "city"?

> Who's to plan, who's to set the property tax? Who's to write and approve a meaningful capital budget appropriate to the territory? The answer today is that this job is relegated to a thousand or more elected officials and their technicians struggling away in a hundred or more local general purpose and special district government offices, all of them hampered by too few resources, too much confusion, and too little power.

That may be just fine to many of the new ruralites and corporate divisions that, like the earlier pioneers who headed west for elbowroom and freedom, have settled far from each other.

Yet there is hope. One senses, listening to the new ruralites, a slowly growing acknowledgment that what they love most about rural life may slip away. In addition, a shift in perspective is occurring among those few individuals and organizations concerned with rural planning. Much of the discussion through the late 1970s revolved around how to stop or slow the movement of people into rural areas, and gave rise to a legislative farmland preservation movement. As a report by the Urban Land Research Foundation says, what these methods for farmland preservation have in common is prevention of development rather than encouragement of better development. Now the focus of the debate seems to have shifted toward accepting rural deconcentration, but guiding it into clusters (rural versions of the urban village idea proposed for the anticities) rather than letting population spread in buckshot fashion over valuable farmland or terrain that would be better left in its natural state. The foundation also suggests a change in how local rural governments deal with incoming migration. Many of these governments, assuming that it is the way to preserve the status quo, have required houses to have 2-, 10-, or or 250-acre lots. Such requirements do nothing to halt urbanization, but do encourage the gobbling up of valuable land.

At least one organization, Rodale Press, is suggesting that deconcentration can actually be good for the land, depending on how it is carried out. "I used to be one of those people who wanted to slow down the number of urbanites moving to rural areas," Robert Rodale told me one afternoon in his office at the large Rodale complex in the little town of Emmaus, Pennsylvania. "I'd go to all the meetings to talk about ways to preserve agriculture. Together, we'd wring our hands over the loss of land. But then it began to occur to me that one of the problems with American agriculture is that there are so few people involved with it. It's just an industry now, and it's in trouble—most of the big farmers are heavily in debt, overdependent on big, expensive machinery, dependent on petroleum-based fertilizers. People in New England are totally dependent on food being shipped to them by truck from Southern California. The whole system is vulnerable to breakdown; I call it the Detroit factor in agriculture. One way of getting back to some kind of regional food self-sufficiency would be to take advantage of the demographic shifts: encourage more part-time farming on small parcels of land, using biological pest control instead of pesticides and herbicides, which would cut down some of the friction between farmers and nonfarmers. So I've come to think that what we've got to do is move toward regenerative agriculture: improving land by having more people care for it. I think now in terms of repopulating agriculture."

An optimistic note is that, for the first time in decades, the number of farms is increasing. This is not an increase in the number of big agribusinesses or large, heavily capitalized family farms—the number of those farms is still falling. The new farmers are primarily part-timers, often former urbanites. This is particularly true in the northeast. The New England states have experienced actual increases as high as 30 percent in the number of farms since 1974. As Stewart Smith, Maine's commissioner of agriculture, told me: "For a hundred years Maine has been moving away from food self-sufficiency, but it's bottomed out. We're on our way back up." The reason, he says, is the big increase in part-time farmers, some of whom are using computers to manage their complicated biological pest-management programs.

THE WISH FRONTIER

The dream of having it all continues: of preserving the land even while people move onto it, of having the best of what is urban and what is rural. Most urbanites seeking refuge in the new country are more interested in high tech than in high crop yields. Yet, many of these people hope that new technology can do as much to save traditional rural life as destroy it.

When I visited South Dakota, I was impressed by the number of people, both long-time local residents and new arrivals, who are grappling with these issues, who want to see a fruitful marriage between what is old and what is young. Consider Rosemary Erickson and her husband, Bud Crow. Rosemary is a sociologist and Bud is a social psychologist, both well known for their crime prevention techniques. In 1959, Crow cofounded the Western Behavioral Sciences Institute in La Jolla, California. They're living the kind of life that millions of urbanites are beginning to dream about living.

Until recently, the couple lived in a large home in Rancho Santa Fe, a planned community designed to re-create a rural atmosphere. It prescribes a certain amount of greenery around each house, and its "dark sky policy" prohibits floodlights so residents can see the stars. But for Rosemary, who grew up on a South Dakota farm and attended a one-room school, the Rancho Santa Fe illusion was always, somehow, unsatisfying. One day, as Rosemary tells it, "we looked around at where we were living, and thought of all that money we were spending for a phony rural atmosphere, and decided, 'Hey, why not try for the real thing?' " So they packed up their computer and headed inland to a farmhouse outside Davis, South Dakota, plugged in their computer and started Athena Research Corp, a consulting business independent of any geographic restraints. Most of their clients are corporations that, as Rosemary puts it, "don't care if they fly you from Southern California or South Dakota." They discovered that not only were they able to cut their living expenses by at least a third, but their professional lives prospered: after the first few months, they were actually making more money than they had in San Diego. In the summer, spring, and fall, they live in South Dakota, thirty minutes from the Sioux Falls airport. In the winter, they flee the gathering snow clouds and head south to Southern California, computer in tow. They call themselves "electronic snowbirds." It may be the ultimate America II fantasy.

I visited them on spring afternoon in Rosemary's girlhood home, which they share with her widowed mother. (Her brother, a farmer and part-time policeman, lives next door with his family.) The house is white, clean, and small, set on a little knoll overlooking rolling farmland and strips of woods, the sky boiling up all around with muscled, white clouds. Rosemary's mother, Opal, a gentle, white-haired woman, was fixing Sunday dinner. The aroma of turkey and biscuits filled the house. Rosemary, who is in her late thirties, sat in her father's rocking chair. "It's not that we decided to drop out, not as much as dropping in," she said. "You can become almost ill on all that information overload. It's almost as if the more information and change you have to deal with in your profession, the more you need to balance it with a quiet life that doesn't really change." She was looking out the front window as she talked, at a clump of trees and a silo far away, and at her husband crossing the front lawn, leaning in the March wind, his pantlegs shoved into the tops of his work boots.

He came in and grinned. "Your brother decided I need to do some real work, a little plowing maybe." Before coming here, he had never set foot on a farm in his life, but he took to it immediately. He helps his brother-in-law plow the fields, listening to classical music over the tractor cab's stereo system. With his hair still disheveled from the wind, he opened a door to a back room and walked over to an Apple II computer set up on an antique table. He clicked on the computer. "You notice there aren't any massive file cabinets in this room," he said. "That's because this little computer stores all of our files and data analysis." He sat down, stared at the screen, and placed his telephone receiver in the cradle of a modem, a small machine that hooks him into such information banks as Lockheed's Dialog Information Search and The Source. These services include current synopses of all major newspapers, academic journals, and wire services, as well as air-line schedules and stock market quotations. He tapped a few keys and a long list of magazine references to small towns flashed on the screen. "These data banks cost about sixty dollars an hour to use, but you can collect all the information you'd ever need in a matter of minutes. We spend about fifty dollars a month gathering information."

Bud and Rosemary are also plugged into a network of their colleagues all over the country. Each evening they check in with their computer for messages, through a computer networking service called POLIS (Greek for community), operated out of the University of California, Santa Barbara. Similar computer bulletin boards, as they are called, are now available for genealogists, astronomers, and other professionals. In Kansas City, a computer bulletin board provides commodities news. And in San Francisco, there's a bulletin board for gays. "It's like sending letters via computer," says Bud. "This helps us avoid feeling out of touch with our profession. We've even made some new friends. A lot of our friends are moving to the country, taking their computers with them. You don't have to have a computer, but it helps. Writers, college professors, scientists, artists. It's just beginning."

With a college and university within thirty miles on each side of them, they feel no sense of intellectual isolation. When Rosemary feels a surge of urban withdrawal symptoms coming on, she gets her "fix," as she calls it, by spending an hour in a Sioux Falls shopping mall.

Bud stopped tapping for a moment: "I was surprised. The mid-American values are still alive and well out here. I always knew that rural people were self-sufficient, but I never really understood the flip side of that, the interdependence. They still have barn raisings here. If a man dies, families from miles around show up to a harvest bee, to help the widow with the harvest. It's an intricate social accounting system. You don't call a plumber, you call a neighbor with the tools. And you repay favors. People keep track, for months, years. I find it really hard to keep track, but if you don't you hurt a lot of feelings. I'm still getting used to that.

"You know," he added, "if someone got in a plane and charted all those empty farmhouses in the Midwest and West, you could move a big portion of the northeastern population out here." They've switched their insurance to a local broker, and they do most of their shopping at local stores, avoiding the chain stores controlled by outside corporations.

Bud had an errand to run, so I rode into Sioux Falls with him, to "take the farm dog into town for a beauty treatment." After dropping the dog off, we stopped at Sioux Falls' computer store. Thirty-year-old Jack Green grew up in Sioux Falls and now manages this store, which sells more computers to farmers than to anyone else. "They give farmers access to the information that previously was easily available only to big agribusiness. How else you gonna compete with all these foreign countries coming in and buying up land? I set these farmers up with a computer, two disc drives, a telephone modem. If they can spend $40,000 on a combine, they can spend $4000 on a computer that can save them the cost of a combine. New programs coming out every day." Ones such as: "Least-Cost Fertilizer Application," and "Pig Production: From Weaning to Slaughter." "For instance, chickens. It'll keep a record of each chicken, which is impossible without a computer. How do you keep records of a flock of 10,000 chickens? You don't just walk into a chicken barn with 10,000 chickens and say, 'OK, who's been slacking off on the eggs?' I've got programs that'll turn on the ventilation when you need it on, and security systems—farmers out in rural areas are real vulnerable. Cow rustling! Chicken rustling! I've got a system that'll monitor a farm and call the police for you." Several state universities now offer centralized sources of information, sophisticated computer bulletin boards, that can guide farmers through a whole season. "Sometime in this decade," said Green, "it'll be feasible for a farmer to work at a part-time job in town and leave his computer in charge of his farm."

A local farmer, Max Anderson, was punching along at one of the display computers. "I'm tryin' out a new program," he said. "Got each field plotted out. Place I buy my fertilizer, about sixty-five miles away, also has an Apple—we communicate a lot over the computer. I have a tax planner, and I want an electronic balance sheet; I own some FHA apartments and need a 'land-lorder' program. Only thing is, I can't program the rain."

Though the recession has pushed many farmers under, the exodus of young people from the rural areas surrounding Sioux Falls has ended. Most of the young people end up working in the burgeoning service sector, but a few stay on with the farms. The farmers talk with pride of the number of college-educated sons and daughters beginning to return to the region, choosing, as one young farmer put it, "to find a way to make a life, not just a living." Just as the home computer has helped liberate Bud and Rosemary, it may be the edge that small farms need to compete with big agribusiness.

An hour and a half from Sioux Falls, we stopped to see Dallas Tonsager, twenty-six, who owns a small farm. He and his wife, Sharon, live in a Victorian-style house ordered from a catalogue fifty years ago. This area of the state, electrified only in the early 1950s, is now being computerized. The roads are still unpaved. He talked of his Ohio Scientific Challenger 4P computer in a detached way. "I want to get into keeping track of accounts, cash flow, credit records," he says in a slow drawl. "I'm going to set up a keyboard in my barn and hook it up to handle my cow feeding operation. In the morning, I'll work on my programming while I'm milkin' the cows."

Back on the little farm near Davis, after Sunday dinner, Bud and Rosemary piled some young fruit trees into their pickup and drove out over a field, past a stream that snaked through a gully and across the land. Rosemary was talking about the price of Eden. "It's hard to know how it'll all turn out," she said, as the pickup rattled and bumped over the furrows. "Maybe it'll all get ruined, all the good things. It just depends on everybody's individual decisions, I guess. Maybe that's what planning really is: just a mirror, or a reinforcement of the kind of decisions people are already making.

"The one negative thing I've really begun to notice is that crime is increasing. When I was a little girl, the plains were all dark at night; but now every farm for as far as you can see has security spotlights. Those are the same type of lights Rancho Santa Fe outlawed in order to create the illusion of country living."

As Bud and Rosemary stopped the truck and stepped out onto the pasture, big thunderheads were rolling over the horizon, shaking the branches in a grove of walnut trees. It was beginning to sprinkle. Rosemary tightened her windbreaker as Bud dug into the rich earth. "It's possible that all these people moving to the country could ultimately save what's left of rural values." He voice had in it a quality of yearning and subtle doubt. "In the process, there could be a real blending of rural and urban values, creating a new way of looking at the world. And maybe that will be quite wonderful." It was raining hard now, and Bud and Rosemary ran back to their truck. They opened the windows a crack and watched the cottonwoods far across the fields bend and sway, and they sat quietly and smelled the rain.

PART FIVE

WORKING IN AMERICA II

Some of our deep-seated American values are inappropriate for these times. The West could accommodate ten thousand John Waynes spread over the vast landscape. But millions of John Waynes employed under ten thousand corporate roofs may not, in the long run, prove workable.
    —*Richard Tanner Johnson and William G. Ouchi,* Harvard
                                              Business Review

Economic security is to modern man what a castle and a moat were to medieval man.   —*Lester C. Thurow,* Newsweek

YOU'RE ON THE BUS OR YOU'RE OFF THE BUS

There was a time when opportunity seemed unlimited in America. Norman Rockwell once put it this way: "I was a high school dropout. I had the feeling, and so did everybody else, that life was full of boundless opportunity. No one was going to stop you, you know, from being a success." The current mood, however, is more like Ken Kesey's slogan, which he coined in the early days of the drug culture to measure hipness: "You're on the bus or you're off the bus." In America II, you're either a Postindustrial or you're left behind.

The landscape of work has changed entirely, the map has been redrawn. The old inner cities are the vestiges of what once were large pockets of population devoted almost exclusively to traditional kinds of manufacturing; these were the magnets of the industrial age. For the poor, they were not particularly pleasant places to live, but in 1880 or 1920 or even 1960, people could travel from rural America to the city and had the potential of finding a job, whether or not they were well-educated. They could obtain an unskilled job with at least the hope of moving up the ladder. The first rung was within reach. The American dream was understandable.

Today, the old magnets have lost their attraction; but out there in the land of the Postindustrials, in the new Eden and the anticities, are fresh, powerful, barely understood new magnets—in Florida's Pinellas County, or California's Silicon Valley, or North Carolina's Research Triangle Park. These new magnets and new jobs are bewildering to those whose training fits another age. The untrained young black or the fifty-year-old former steel worker has little chance of reaching the first rung on this ladder, a ladder levitated beyond his or her reach by the new technological forces. They can see it, but they cannot reach it; yet if they listen closely they can hear the Postindustrials speaking their new and alien language, murmuring "megabytes . . . buffers . . . ram-card. . . ."

By now, most Americans realize that a whole way of work-life is dying, and that a new one is rising. At a grade school science fair, a computer teaches children about exponential growth; the name of the display is "Survival of the Fittest," an apt lesson for budding young Postindustrials fresh on the scene. The new economy is Darwinian indeed. The steel mill workers who once were the backbone of the nation's "arsenal of democracy" are giving way to computer systems analysts, to french-fry scoopers and special sauce specialists squirting orange goo from preset guns. Big Mac is supplanting big steel. America will produce services and information for the world; less-developed nations will take over the basic manufacturing industries. That, by most accounts, is the new road map.

GETTING THERE

In the process of this change, millions of workers, largely over forty-five, are being shoved out of the work force. One woman, who went to work at a McDonald's after her husband was laid off by U.S. Steel, told a reporter for the *New York Times,* "You don't know what's going to happen one day to the next. I'm afraid for my kids. You don't know what the future is." And a new generation of Americans, many of them black and functionally illiterate, are entering adulthood with little hope of being trained in the new industries.

An America I job may disappear completely, be supplanted by an entirely different kind of opportunity, or may be changed radically enough to demand different kinds of workers, ones whose center of gravity is in their brains, not in their bodies; and ones who get along with computers as well as or possibly better than with people.

Some estimates of the number of jobs to be dislocated by high technology range as high as 45 million, with as many as 15 million positions permanently eliminated. The Congressional Budget Office projects that 3 million jobs, 15 percent of the manufacturing work force, may be lost by the end of this decade because of computerized laborsaving technology, which reduces the need for workers in older industries. The pace of change will likely accelerate over the next decade. The number of working robots is expected to increase from a few thousand in the early 1980s to possibly 100,000 by 1990. During the same period, electronic work stations may increase from 4 million to 30 million.

So far, employment dislocation has been chiefly among blue-collar workers. As of June 1982, the unemployed were 46 percent blue-collar, and only 26 percent of the unemployed were white-collar workers—even though white-collar jobs already outnumber the blue by a five-to-three margin. Blacks, especially, are being left behind. Even though they are only a tenth of the U. S. population, they make up a fifth of the nation's total unemployed.

However, the coming dislocations will not affect just over-the-hill blue-collar workers. The next frontier of job transformation and displacement may be among office workers, clerical workers, and middle managers who no longer will be needed now that computers can track and report departmental activity. (The Europeans are far ahead of the United States in studying the social impact of new technology; the French finance ministry predicts that the banking and insurance industries will require 30 percent fewer workers by 1990 because of new technologies.) In the United States, clerical workers—secretaries, bookkeepers, file clerks—may find themselves replaced by computers operated by minimum-wage employees. In addition, these clerical jobs will also become more portable because of the technology, effectively moving many clerical jobs out of the older downtowns and into private homes or small branch offices in suburban or rural areas —or even to foreign countries.

Will there, down the road, be enough jobs to go around? The Arthur D. Little research firm in Cambridge, Massachusetts, thinks there will be plenty, about 1 million new jobs in computers, electronic equipment, and consumer electronics by 1987. The problem, according to this firm, will not be a dearth of jobs, but a scarcity of skilled workers. The Bureau of Labor Statistics makes a similar prediction of plentiful jobs, with a labor force growing from 105 million in 1980 to between 122 million and 128 million in 1990. Neal Rosenthal, director of the BLS occupational outlook division, says there is already "unbelievable movement" from America I jobs to America II jobs. But Harvey Shaiken, a work and technology specialist at Massachusetts Institute of Technology, who once was a consultant to the United Auto Workers, says industry is moving at a snail's pace toward training programs that would avoid the severe employment dislocations brought by the new age: "Here we seek to deal with the problem by denying it exists. The invisible hand that is supposed to take care of things like this may already be arthritic and may well be paralyzed by the time we're through with this." So far, most government training programs have focused on young, disadvantaged Americans who have not yet entered the work force. These programs have little relation to the coming job market. Too often, they can be compared to the one in Los Angeles in the early 1960s that spent federal money training young blacks to be elevator operators, just as automatic elevators became the standard. Few federal or corporate programs have dealt with the displaced worker, whether former auto worker or middle manager.

Just because someone is on the bus today does not mean he or she will be on the bus tomorrow. American who already have postindustrial skills will need continual retraining to keep up with the changing job market. For example, computer programmers may eventually find themselves displaced by the technological change they have helped create: "We are on the verge of developing self-programming computers," says Victor Walling, director of the business futures program at SRI International, a leading research firm based in Menlo Park. Quoted in the *Los Angeles Times*, Walling says, "It is crazy to be talking about the need to develop computer programmers in schools today when the need for them is going to shrink dramatically within a decade."

One thing is clear: hundreds of thousands of the workers now displaced will never return to their old jobs; their roles are done, finished. For many, the best that can be hoped for is to become what *Fortune* magazine terms "foot soldiers in the armies of the service economy," low-paid fast-food workers, janitors, and low-skilled clerks. A real danger, according to Harvey Shaiken, is that the information age will produce a polarized work force. Shaiken, according to the *New York Times*, is one of the first experts to explore the subject. His vision of the work force is one in which a small number of highly skilled, high-paying jobs exist alongside a much larger number of routinized, low-paying jobs. And that, says Shaiken, is a recipe for social ferment.

This debate over the effect of new technology on the work force is nothing new. It occurred during the development of the nineteenth century industrial revolution, which ultimately led to dramatic advances in living standards, democracy, and a greater degree of social equality in Europe, Japan, and North America—though a heavy price was paid along the way, in exploited workers, the destruction of some traditional values, and the creation of huge slums. In the early 1960s, *automation* was the buzzword. Somehow, most of the people have survived and, in most ways, prospered from each technological surge. But there is the feeling this time that this new revolution is different, more powerful, more difficult to grasp than any before.

FINDING SHELTER

In such a rapidly changing economy, the need for a sense of belonging and control is intensified—especially in the workplace. Given a national atmosphere in which public education is devalued and egalitarianism out of favor, it could be expected that those with the appropriate knowledge and skills would protect themselves by circling the wagons (or, to extend the metaphor, the buses). The more vulnerable we feel, the more we fragment into smaller work units, adopt new management methods, embrace entrepreneurship, whatever it takes to feel protected from the waves of job market change. We devise socially insulated, technologically secure working places: the company as home, the company as cult. These work enclaves take a variety of forms: from Hewlett-Packard's familial management approach; to self-contained work/residence communities, such as Apple Computer's Supersite, a planned merging of residence and work; to huge, relatively out-of-the-way chunks of the new country, such as North Carolina's pristine Research Triangle Park, or the research and development parks and condo complexes of Fairfax County, Virginia. You're either on the bus, or you're off the bus; and, more and more, if you're on the bus, you live and work with your own kind.

Further, in the sunrise industries, especially in electronics, where companies vie for qualified technical and professional employees, they have had to become quite creative in their recruitment techniques, appealing to the employees' deepest hungers for home. Mitchell Energy & Development Company will finance homes for new workers through its own mortgage company at subsidized rates for up to six years. Many California companies, especially those in the sunrise industries, provide housing for their personnel to stem the serious "brain drain" brought about by the state's high housing costs. This new tactic includes campus housing on universities, campus-style housing near some companies, company-leased condominiums, and joint company employee investments in homes—all at below-market prices. In Orange County, California, companies have banded together to offer condominium office complexes with fireplaces, wet bars, vaulted ceilings, private balconies, and patios with views of the lakes and streams. All of this is happening, remember, in a nation in which the unemployed and homeless of America I are found sleeping on the sidewalk grates of heating ducts, in tent cities, or in their cars.

The need to make the workplace a home comes at a time when work itself is increasingly difficult to conceptualize. It is easy enough to imagine the product of the industrial age—a steel ship hull comes to mind. In the information age, what come to mind are flickering letters on a video display terminal, or the transient statistics of an investment newsletter—all ephemeral, impermanent. The assembly line stripped manufacturing of much of its satisfaction long ago, but the information age removes even more of the tangible proof of our labor. If what we make does not seem real or solid, or even semipermanent, then our connections to our work do not seem real or solid. Work is the glue that holds society together: identifiable, role-producing, understandable work. Much of the sense of purpose and commitment that comes out of work is its constancy: a parent passes his or her trade or skill on to a child; a company proudly manufactures the same quality item decade after decade; towns and cities come to assume that the plant out on the highway will be there years from now, and plan accordingly. The stability or disappearance of a workplace can make or break a town. When the economy shifts so quickly, when companies that have for years been the focal points of communities suddenly move to South Carolina or Taiwan, the chance is greatly lessened that any real sense of community will flourish or even survive.

When a person's skills are no longer needed by a society, that person no longer feels any community role. This can be true not only for steel workers, but for a Postindustrial as well. Workers who ride the crest of the high-tech wave are expected to update their skills continually and shift their job assignments frequently. Such a demanding degree of flexibility and change does little to engender a sense of constancy and community—in the plant, in the community surrounding it, or in the worker.

What this atmosphere of uncertainty suggests is the need for radically different workplaces. One option is to work for yourself, to be an entrepreneur. In an economy that demands flexibility, self-employment can be a way to get a sense of selfhood and potency. While one way of working in America falls, another rises. An America full of self-satisfaction is doing everything it can to create the illusion that work in the future will be full of wonder and security, in places worthy of coming home to. The truth may be different.

The key to these new workplaces, whether in the home or in an office building or factory, is not just job security, but identity. During much of the industrial twentieth century, only the relatively few remaining craftsmen and the economic elite demanded much more from the workplace than a paycheck. But in the healthy economy of the 1960s and early '70s, Americans began to expect more from the workplace. The counterculture was, for the most part, antithetical to the old Puritan work ethic: work had to be more than just a job; it had to be liberating, it had to have "meaning," "relevance." Yet the workplace just didn't seem to fit our expectations. By the late 1970s and early '80s, surveys showed that most Americans did not like their work; just as they wanted out of big cities, they also wanted out of their jobs. Appropriately, one of the most popular songs of the era was Johnny Paycheck's "Take This Job and Shove It."

At least part of this resentment, even if it was only subconscious, was toward a corporate ethic that demanded of Americans their loyalty, while stripping from them their identity. Over the years, the physical landscape of America had become "placeless": one town looked like the next, so many golden arches and

Holiday Inns stretching across the horizon. It was the kind of environment that worked hand-in-hand with a corporate ethic. People could be transferred with a minimum of upset because Wichita looked just like San Jose. Writer Ralph Keyes calls it the "national hometown." You can move anywhere in the nation and still get a quarter ounce of onions on your 1.6-ounce McDonald's hamburger. "The more sameness you're selling someone," Keyes quotes one franchiser, "the more secure he will feel." Not quite secure enough, though, or else so many Americans would not have gone off searching for real hometowns.

Even as corporate American was undoing regional diversity, it was beginning to create a workplace culture that felt like home: companies such as Kodak, IBM, Cummins Engine Company, Levi Strauss, National Cash Register, and Proctor and Gamble. As financial writer Adam Smith tells it, IBM managers used to line all the salesmen up every morning for inspection: "They wore identical charcoal-gray suits, white shirts, conservative ties. I watched the inspection once or twice, and so help me, the division manager inspected everybody's fingernails. But it was unheard of to get fired." What has developed, over time, is an expansion of the old idea of the company town. Management experts William G. Ouchi and Alfred M. Jaeger point to the early incubators of the insular community/company:

> In a few cases, companies grew up in small towns, or in places like California that were populated by emigrants, or in industries that required frequent relocation of employees. In all three cases, one side effect was that people had no immediate form of social contact available except through their employer. The extreme case is the military base, which looks, feels, and smells the same whether it is in Hawaii, Illinois, or New York. To make life possible under conditions of high geographical mobility, the military has developed a culture that is immediately familiar and secure no matter where its employees go. These organizations, public and private, created a social vacuum for their employees and then had to develop internal sources of support to replace what had been taken away. Now the rest of the country is "catching up" with them as stable sources of support disappear elsewhere.

In the early 1980s, when the economy began to dip and sputter and change, most people were happy to have any job at all. In this atmosphere it was quite natural that Americans would begin to look upon the workplace as a haven, as a home. For one thing, our attitudes about work have not yet returned to the notion that a job is a necessary drudgery; currently, the workplace is seen as a potential safe zone.

THE COMPANY AS CULT

As a young man, Arthur Jonishi was drafted into the Japanese army two months before the end of World War II. These days, as a top executive in one of the most successful electronics companies in the world, Jonishi sounds like General Douglas MacArthur advising the vanquished. "Looking at you all here," Jonishi said to a packed audience of American executives, "I feel encouraged. You all look Oriental." In a soft, hesitant voice, Jonishi described Kyocera International's "deep moral principles and respect for the Divine," a semireligious approach to management: the company as cult. And the Americans listened intently.

From the San Francisco Bay area's Silicon Valley to San Diego's Computer Row (the two largest concentrations of Japanese companies in the United States, with San Diego having the edge), executives in the electronics industry are seeking ways to increase productivity and avoid unionism. In the past, especially in the industrial northeast, workers had been treated as expendable commodities. So they turned to unions. But the southern and western United States and the rural areas, where much of the population is moving, don't have quite the long history of labor organizing and industrialism. The electronics industry lends itself to a more humane working environment than, say, a dangerous steel mill in Pittsburgh. Still, labor unions and a shortage of skilled high-tech workers are providing the impetus for change. As the focus of American industry shifts from steel mills to high-tech industries, a chance exists for something new in labor management relations. A real question is whether Japanese management methods are culturally appropriate in America, or if a handful of progressive American companies, such as Hewlett-

Packard, just might have a better idea. Nor is it clear whether these management methods are as humane as their promoters suggest they are.

THE KYOCERA MODEL

Kyocera's egalitarian psychology begins each workday at 7 A.M. On a morning when I visited the Kyocera plant, seven hundred employees—assembly line workers as well as supervisors, including Jonishi—filled out onto a parking lot in the dull morning haze. The workers wore differently colored jackets to signify rank. Each worker stood on one of the evenly spaced yellow dots painted on the asphalt. They turned and faced the dais.

On this morning, Bill Polumbo, an employee of the materials and purchasing department, was providing the inspirational message. He spoke of honesty, cooperation, and spirit. Then a supervisor stepped to the microphone and led the employees in group exercises. They lifted their arms up and down in unison, middle-aged women with teased hair and expressions ranging from cynical to enthusiastic, a few Japanese engineers, young Filipino women, and a sprinkling of young, tough-looking men—the kind you would expect to find in a Youngstown steel mill. One sad-eyed fellow from Texas stood at the back of one line, on his yellow dot, wearing his blue smock and frayed boot-cut jeans and a bull-rider Stetson with a purple feather dangling off the back brim. His Adam's apple stuck out. He lifted his arms up and down, like some kind of large, anemic eagle going through the motions of trying, unsuccessfully, to fly.

Jonishi told me later in the day that this exercise period is "like the huddle of a football team—to set the momentum of the day." Indeed, the Kyocera team must be doing something right. Established in 1971, the San Diego plant manufactures 70 percent of the ceramic semiconductor packaging made in the United States. Its parent company, Kyoto Ceramic Company, in Japan, enjoys what *Fortune* magazine calls "an identical commanding share of the world market." Sales have increased 607 percent in the past six years. Kyocera's labor turnover is a third of the typical rate for U.S. factories.

In the San Diego plant, all decisions are made by consensus, in what one employee calls "a series of never-ending meetings." The contrast with traditional American management is startling.

"The involvement is much more horizontal and democratic," Jonishi explained to me from behind his modest desk. He was wearing one of the little blue smocks. "Americans use a vertical chain of command, going from top to bottom, where subordinates just follow the decisions. At Kyocera," he said, "we have a chain of command, but it is from the bottom up." For instance, the organization is divided into small "amoeba" units. Each amoeba is a profit center, and the role of each amoeba leader is that of a president of a small company. The amoebas buy and sell to each other, measuring their performance in terms of profitability. "If the manager accepts entrepreneurial responsibility for his department, he will feel a greater sense of urgency about the success of his entire group, not just himself," said Jonishi. "The individual entrepreneur will measure himself much more stringently than a boss ever could."

A few weeks before my visit, one amoeba had decided that it could improve its profit margin by purchasing materials from a San Diego source rather than ordering them from Kyoto Ceramic in Japan—much to the Japanese parent company's dissatisfaction. This was explained to me by Laura Elfenbein, who supervises the advertising services department, which recently became an amoeba. "We turn a profit by charging other amoebas for our services. But another amoeba decided that, by going to an outside printer, it could produce a brochure cheaper than we could. We're trying," she added, with some embarrassment, "to win that account back."

In the Kyocera plant the carpeting is frayed, the furniture old. Departments have learned how to increase profits by cutting frills. The members of a profitable amoeba are not, however, rewarded with quick promotions or more money—at least not directly. The reward is public recognition at the morning meetings and, as Jonishi puts it, "internal spiritual reward." And no layoffs. Even during the 1974 recession, when the market faltered, excess employees were kept on the payroll and put to work cleaning floors or polishing machinery. "U.S. companies generate profits for shareholders first," said Jonishi, "but for Japanese firms, the employees come first. We would cut into retained earnings if the situation became critical."

In the company lunchroom I talked with some of Kyocera's employees, asking especially about the no-layoff policy.

"It's right there, written into your contract," said a young kiln worker, pushing the brim up on his cap. "I'd like to see 'em pay a little more money here. But the no-layoff policy is worth a lot of money; you know you're secure here. None of this hire-and-fire stuff. No union can get us that kind of security; they're just a racket."

Some workers, though, complain of a cultural gap between American workers—especially women, Hispanics, and blacks—and workers from Japan, who somehow have an easier time achieving the correct Kyocera attitude. That attitude is defined as spirit, loyalty, zeal, and cooperation, qualities that Kyocera's semiannual performance reviews place above job knowledge and performance.

A woman who had come to Kyocera from another San Diego electronics company had no such complaints. "If your work isn't that good, they take your attitude into consideration," she said. "At the company I used to work for, people meant nothing to them. As for the exercise period, at first I said, hey, this is America, not Japan. But the exercise period is part of the Kyocera philosophy, and now I kind of like it."

Another management tool is the "compa," a frequently held brainstorming meeting at a company house in La Jolla. At a compa, light liquor is served to "open people up, create a relaxed atmosphere," Jonishi had explained. "Through compas we exchange information, solve worries of the employees, help employees understand the company philosophy."

The San Diego plant's management techniques are mild compared to those of the parent company, which was recently judged by Japan's leading business newspaper in 1981 as the best-run company in Japan. Workers there put in an average of twelve hours a day. Foremen report to plant managers with military salutes. Workers do not walk, they run. And the names of absentees are read aloud before the morning assembly, so that workers without the correct attitude lose face. Although Kyocera did not bring this kind of regimentation to San Diego, it did import the long hours. Most employees at the San Diego plant start at 7 A.M. and work an average of eleven hours a day; many work on Saturday. While the workers are treated like a family, essentially they are asked to sacrifice their own family life—which fits in with traditional Japanese sex roles: the male is married to his job; his wife is wedded to the kitchen. "Managing wives," as Jonishi put it, "has always been more difficult than managing subordinates."

"I resist the long hours," explained an athletic, intense man in his early thirties who holds two titles at the plant. "I work about ten hours a day instead of eleven. That hour is my family's space." Nonetheless, he remains committed to Kyocera. This man, who is highly educated and once wanted to become a minister, leaned forward intently.

"See, we think about literally preserving this company for posterity, for our children or someone else's children. I'd like to think I'm not substituting one religion for another. But maybe I am."

THE HEWLETT-PACKARD MODEL

When entrepreneurs Bill Hewlett and David Packard founded their electronics company in 1939—in a garage that still stands in Palo Alto—they decided not to run a hire-and-fire operation. Their goal was to "make meaning" as well as profits. They established a generous profit-sharing program and began imbuing their employees with the Zenlike precepts that became known as the "H-P way." The results have been similar to Kyocera's: employee turnover is low and sales triple every two years.

"It's hard to define the H-P way," said Joe Costa, the burly employee relations manager at H-P's antiseptic Rancho Bernardo plant, near San Diego, which designs and manufactures computer plotters. Costa went to work for H-P in 1947, drilling holes in mahogany component boxes. He moved up in the company, he says, because he developed an allergy to mahogany. "There's a lot of similarities between H-P and what people consider the Japanese management style. Lifetime employment, for instance. But we're, well, different. The individual counts more. We're egalitarian, but nobody stands on any little yellow spots." Nor does anyone wear a uniform. Or, for that matter, a tie. There are no morning inspirational speeches or calisthenics. And workers are not expected to stay long hours.

At Kyocera, everyone except honor employees (workers who have proved their dependability) must punch a time clock. But at H-P there is no time clock. H-P workers can also earn merit raises based on their teamwork and ability to meet or exceed their individual quotas. Faced with possible layoffs during the recession of the early 1970s, H-P decided to experiment. "Everyone —all the way up to Bill Hewlett—took a 10 percent pay cut. No one was laid off. And productivity actually increased," said Costa. "Then we tried a 'fortnight program,' in which employees worked eight-and-a-half-hour days, with every other Friday off." That program was ultimately scrapped. "Federal laws stipulated we had to pay time-and-a-half after eight hours. And figuring out accrued benefits, vacations, all that was a nightmare. Seems like everything is controlled by a stupid computer." H-P ultimately settled on what it calls its flexible work hours program: all employees are expected to work eight hours a day, but they can select their own hours within a work "window" (between 6:30 A.M. and 8:30 P.M.).

Beyond these differences, Kyocera and H-P have a lot in common. Although H-P's lifetime employment policy is not written into a worker's contract, employees believe, as a matter of faith, that they will never be laid off.

"Look, they take care of you here," said Michael Graniero, fifty-one, a machine operator. He pointed to the rafters. "Acoustic tile. I worked in other shops for fifteen years, and they never cared about the noise, or the cold, or the heat. So why do I need a union if my company is like family—one that looks out for you?" He leaned over and added, a bit conspiratorially, "Hey, you oughta come up here some Friday when we have one of our company beer busts if you want to see a bunch of happy people."

Even the machinery is set up to allow individuals to work at their own speed. "At Sony, across the street, they use gravity-feed assembly lines," explained a young assembly-line supervisor sitting in the company's cafeteria. "But we use a carousel assembly line. It's like a bunch of shopping carts going around in a circle. A worker can reach in and grab what he needs as the carousel goes around. With the gravity-feed system, though, you have to keep up with the machine, or the pieces just keep piling up." A forty-year-old assembler cut in: "I worked across the street at Sony before I came here. If you had to go to the bathroom, or got sick, you were supposed to turn on a red light and wait for a supervisor to come. Here, you just go. The unions are handing out leaflets at Sony all the time, but not here. I don't like unions, but if I was still at Sony, I'd want one. You're not paid as well over there, but there's more to it than that. Over there, you're just a part of the machinery." As at Kyocera, H-P employees work in large, open spaces. Only one office, the personnel office, has a door on it.

A few minutes later, Costa, the employee relations fellow, talked about a theory that had occurred to him: "We try to be a family, but a family of individuals," Costa said. "People move out to California, they've cut their social attachments to churches or towns, but they still want to belong to something. Because of the way society is changing, I think the workplace is going to have to provide these social connections. So we keep the size of our plants down—if one exceeds about 2000 employees, it usually splits into smaller plants." The San Diego plant now has about 1500 employees. Pretty soon, said Costa, it would probably have to split, like an amoeba.

As at Kyocera, H-P encourages decision making at the lowest possible level. Recently, the company decided to try a Japanese management technique called the "quality circle," originally introduced to Japan in 1941 by an American management consultant, W. Edwards Demming. Quality circles have already saved H-P hundreds of thousands of dollars, according to Fred Rilely, an H-P employee in Palo Alto and president of the International Association of Quality Circles. A quality circle in H-P's Loveland, Colorado, plant saved the company $100,000 by devising a simple way to keep the tip of an automatic screwdriver from falling out. The idea is catching on. Nationally, at least 500 companies now use them.

Bob Schultz, H-P's San Diego quality circle expert, told me late on the afternoon of my Hewlett-Packard visit, "What we've found out through a lot of studies is that money is one of the least important motivating factors in a job. People need to be recognized as team players *and* as individuals. And they need to feel good about what they accomplish. Maybe Americans have placed so much importance on making money that we've forgotten these other, more important motivators. Well, we're learning them again. And when the dust settles, I think you'll see Americans devising management systems that are far more competitive than anything the Japanese have come up with."

EFFICIENCY AND COMMUNITY

Among the leading proponents of a new management style is William G. Ouchi, a professor at University of California, Los Angeles. Ouchi is by no means a full-bore Japanophile: "Probably no form of organization is more sexist or racist than the

Japanese corporation," which he calls the "type J" organization. "They do not intentionally shut out those who are different nor do they consider male Japanese to be superior. Their organizations simply operate as culturally homogeneous social systems that have very weak explicit or hierarchical monitoring properties, and thus can withstand no internal cultural diversity." The Japanese accept ambiguity, imperfection, and uncertainty as a part of organizational life. Americans expect their dealings with management to be much more straightforward. Americans, because of the influence of labor unions, believe in honoring seniority in the workplace. Ironically, the Japanese style is not so respectful of age and experience; it encourages the hiring of low-paid, unsophisticated young workers who are indoctrinated into the system. The Japanese style, then, is not particularly adaptable to American culture.

Until recently, what Ouchi calls the "type A" organization was the most successful work form in American society, characterized by high rates of interfirm mobility, a short average tenure of employment, and the need for specialization. This system worked well until the traditional society networks and affiliations were so fragmented that the work ethic itself, which depends for its survival on generation-to-generation socialization, was in question: "When people had relatives, neighbors, and churches, they did not need Dr. Spock to tell them why the baby was purple, and they did not need a company that provided them with a rich network of social contacts." The management style that had helped destroy community now feels compelled to create it within the walls of the workplace.

Ouchi has been a leading voice in working out a new American equation, suggesting a form mixing Japanese and American styles that would permit both individual freedom and group cohesion. In Ouchi's view, many American companies, such as Hewlett-Packard, already exhibit many of the characteristics of this mixed-model, which he calls the "type Z" organization. The ideal type Z organization, according to Ouchi and associate Alfred M. Jaeger, "combines a basic cultural commitment to individualistic values with a highly collective, nonindividual pattern of interaction. It simultaneously satisfies old norms of independence and present needs for affiliation. Employment is effectively (although not officially) for a lifetime, and turnover is low. Decision making is consensual, and there is often a highly self-conscious attempt to preserve the consensual mode. . . . But the individual still is ultimately the decision maker, and responsibility remains individual. This procedure puts strains on the individual, who is held responsible for decisions singly, but must arrive at them collectively."

Management experts like to talk about efficiency; employees talk about community. Apple Computer is probably the most visible of the new, young postindustrial companies. It is not known for a particularly progressive management style; rather, it represents the kind of insulation common among the postindustrial companies. The employees (who are each given an Apple) are imbued with a feeling of corporate community—a type of community that works to replace the lack of community beyond the walls of the company. Apple, in California's Silicon Valley, the heart of the semiconductor industry, consists of a cluster of office/warehouse buildings that could best be described as neo–Taco Bell. If all the buildings that looked like these were suddenly whisked away, the valley would be practically barren—except for all the singles bars. Silicon Valley is a good example of the kind of placeless urban landscape that makes the company a home.

In Apple's small company cafeteria, Phil Roybal, public information director, and Susan Jacoby, who works in marketing, were talking about their loyalty to their company. Both are young: Phil is in his thirties, Susan in her early twenties. "Silicon Valley isn't a community," said Susan, "it's a place you drive to in order to go to work. It's a place to come and work and a place to live, but it's not a community. There's an enormous amount of lonely people in the Valley. It's really hard to meet people outside the company you work for, unless you go to singles bars. I used to live in Boston and it was a lot easier there."

"You ought to try Dial-A-Match," said Phil, referring to a computer dating service now available to people with home computers.

Susan smiled and arched an eyebrow. "I play the violin and the viola, and I've been thinking about joining the Los Gatos Chamber Orchestra. It's taken me two years. Ever since I started working here I let it go, and I shouldn't. But you get into your work. The workplace becomes your whole community. A while back I went to an Apple party. It was a castle-warming party—Steve Wozniak, one of the founders, had just bought this castle up on

Skyline—and I brought a friend who worked outside of Apple. I went around bragging to people about that: Look at this! A friend!"

As Phil Roybal said, "Apple is a way of life. I think that there is a kind of cult aspect, or at least there was in the earlier days."

Susan interrupted: "But there still is. We all have Apple T-shirts and Apple pens and Apple labels on our cars."

"People honk at me in my car."

"That's just because you're cute, Phil."

"Well, it's guys. Well, it's San Francisco," he said, laughing. "But there really is something to the cult idea. We've been buying back the very first Apples, which are numbered. We're going to put them under glass so everyone can pass by and see them. You know, kind of like religious relics."

This kind of workplace social insulation is by no means limited to the postindustrial companies. Most television sitcoms, of late, revolve not around the family or neighborhoods, but around the workplace. But in America II, the companies are taking the next logical step by withdrawing further into their own culture. Apple, for example, is planning to move its operations to a Supersite that will be a recreation-oriented, Disneyesque postindustrial park and residential condo community. Not only will the employees' employment and continued training needs be taken care of, but their social ones as well. One can imagine a sign at the gate: "If you worked here, you'd be home by now."

A clear linkage exists between the new workplace and the move to postindustrial parks in regions with fewer unions and fewer traditions: what they have in common is the feeling of membership and the structure of forts.

SECOND THOUGHTS

Whether this approach leads to an enlightened society where work has more meaning, or to a kind of workplace feudalism, depends on one's point of view.

The new management style has drawn praise from some unexpected quarters, including Tom Hayden and liberal economist Lester C. Thurow. Writes Thurow: "Historically, the United States has tried to meet the demand for economic security through its social-welfare system." But now, he says, we should start looking to the company to provide some of that welfare.

Thurow's notion is that, as the social safety net contracts, the private safety net will have to expand. On a trip to Japan, Thurow was intrigued by the Japanese hesitancy to fire anyone:

> Every firm I talked to admitted that it had some bad workers who were not performing adequately. They were described in very unflattering terms and, according to company officials, immense social pressure was brought upon them to start working. But they were not fired even if they had "not worked in years," largely because management did not entirely blame them for their failures. As the Japanese see it, the entire system somehow shares the blame for inadequate performance: either it has not provided the right job for the individual worker, or it has failed to motivate him properly.

Such a system of "private welfare" might work in the United States, but, as Thurow points out, "If the private safety net is not expanded, voters will quickly turn back to government in pursuit of economic security."

Labor unions have also shown interest in the new management methods—particularly the no-layoff policy. In the early 1980s, the United Auto Workers made a $3 billion concession to management: at General Motors, workers negotiated for and got a guaranteed income stream (GIS), which gave workers continual wages even if they were laid off. However, as part of the agreement, the workers had to accept alternative employment provided by GM. In 1983, workers in South Gate (near Los Angeles) were being forced by GM to relocate to Oklahoma or lose GIS benefits forever. The problem was compounded by the fact that they were not guaranteed continued employment in Oklahoma. There, they would have the least seniority, and would be the first ones to be laid off in the future. General Motors had, in some cases, offered employment in Oklahoma to one spouse who worked at GM, but not to the other, thus dividing the family. Some workers who had believed that they had finally negotiated a little security considered themselves, as one put it, "slaves that can be moved at will from one GM plantation to another."

Doug Woodbury, president of CWA Local 11509 in San Diego, is all for the kind of management methods used by companies like Kyocera and Hewlett-Packard—as long as they follow through on their promises. "If these things work, then I guess the companies won't ever need a union. But that's not human nature. The new techniques may just be window dressing. Management usually ends up abusing worker rights."

Indeed, what management gives, management can take away. "People are not given freedom, equality, or self-respect; they must organize, fight for, and take it," says one Los Angeles organizer. "What they get from these management policies is the illusion of importance." The America II company may look like a family, he says, but "in the final analysis, it's a family in which primogeniture still holds, in which the threat of disinheritance and banishment are real."

Consider the case of Emcon, a subsidiary of Kyocera. In 1980, when Kyocera took over the struggling plant, the workers, mainly middle-class Midwestern transplants, tough, gum-popping women with teased hair and a firm belief in the American dream, were elated. They thought the idea that the company could be a family was a great idea. Kyocera first trimmed the work force by more than 100 employees. These workers were offered what they considered generous separation pay: one week's salary for every year they had worked at the plant, to be paid by the plant's previous owner. Employees who were asked to stay were assured by the new management of Emcon that there would be no further layoffs, according to Sherry Alvarez, a former sales representative, and other former Emcon employees. A folder of information on Kyocera's philosophy was handed out at Emcon, explaining that policy. Several times over the next few months, Arthur Jonishi, the ex-workers say, spoke at their morning meetings in the parking lot, assuring them that, in return for their devotion to the company, they would be protected by the no-layoff policy. Jonishi, as the ex-employees tell it, told Emcon employees that if the company hit hard times, they would be absorbed into other Kyocera concerns in San Diego.

The employees believed an agreement had been made and they set about fulfilling their end of the bargain. They worked ten to twelve hours a day, the kind of hours common at Kyocera-owned concerns. One woman later claimed that she worked sixty hours a week, pregnant; others reported that they were asked by Emcon managers to take work home, and that secretaries were asked to assemble electronic parts at their desks. And, during July and August, the employees went on a voluntary four-day work week, drawing on accrued sick leave or vacation time, or simply taking a pay cut. Although Emcon's management was "paranoid" about possible union activity, according to Alvarez, "we weren't interested in belonging to a union, not with the no-layoff policy."

The company, the employees were told, was going to make it. But on August 27, uniformed guards walked into the plant and a voice came over the intercom instructing the employees to turn off their machines, leave their posts, and assemble in the parking lot. There, the 350 employees were told that the plant was closed, and that they had ten minutes to return to their desks and lockers, accompanied by the guards, to collect their possessions. "Here I'd been assuring my people, telling them they could trust Kyocera," recalls Leslie Nawl, a production supervisor. "They were crying, men, women—some of whom had come to the plant as teenagers, working fifteen, seventeen years—so devoted that they were coming to me and asking if they could go back to their machines to finish their morning quotas."

Four days later, the plant reopened its doors, changing its corporate identity from Emcon, a wholly owned subsidiary of Kyocera, to Emcon, a division of Kyocera. During the four days, Emcon phones continued to be answered, and, the ex-employees say, orders were taken and some machines continued to operate. Approximately forty of Emcon's employees, most of whom had earned just above the three dollar and thirty-five cents per hour minimum wage, were rehired within a few days. Some employees, who had earned six dollars or seven dollars an hour previous to the liquidation, were rehired at wages below four dollars an hour. Over the next year, according to the exemployees' recently hired attorney, the plant never lost a day of production, continued to operate three work shifts per day, and now has about the same number of employees in December as it did on the day the ex-employees were fired: "The only difference is that the present employees are paid lower salaries."

Jonishi sees all of this differently. "I've never said that they would not be out of a job. We do have people leave. Bankruptcies are quite common in Japan, too." He insists that no promises were ever made, and that there was no layoff. Emcon, he says, was a failing company, suffering losses of over $2 million in seven months. "It was a liquidation—a bankruptcy, really." State records, however, show that Emcon and Kycocera were formally merged. In the months following the controversy, there was no record of a formal liquidation. Nor did the U.S. Bankruptcy

Court register Emcon as having filed bankruptcy papers. And, even though Jonishi asserts that the management of Emcon is "totally autonomous" from Kyocera or Kyoto Ceramic, the final decision to shut Emcon down was made, he says, by Kazuo Inamori, Kyoto's chairman of the board—in a long-distance phone call to San Diego.

The former Emcon employees have filed a class action suit charging, among other things, fraud, that promises were made without intent to perform, and that emotional distress was intentionally inflicted on the terminated employees.

If their claims prove to be true, the case could, according to some legal experts, alter the relationship between workers and those employers who promise a safe haven in the shifting economy. Most of the employees have been unable to find jobs in the electronics field at the level of their Emcon salaries. "What it comes down to," says one ex-employee, who had worked at the plant for nine years, and lost her house after the shutdown, "is the value of a promise. I guess the promise is only good if you're a computer whiz or willing to slave along for the minimum wage. The rest of us are on our own. I'm a lot more likely to join a union now, but what good would joining a union do? Management would just move the plant to another state or another country. One of these days, they're just going to push us middle-class people too far."

THE ROLE OF UNIONS

Perhaps the most important workplace affiliation of past decades, the mainstay of collective worker identity, was the labor union. Organized labor has been in decline for a decade—though more people belong to unions than ever before, the proportion of the work force with union membership has been dropping precipitously as the work force shifts from blue- to white-collar. Industrial decline is occurring where unions are strongest, and unions have made few inroads into the emerging America II job market. The United Food and Commercial Workers Union has found it almost impossible to organize fast-food chains, because the franchises are so physically decentralized, with thousands of small separate facilities with high employee turnover. And for some of the same reasons, unions have moved extremely slowly toward any kind of effort to organize the increasing number of people working out of their homes, either as employees or independent contractors. The growth industries, such as computers, electronics, clerical, and service occupations, have relatively little union representation. The decline of unionism is also linked to the rise of big government, supported by big labor, which emerged in the 1960s and '70s as a competitor in the same arena, with federal and state agencies battling for occupational safety, equal opportunity, and higher minimum wages. The final reason for its current decline is the very success of the labor union movement, which has forced many companies who wish to avoid unions to adopt more humane management techniques. Of nonunion companies, 30 percent now have some kind of formal grievance procedure. Fred K. Foulkes, a professor at the Boston University School of Management, studied the personnel policies of twenty-six large, nonunion companies, and concluded that these companies were offering blue-collar workers the best of both worlds. Many of the companies were limiting their managers' freedom "beyond anything that a union would be able to negotiate," and some employees of these companies had retained "some undefined intangibles that . . . relate to morale, trust, confidence, spirit, good faith, an identification with management, and a consequent avoidance of the we-they adversary relationship that can so frequently characterize the union-management relationship." All of this, of course, depends on the continued threat of unionization.

The labor movement is adapting to the new realities. Some unions are shifting their bargaining power to goals other than trying to gain more wages and benefits in an era of limits, demanding that workers be trained in the new technologies instead of just dumped. A new kind of union member, epitomized by air traffic controllers, is emerging in the fields of communications and other technical areas. "Computer technology creates the false illusion that problems with the workplace are over," says Harvey Shaiken, a research associate at Massachusetts Institute of Technology. Shaiken also specializes in advanced technologies. "But the controllers [exhibit] old attitudes, the attitudes of coal miners." During the 1981 air controllers' strike, ninety-four controllers at the air control center at Gander, Newfoundland, were able to stop most American air travel between the U.S. and Europe. "That's scary," said Robert Shrank, an expert on work with the Ford Foundation and a former blue-collar worker, "but that's the computer. Folks better think twice about how much power they put in the hands of a few people." According to Shaiken, as computer technology grows, "small groups of workers will increasingly acquire great power. . . . Any workers who operate a large centralized computer operation are sitting on a source of exceptional power." The air traffic controllers were the first of this new breed of workers to cross the line: "Here you have guys making $30,000 a year or more and their basic complaint is the insensitivity of management." The strike, he said, was historic because it was the first time that American workers "have given up their jobs because they have been mismanaged." These kinds of demands can be expected in the future from new expanding areas of the economy, where people often work at repetitive, menial, or boring jobs. Such workers are defined by Shrank as "anyone who works with computers, with symbols, with video display terminals; people who never get near a shovel or a wrench."

Indeed, the most militant unions in recent years have been made up not of typical blue-collar workers, but of air traffic controllers, movie and television writers, baseball and football players. These people, as Stanley Aronowitz, writer and labor activist, puts it, are "in the new, key areas of society, communications, recreation, not manufacturing. These people are beginning to sense they have power." If organized labor comes to understand this new group, then unionism has a bright future. But the language of collective bargaining must change. For instance, the new work force, as shown by the controllers, is especially concerned about stress in the workplace. Says Aronowitz, "Stress is the black lung of the technical classes."

Companies that ignore worker stress do so at their own peril. In the past, worker compensation awards were limited to cases involving physical injury; but in the last twenty years there has been an increasing number of judgments allowing worker compensation payments in job-related cases of depression, anxiety, and other disabling mental disorders, many of them due to what can be loosely defined as stress. Twenty-one states, including California, have ruled that stress is a valid factor in determining disability eligibility. In six states, courts have extended coverage from simple dramatic incidents of emotional trauma to emotional illness caused by "cumulative" injury from work stress. One secretary with lung cancer successfully sued her company, claiming that the stress under which she had worked for years caused her to smoke continuously.

These suits have not been solely responsible for changes in management style, but they have encouraged many companies to institute corporate psychological-counseling programs—often the first step toward shifting the management style toward a more humane, familial approach. The problem is that this works fine for those workers with skills that are in demand, but as former employees of Emcon found, promises and new management methods do not mean much when workers are easily replaced, or when companies threaten to move to another country.

THE FAITH OF
ENTREPRENEURIALISM

Marjorie Ulloa, now fifty-two, was forty-nine when she made what she describes as her "commitment to the machine." As a result, her house has been virtually gobbled up by a Xerox 860 word processor. The machine is the focal point, the magnet. When her family talks, they talk around the machine: it hums, they talk. When company drops over, they drift toward the machine. The machine is the priority, and brings with it a new freedom and new priorities.

"I was a housewife for twenty years," she says. "I started working again by doing temporary typing for companies in their offices, but I decided to buy a word processor and work out of my home when I realized that was possible. I figured that I could make more money at home. Another reason I wanted to work out of my home—people look at me funny when I tell them this—was that, since I was married and really didn't have to work, I didn't want to displace any of the women who do have to work, who are the sole supporters of their families.

"I'm at the stage where the children are grown and I want to do something for myself. When you're at home as a housewife, no one in this country puts much value on it. But when I walk out of this house wearing a good wool suit and look like I'm making money, people listen to me. Now, I'm *hiring* people. Several part-time women. I'm really proud of that. I've grown a lot; I feel a lot better about myself. At my age, you just don't have a future in an office, unless you've got an outstanding educational backround. By working at home I'm making an end run around that.

"I've moved far beyond simple word processing. I've put together financial programs for other women, put together a lecture service to help women become entrepreneurs. All of this has put a real strain on my family; I guess I've become all work and no play. But you make priorities. Working in your own home, you can look around and see all the housework that needs to be done. A few years ago, I couldn't have tolerated this mess. I used to try to do both, my work and the housework. Not anymore."

Maybe, she says, the undone housework is "a kind of metaphor" for putting aside involvement in church, causes, family. The machine's hum fills the house, but it's worth it, she says. She thinks how much being an entrepreneur is worth every time she walks out that door wearing that good wool suit.

Entrepreneurialism is the latest thing, the way out, the escape clause in the postindustrial economy. Through the 1960s and 70s, those people who owned a small business enjoyed no particular distinction. In the insecure 1980s, though, it's the new faith —a paradoxical faith indeed, because starting a small business is among the most insecure of endeavors.

Paul and Sara Edwards have set out to make a career of helping people who work for themselves at home. They live in Sierra Madre, a town of about 10,000 on the edge of a mountain range overlooking Pasadena, California. They chose to move to Los Angeles because, as Paul told me on a hot, smoggy day as we drove toward his home, "Back in Kansas City, they wait for ideas to be tried out everywhere else first; here, ideas get tested," and they chose Sierra Madre because it was the closest thing to a small town they could find near Los Angeles. Paul is a lawyer and former Kansas City neighborhood activist. His office is now in the living room, and Sara is a psychotherapist who still does therapy in the back room and is "transitioning," as she puts it, into full-time consulting. Entrepreneurialism, in Paul's words, "is a real escape," an escape from a traditional job market that doesn't have a lot of room or flexibility any more. But something else is going on here as well. Both have been active in the human potential movement, and entrepreneurialism, they say, is the logical and emotional extension of that movement.

Says Sara, "The question we've started wondering is, where are people going after they've had this inculcation? We think it's entrepreneurialism. One woman I know became a minister in one of the alternative religions, and then started her own enterprise. In my practice, I see that more and more. People take all this energy they used to put into est, or whatever, and pour it into their own businesses. People seem to have turned from interior excavation to exterior improvements. Entrepreneurialism is kind of a new religion. In the sixties, social activism became a religion, and the decline of organized religion began. Then in the seventies, the human potential movement and psychotherapy took off. When they come out of psychotherapy they frequently change their jobs—and usually end up working for themselves. So many of my clients who are teachers leave their profession. They say, 'I'm not going to do what someone else wants me to do anymore.' And they go off and do something they've always wanted to do. . . . Not only do they become entrepreneurs, they leave. They move up north to Marin County, to some small town."

COMES THE ENTREPRENEURIAL REVOLUTION

So many people are calling themselves entrepreneurs these days that the meaning of the word has become rather hazy. The classical definition of an entrepreneur is an innovative capitalist, as opposed to the garden-variety capitalist, who uses other people's innovations to make money. But the word has come to have broader meaning, especially now that some businesses are adopting entrepreneurial techniques, dividing employees into competitive teams, virtual minifirms, that assume some of the risk of their particular product or service. *Webster's New World Dictionary* defines an entrepreneur as "a person who organizes and manages a business undertaking, assuming the risk for the sake of the profit." In any case, never before have so many businesses been started: in 1950, 93,000 new businesses were being created each year, but in the early 1980s, over 600,000 new businesses were being started annually. The death rate for new businesses is higher now, but the birth rate is also much, much higher.

Until quite recently, the common wisdom was that companies, like cities, would grow and grow, and that small businesses would fade to an insignificant number. In the 1940s, Joseph Schumpeter, in the widely quoted *Capitalism, Socialism and Democracy,* predicted that several tendencies would ultimately cripple the "capitalist engine." Schumpeter believed that the entrepreneur —who is undeniably essential to capitalism—would disappear, swept away by the advantages inherent in large corporate organization and capitalization, what he called "monopolized capitalism." But things didn't quite work out that way. What has happened since Schumpeter's pronouncement is that the huge corporations of the 1930s—Ford, GM, RCA, and many others—are still thriving, but "the economy's cutting edge has since moved to firms that were hardly known to the public in the 1930s or didn't as yet exist, among these Xerox, Hewlett-Packard, Texas Instruments . . . most founded during or after World War II by solo entrepreneurs and entrepreneurial teams," according to sociologist Edwin Harwood, who is a codirector of the Entrepreneurial Studies Program at the University of South Florida.

Since the mid-1960s, the 1000 biggest U.S. firms have gradually been reducing their labor forces, and most private-sector jobs created since then have been created by smaller firms. According to British economist Norman Macrae, the majority of the new extra jobs at any one time have been in firms less than five years old, even though more than half of new small American firms disappear in those first five years. Macrae's analysis is confirmed by research at the Massachusetts Institute of Technology: MIT research scientist David Birch contends that a fundamental shift is taking place in the nation—a shift from large-scale enterprises to small-scale enterprises and from bureaucratic to entrepreneurial styles of management. Birch's research shows that nearly two-thirds of all new jobs in America are created not by major corporations but by firms with fewer than twenty employees, and that in the 1970s, companies that had fewer than 100 employees accounted for 80 percent of the new jobs, with most of these companies concentrated in the economy's service sector. According to a study at the University of Southern California, since the early 1960s, investors in small companies have done far better than those who invested in larger firms. One dollar invested in 1963 in a firm with less than $5 million in capital would, by 1980, have increased to about forty-six dollars; but the return on a dollar invested in companies with over a billion dollars in capital would have been only four dollars. Clearly, investors have found that small is beautiful. A torrent of venture capital is flooding into small entrepreneurial firms, particularly in the electronics field. And the pace is accelerating.

WHY ENTREPRENEURIALISM?

Why is entrepreneurialism expanding, even in the worst recession since the 1930s, even in the face of an unprecedented number of small business failures and corporate mergers?

The reasons are complex. First, the trend fits the shift from a manufacturing economy to a service/information economy. As a general rule, it takes relatively less capital investment to set up shop in an information or service business than it does to establish a manufacturing plant with the necessarily large operating facility. The small entrepreneurial firm can move faster in a changing economy, since it lacks the decision-delaying bureaucracy of the large corporation. In the entrepreneur, the smaller firm has a natural product salesman and champion. And also, a small firm has no vested interest in any older product line. As Harwood writes: "Texas Instruments, when it launched its transistors, did not have to worry about transistors cutting into vacuum tube sales, unlike RCA, which dominated the vacuum tube business."

Population deconcentration is both a stimulant and a result of the new wave of entrepreneurialism. The anticities of the South, West, and rural areas—with looser zoning regulations, lower taxes, and an atmosphere of boosterism—are more attuned to entrepreneurialism. "The smart entrepreneur can sit in L.A. and look at something new, like tanning parlors springing up all over town, and immediately export this to Sioux Falls and the rest of the world," says Howard Shensen, a Los Angeles consultant who bills himself as the "consultant's consultant." This is particularly true of those businesses that use the new technologies: sixty-minute photofinishing shops, delis, photocopying shops, word processing. Population deconcentration does not, however, help the black entrepreneur. According to demographer Cheryl Russell, writing in *American Demographics,* most black-owned firms are located in the central cities, serving low-income clientele. Well over half of all black businesses of New York, Illinois, and Michigan are located in the central cities of New York City, Chicago, and Detroit—all cities that are losing population. Between 1972 and 1977, the number of black-owned firms grew by only 12 percent, compared with the increase of 31 percent for the total number of minority firms. Nonetheless, the most successful places for minority entrepreneurs are in the South, the West (particularly Texas and California) and to a lesser extent, rural areas.

The trend away from mass-produced goods and a shift toward individual goods and services is also stimulating the growth of entrepreneurialism. Demographers and marketers believe that, because of the aging of the population, the demand for many durable goods will drop off, and is, indeed, already decreasing. A good portion of the money now spent on mass-produced goods will likely shift toward specialized cottage industries, producing crafts and other more personalized products. According to William A. Cox, deputy chief economist for the Department of Commerce, "This trend will be fostered by the rapidly rising number of affluent middle-aged people with few children to provide for, who are able and willing to pay the price for convenience, personalized style, and enjoyment of life. It could be furthered also by people looking for jobs outside large corporations. . . . In effect, we may see a return to patterns of production typical of our past, when more labor was invested in products." Evidence of that shift can already be seen in the proliferation of personal services—marriage counselors, consciousness-raising seminars, private schools—and the rising number of craft shows around the country. These shows, which are now quite popular in shopping centers, are primarily a middle-class phenomenon, but to attend some of them is to step backward in time. Hundreds of counterculture entrepreneurs are earning part- or full-time livings making and selling pottery, macramé, wood carvings, and custom furniture—the kind of goods that most affluent people of the 1950s and '60s would have scorned. (Many of these people, incidentally, live in rural areas but sell their wares at craft fairs in large cities.) As Robert Schwartz, who established a school for entrepreneurs at the Tarrytown Conference Center in New York State, puts it, the counterculture entrepreneurs believe that work should "not only provide a living but also develop selfhood, foster companionship, and nourish the earth."

The two-paycheck family is also influencing the surge in entrepreneurialism. Men whose wives work have a higher frequency of changing jobs for higher wages and of taking chances, according to a study by Marta Mooney, assistant professor of management at Fordham University's graduate school of business in New York. Says Mooney: "A two-earner household definitely relieves the economic pressure on the husband. This enables him to take risks and to work in occupations he would prefer to work in, rather than at the highest-paying job. It gives him a little something behind him so that a catastrophe isn't waiting if something goes wrong at work. It's easier for the two-paycheck husband to

change jobs, to start his own business, to take an earlier retirement—and he does." Among two-paycheck families, Mooney
found that men earn 20 percent less income than husbands in
one-paycheck families. White-collar husbands work less because
their wives have jobs, cutting their average annual work hours by
up to 14 percent. All of this means more ability to step out of the
corporate ranks to start up that always-dreamed-of small business, even if only part-time. It is unclear whether husbands are
quite as much help to entrepreneurial-minded wives. As Jill Charboneau, managing editor of *American Demographics,* writes, "Good
statistics on women entrepreneurs are hard to find." What is
known is that the number of women entrepreneurs has more than
doubled since 1972, according to the Census Bureau, and the
share of self-employed women grew from about one-fifth of all
entrepreneurs in 1972 to one-quarter in 1972. The typical
woman entrepreneur is an unmarried, white, college graduate
who is about fifty-two years old. Especially for women reentering
the job market after raising a family, as Marjorie Ulloa found,
starting a business can be a way to gain self-confidence, to get
control of one's life.

Despite the failure rate of small businesses, working for oneself
offers a peculiar kind of security in a changing economy. As
author Ralph Keyes, who is writing a book about risk, puts it, "I'd
rather be an entrepreneurial free-lancer than risk getting fired."
Says Shensen: "A lot of people will say consulting is very insecure. They say they'd rather be plugged into the corporate welfare system; but they soon discover that it's much more secure to
be a consultant, an entrepreneur. If a consultant loses three
companies he's still got the majority of his business intact."

The psychological attraction to entrepreneurialism is based on
economic reality, not necessarily any particular nostalgia for the
rugged individualism of Horatio Alger. Entrepreneurialism is,
increasingly, a pressure-release valve in an economy that, because of new computer technology, has less and less room for
middle managers—particularly those born in the post–World
War II baby boom. The economic impetus for the growth in
self-employment is linked to deep demographic change. Over the
next decade, America needs to generate 15 million new jobs,
according to MIT researcher Birch. There just isn't enough room
for all the baby boomers who want to be executives. Studies by
the Rand Corporation and the Bureau of Labor Statistics show

that the number of persons thirty-five to forty-four years old (the prime candidates to become middle managers) will increase by 42 percent between 1980 and 1990—while the number of jobs for managers and administrators will increase by only 21 percent. The result: mounting stress, burnout, and personnel problems of a scope never before faced by U.S. industry.

So what happens to white-collar baby boomers stalled and frustrated in their most potent years? One option: they seek retraining in a technical field, giving up the perks and status of management, but gaining some job mobility. A second option: they stay stalled, but seek one of the increasingly popular company counseling programs that helps workers find more satisfaction outside the job. A third option, for the ambitious and creative, is the most exciting: do an end run around the big companies, adopt the entrepreneurial ethic. If you can't join 'em, start your own company.

HOME WORK

The easiest way to become an entrepreneur, with low overhead, is to work out of the home. For much of the nation's history, most people worked at home as self-employed farmers, entrepreneurs, or independent contractors. This continued well after the mass migration of rural people to the big industrial cities began. Even in the nation's largest industrial city, New York, only 23 percent of all workers in 1840 worked outside the home. In 1980, *Business Week* estimated that, because of the entrepreneurial endeavors, as many as 5 million people may be working out of their own homes. The number is growing rapidly, suggesting that many Americans may prefer nineteenth century work habits to twentieth century office politics.

"We believe our values will change because of working at home," says home–work consultant Paul Edwards. "Because of the rise in home entrepreneurialism, Americans are going to be doing a lot of bartering: trading piano lessons for business advice, that kind of thing. As more people work at home there will be a revitalization of community activity. More networking, more support groups. A lot of the old glue is gone, the kinds of loyalties people shared through large families or churches, whatever. But our basic needs remain the same. When people no longer have the social connections provided by the office, they're going to replace them, and computer networks won't do it. We'll be forced by necessity to put more effort into our most personal relationships, because working at home puts so much pressure on them. Another potential we see is for a revitalization of community activity. Suddenly your neighbors take on some importance. I could envision neighborhoods—you know, bedroom communities—coming to life, and whole condo communities populated with people who work at home who share communal computers for their work."

There are caveats to all this enthusiasm. What tends to be forgotten, in the general enthusiasm about working at home and entrepreneurialism, is that, during the rise of the industrial age (and well into the twentieth century, especially in the rural South) working at home was often associated with labor exploitation. This was particularly true in the garment industry, which thrived on the labors of thousands of poorly paid, nonunionized women isolated in their homes. Today, businesses are beginning to farm out more and more work to independent contractors, who often work at home. The company profits from this: full-time salaries, benefit packages, and unions can be sidestepped. The entrepreneur profits, too, by having work, but eventually the price could be considerably high.

Karen Nussbaum is president of 9 to 5, the National Association of Working Women, and of the Detroit district of the Service Employees International Union. As Nussbaum sees it, all this futuristic talk about entrepreneurialism and the electronic cottage hides some disturbing realities. One of the reasons it's difficult to define what an entrepreneur is, she says, is that "ultimately, entrepreneurialism is a class distinction. Home work is a completely different story depending on your income. For the professionals who, by the nature of their work, make good money, it's a boon. But for the low-paid, lower-level worker, primarily the female clerical worker who is now being slated for home work, entrepreneurialism is just a fancy word for the kind of working conditions we tried to get away from a hundred years ago—piecework in the home. One of the reasons people choose to do home work is that they can't afford good child care; and this means that many women are doing two jobs at home, their regular work plus child care."

Indeed, when computers are used at home by clerical workers contracting with large organizations, some interesting possibilities arise. Though Nussbaum says statistics are difficult to come by, some companies, particularly in data processing, require that their subcontracters pay rent on company computers installed in the home. Further, some of these computers come equipped with worker monitoring capabilities. The machine keeps track of the home worker's productivity, counting the worker's keystrokes-per-minute. In some cases, the home workers are paid only when the machine is turned on; in others, by the line rather than by the hour. The computer is not only capable of keeping track of this, but also of flashing on the worker's video screen a running report of the worker's productivity—whether or not a quota is being met. This places the home worker under tremendous pressure, and the pressure may, in fact, be counterproductive. A study by the National Institute of Occupational Safety and Health showed that when machines are used to pace workers, productivity can drop dramatically. Nonetheless, such a drop in productivity may be worth it to companies that wish to avoid paying benefits and high salaries to permanent office workers. (In Canada and some Scandinavian countries, legislation has been introduced to ban machine monitoring.)

In the long run, the isolation of the home worker, whether an entrepreneurial independent contractor or an employee stationed at home, will probably have a depressing effect on wages and benefits of all workers. "When people are isolated from each other, particularly when they're not selling a high-priced skill," says Nussman, "working conditions almost always deteriorate because they don't have collective action as a tool." This social isolation not only affects union organizing but potentially the mental health of some workers. While working at home can be a liberating experience for some people, others find the lack of social contact oppressive—particularly lower-income workers, who, because they have less income to spend on social activities, have traditionally depended on the office for socialization.

Marilyn Montanez, who runs a typesetting business out of her two-bedroom apartment in San Diego, describes this phenomenon: "I'm working all the time, sixteen hours a day, weekends, and sometimes I sure feel like one of those women who used to sit at a sewing machine at home all day. Only I'm sitting in front of a video display terminal next to my kitchen. This could be a depressing situation, I guess, except last month I made a proft for the first time. And that's exciting; it makes up for some of the isolation." Marjorie Ulloa, who has found her home work to be such a liberating experience in so many ways, also complains of the lack of social contact and the serious strain her work has placed on family life. "So I'm forcing myself to get out of the house more," she says. "I'm, joining a word processing organization."

Entrepreneurs have realized that other entrepreneurs feel isolated, and therein lies an entrepreneurial idea. Peter Bahnsen of Alexandria, Virginia, started a business solely to provide these people with a place to network. E-Net, as he calls his business, provides a weekly forum where entrepreneurs can interview an innovative business owner, or learn about specific services offered by other entrepreneurs, or disperse into small groups to discuss projects. E-Net is a place to exchange ideas and offer support, to fill the stimulation gap that some entrepreneurs feel, whether they work at home or in a small office. Further, this problem of entrepreneurial isolation has some interesting political implications. Gordon Bizar, founder of the California-based International Business Network, a membership association that provides entrepreneurs with business advice, says that because entrepreneurs and small-business people are independent by nature, they're not politically organized: "They're nonjoiners, the last of the rugged individualists. They see themselves as problem solvers and tend to have action/response coping mechanisms. That person isn't into long-term planning. But government change takes time. So problems never get dealt with until they're immediate."

Tom Fatjo, whose private garbage business serving Houston's condo communities made him rich and famous (at least among other entrepreneurs), now operates the Houstonian, a plush getaway resort offering rest, exercise, and motivation seminars for wealthy entrepreneurs. Says Fatjo, "One of the hazards of being an entrepreneur is it's pretty essential to put blinders on and really give an all-out commitment. What normally happens is you sacrifice your knowledge of the outside world. I have a real appetite, now, to be better informed, to figure out how to take some of that creative enterprise and apply it to public problems. There was a feeling of responsibility people had a hundred years ago, that a person had to have a sense of private and public responsibility. The entrepreneurial-type persons, me included, have ignored our public responsibility." So Fatjo has established, in addition to his spa, the American Leadership Forum, headed by Joseph Jaworski (the son of Leon Jaworski, the Watergate special prosecutor). The Forum is another inspirational, motivational endeavor that collects entrepreneurs from around the country and "prepares them for involvement in the leadership area." Fatjo is one of the few entrepreneurs talking about public responsibility. Apple's Steven Jobs and Stephen Wozniak are two others: through a bill passed by the California legislature, Jobs wants to give an Apple computer to every school in the state— a nice tax write-off and promotional scheme, but certainly in the public interest; and Wozniak has organized a series of neo-Woodstock rock concerts under the banner of UNISON (short for "Unite Us in Song"), with the vague theme of working together for the public good.

It is unlikely, however, that entrepreneurs are going to band together in a collective national conscience. An ironic aspect of the newest wave of entrepreneurialism is that it creates growing resentment to government regulation among some of the former counterculture baby boomers, who in the past were so idealistic about what government should do for the common good. Now that they're entrepreneurs, things look a bit different. One day I stopped at a small bakery in Seattle, bought a doughnut and a cup of coffee from a young woman whom I imagined to be quintessentially liberal and socially conscious, and I sat down in a window seat. I asked her for a napkin. Hand on her hip, she glared —perhaps more at herself than at me.

"If I had a napkin," she said, rolling her eyes, "I'd be a restaurant. If I were a restaurant, I'd need a toilet for the handicapped."

CUTTING LOOSE

There is another kind of entrepreneurial isolation and withdrawal. As people are forced out of traditional employment, not all end up with kitchen table electronics companies or Marin County boutiques. The same forces propelling the growth of tax-paying independent contractors is also fueling another kind of growth. Getting control in America II can mean going underground. The Internal Revenue Service estimates that upwards of $300 billion of income in 1981 went unreported. The underground economy is growing so fast that policymakers and forecasters no longer can accurately describe the health of the nation's economy. The growth of this subterranean cash economy is perhaps twice as fast as that of the recorded gross national product; some estimates place it at about 14 percent of the recorded GNP. This growth, as *Business Week* reported, has "made a mockery of forecasts that the United States, propelled by the surge in credit cards and electronic banking, is headed toward a cashless society. America's appetite for cash is proving to be insatiable." The underground economy includes doctors, lawyers, electricians, cabdrivers, retailers, and restaurateurs who work part-time "off the books."

Indeed, the most profitable underground entrepreneurial activity in the nation may revolve around drugs, not microchips. In much of rural America, marijuana is the number-one cash crop. In northern California, with the decline of the lumber industry and commercial fishing, the resurrection of whole neighborhoods of Victorian homes and the germination of many of the new crafts entrepreneurships began with grass profits.

In Humboldt County one evening, Wesley Chesbro, a thirty-year-old former community activist, now a county supervisor, told me of the impact of this economic trend: "Some of the conservative old-timers are even growing pot. It's just a way to economically survive here." Which would be fine, Chesbro added, "except that so many armed bands are having shoot-outs in the hills, not police against pot growers, but pot entrepreneurs against pot entrepreneurs."

Many observers credit the growth of the underground economy to high taxation. If high taxation were the only reason, why then does Sweden, with the highest tax rates in the developed world, have such a relatively small underground economy? An equally appealing explanation is that many Americans have simply lost faith in big government and other institutions and no longer feel wanted by American business or the general economy.

Entrepreneurs are taking the country in quite divergent directions: toward an entrepreneurial ideology that maintains that good old American self-reliance can bring us back a civil, controllable society; toward an underground entrepreneurial ideology that has more to do with rebellion and distrust; and finally, in some cases, backward to a time of sweatshops and worker exploitation. Perhaps most of all, the entrepreneurial revolution signals the coming of a frontier economy, where all the rules are up for grabs. But then, pioneering entrepreneurs have always tended to reject old civilizations for the frontier—and the more primitive and brutal the frontier the better.

In Peterborough, New Hampshire, I met a prototypical pioneer: Carl Helmers, a bearded and bearish man (more Pooh than grizzly) who lives in a ranch house in the woods. Until recently, he was the founder and publisher of *Byte* magazine, which in a few years grew from a newsletter to the largest computer magazine in the world. A few months ago, he sold it to McGraw-Hill publishing company. The sale made Helmers a very rich man, but soon he was chasing another venture, starting up a national magazine called *Robotics Age.* Robotics, Helmers figures, is the next wave, and he's in a good position to catch it. Listen to Carl Helmers for a while, and you can hear the anthem of the American entrepreneur.

"Everything comes in waves," he says, wheeling his sports car, equipped with radar-detecting Fuzz Buster, though Peterborough. "There's a new wave of entrepreneurialism, but it's been around right from the start. I read my genealogy a while back and found out that this ancestor of mine in the 1690s had a brick factory near Troy, New York, and he was fighting off Indians. We're doing the same thing these days. As a kid, I ate up the stories about Henry Ford and Thomas Edison. Well, Ford and Edison became very big, and every entrepreneur dreams of getting big. Companies get too big and stale and so new ones come up to replace them. I worked for NASA for a while, before I started *Byte,* and there were a lot of bureaucrats around the base always trying to start their own little businesses on the side. They were addicted to the government paycheck, but they were all dreaming about their own companies.

"There's always that frontier out there, you know. Computers lead to robots, robots lead to space. See, it's dreams that it's all about. I always had these science fiction dreams. I had the most complete *Tom Swift* collection around (which I eventually donated to my elementary school library because there were too many hamster turds all over them—course I didn't tell them about that).

"Entrepreneurialism is the whole difference between the European mentality and the American mentality. The American mentality is, 'Grab your hands onto whatever you need to do to get it done and go do it.' The European mentality is, 'Check with the authorities first.' That's my American dream: the independent contractor who doesn't check with the authorities first, getting rid of artificial barriers to flexibility—rules that say you can't stop this production line, rules that say you can't do things the way you want. I'd love to see the day where just about everybody is an independent contractor to everybody else."

His Fuzz Buster started beeping and he turned off on a side road. He was grinning at the thought of his brave new entre-preneurial world. "I can see independent entrepreneurs running efficient job shops, operating whole factories by themselves using computer simulations and robots. All by themselves. That's the real frontier."

WINNERS AND LOSERS

The new technologies may yet make for us a new world, with workerless entrepreneurial factories and a twenty-hour work week for everyone, but as we lurch into the information age, the nation seems adrift. In a sea of information, we do not seem to have enough information to devise a public policy that brings Americans into this new age in a way that does not widen the gap between the rich and the poor. Our security seems threatened as never before, not only by our dependence on factors outside our border (now that we are becoming an information exporting country dependent on other countries for our basic industrial needs), but also by the rising postindustrial inequalities within our borders. The new technologies and the new jobs do liberate many people from some of the drudgeries of work; but for others, the new economy spells disaster in the workplace.

According to Richard McGahey, an economist at the Urban Research Center of New York University, "instead of bringing economic salvation, lower-paying service and high-tech jobs may be a Trojan horse, bringing continued decline in the quality of American life through polarized incomes, growing poverty, and increased class tensions. The shifting American job market is already polarizing wages and income, contributing to the highest level of poverty since 1967. Service and high-tech jobs may be adding to this poverty instead of curing it, for they pay less and offer less mobility than older manufacturing jobs." As McGahey points out, computer assemblers earn about 70 percent of the hourly wage of auto workers. In Silicon Valley, starting wages for engineers grew 33 percent between 1974 and 1978, while wages for beginning production workers grew only 7 percent.

In many of the emerging industries, workers are treated, as the management experts like to say, "as humans," especially those with the sought-after skills. Engineers are rewarded, in the meritocracy system, with large annual bonuses, often as much as 10 percent of their gross annual salary. At the other end of the scale, skilled manual workers, the electronics assemblers, are paid poorly; their annual pay is one of the lowest salary rates in any major industry in the United States. Everett M. Rogers, a professor of communication at Stanford University who has studied the Silicon Valley social structure, is amazed at the disparity between what he calls the "two classes" of high-tech workers in what he had thought was one of the most economically successful spots in the nation. "When a typical engineer changes jobs in Silicon Valley, it usually means a 15 to 20 percent salary increase," he says. "But at the other end of the scale, the high-tech companies prefer to hire as electronics assemblers Third World women, boat people, Filipino and Mexican nationals, many of them undocumented immigrants. Part of the reason they hire them is they're docile, they don't even think about unions. So there's a two-class structure. The professionals, who live in the north part of Santa Clara county, are paid very well. But the assemblers live in a very poor district in the south county. These are very, very different worlds. Two worlds: one is the Third World, the other is the high-tech future scenario."

THE UNEQUAL EQUALIZER

No workplace tool is more important than the computer. Computers may yet be the great equalizers, freeing us all of burdensome chores, but so far greater dependence on computers is creating greater inequality.

A survey in twelve Silicon Valley elementary schools showed that 40 percent of the children have computers in their homes. In a school in a poor neighborhood just ten miles away (where many of the electronics assemblers live), fewer than 1 percent of the children were found to live in homes with computers. The number of microcomputers in American public schools tripled between 1980 and 1982, according to the Department of Education, but the number of schools with computers has risen by only 8 percent, leaving two-thirds of the nation's schools without access to a microcomputer. United States Senator

Frank Lautenberg, who built a personal fortune by founding Automatic Data Processing, the largest data-processing company in the nation, has warned his colleagues in the Senate that the increased use of microcomputers in well-to-do school districts is driving a wedge between the haves and have-nots in an information-based society. Computers, he said, threaten to create a new class of poor people: "In an age that demands computer literacy, a school without a computer is like a school without a library." Computers are also, according to several studies, associated with gender inequality: in a study of one computer camp, for instance, Rogers found that out of seventy children, only ten were girls.

Bonnie Johnson, a visiting scholar in the Institute for Communications Research at Stanford, studied users of work processors in offices in several cities: "There's a lot of conflict between secretaries and word processing operators, whose work is now perceived as being more valuable. The secretaries were very resentful of the word processing operators, and the operators were quite protective of their skills, not interested in helping the secretaries learn computer skills. When you're at the bottom, it's the people closest to you that you see as the greatest enemy. Word processing takes continuous on-the-job training, so [the secretaries] need a lot of help—the natural people to train them are the operators, but they feel threatened by these potential competitors. And there are, of course, people who are better word processors than others—they fall in love with the equipment, they understand that it's much more than just a fancy typewriter. And some people just can't. That's where you see the two Americas. I've heard the one type of worker called a 'Techie,' and some operators have called their computer talent 'savvy.' A very common phrase we hear from word processors is that a person is or is not 'machine oriented.' "

As part of her study, Johnson looked at many government agencies in Washington, D.C. "No place else was it as clear that clerical people would be replaced by machines," she said. "In Washington, the lowest level of the work force is young, 'jive' black women. 'Jive' and computerese just do not seem to go together. So these agencies are putting in expensive computer equipment, a very simple system that the professionals can use themselves. The largely black, female work force won't be needed anymore." And so, as Johnson puts it, "there are two cultures, the professional culture—the Techies—and a culture that is not 'machine oriented.' "

At the same time that the gap is widening between the information-rich and the information-poor, postindustrial workers are becoming more alike. This is true even for those whose work is not purely technical. The Postindustrials (or Techies, as Johnson calls them) now have a common language: the jargon associated with computers. Before computers, for instance, a reporter had little in common with a worker in classifieds who takes phone calls all day and turns these into ads. Now they talk about computers, VDTs, the eyestrain that comes from them. More and more, they talk their own elite language. And this raises the possibility not only of an economic gap between the two kinds of American workers, but also a conceptual, linguistic gap.

Ely Able, a professor of communications at Stanford, told me how frustrating it is for him to communicate with some of his computerized colleagues: "I find it really difficult getting in touch with some of these guys. I'll try to call a colleague for five hours and his line will be busy because his computer is talking to another computer, which doesn't do much for interpersonal communications. No one really has it all together on how all this is going to change communications, whether computers help people communicate or hinder communication, whether working at home will create new connections or just isolation."

The language gap has occurred before. When people learned to write, they went through what philosopher Walter Ong called the evolution of a "secondary oral culture." Those people who could write better came to a certain ascendance in society, an ascendance that they would not otherwise have had. The new language is technical, and so people with technical abilities will have more of a direction in the shape of organizations, in the shape of who gets elected to public office, in the shape of the nation. The most promotable employees will be those with technical professional skills. The fellow who designed a computer program that saved the company millions of dollars may not be particularly good at dealing with people, but his program was impressive, so he moves ahead.

Not only do those with the appropriate skills have a better chance to find a job, they even have a better way of looking for one: several new services now allow people with personal computers to look for jobs via their phone hookups, and, if they scroll up something they like, to make an initial application. Another on-line computer service allows people thinking about taking a job in one of the hot high-tech geographical areas to investigate school systems, check the cost-of-living, and even shop for a house.

The computer gap, troubling now, may not last. The price of equipment may fall far enough to make it readily available to everyone, and the simplicity of the programs is increasing, making the computers easier to use, less demanding of a special language and expertise. In the meantime, though, the gap widens between those with postindustrial skills and those without.

HIGH-TECH VULNERABILITY

Even if it were possible, turning back the clock is not a realistic option. Nearly every expert who has studied the potential of microelectronics has concluded that more jobs will be lost in the countries that do not pursue the new technologies vigorously than in those that do. The reason: microelectronics will so enhance productivity that the industries that swiftly move to adopt the technology will have a competitive advantage in international markets.

Without doubt, high-tech training should be available, through public education, to every child. But there's a catch: there is a growing realization that the pursuit of high technology does not guarantee salvation, even as states from Washington to Massachusetts pin their hopes for economic recovery on attracting high-tech industries.

Every valley in the United States, it seems, wants to become another Silicon Valley. There may not be, however, enough high tech to go around. Aaron S. Gurwitz, an economist for the Rand Corporation, compares high tech with past development fads, like the hotel-building boom and the downtown pedestrian malls of the 1970s, which failed to ignite local economies. Gurwitz predicts the same kind of failure for many areas trying to climb aboard the high-tech bus, largely because high-tech companies prefer to set up shop near leading universities. If each region tries to emulate Silicon Valley, Gurwitz worries, they will overlook and finally lose opportunities for economic development better suited to strengths and characteristics of the local areas. High-tech salvation is simply not guaranteed. The Japanese have yet to fully enter the market for semiconductors, a field traditionally dominated by Americans, but their sales in the United States jumped from $62 million in 1977 to $370 million in 1980. By 1980, the U.S. share of the chip market had plummeted from its early-1960s high of nearly 90 percent to 60 percent. Great Britain and Korea are now investing heavily in developing their semiconductor industries. In the coming years, the United States will have to move quickly indeed, to keep out ahead of the pack. While it is certainly true that keeping ahead of the pack is worth the investment, the major mistake of America II may be that it repeats the major mistake of America I, the Detroit Factor: overdependence on a handful of specialized industries.

The truth is that no one knows what is going to happen to the world's economic structure as we enter the twenty-first century. The current wisdom is that the postindustrial Western World will process and sell information, while the industrializing developing world will make the widgets and the car parts, and mine the raw materials. Even that commonly held assumption is up for grabs.

Without much fanfare, the International Labor Organization warned in 1979 that the revolutionary silicon computer chip could eventually spell disaster for the Third World. "For the Third World," an ILO report said, "the chips are down." The organization's reasoning: since chips enable machines to perform an increasing number of complex functions more efficiently and cheaply than manpower—especially with the arrival of serious robotics—microprocessing will eventually steal back the labor-intensive industries on which developing nations are pinning their hopes. Textiles, footwear, garments, and electronics industries, according to the report, are already being affected:

> The process of industrial development in the Third World may now go into reverse in some areas, with the industrialized nations recapturing old industries, thanks to the microprocessor . . . . So, instead of a more balanced interdependence between the North and the South, this reversal of shifts in the international division of labor now threatens the developing nations with increasing dependence.

Such a scenario is probably unlikely, but another reversal of the common wisdom is already occurring. In February 1983, Atari, which had become the symbol of the potential boom in American high-tech jobs, shut down part of its American organization and shipped the 1700 jobs to the Far East. The AFL-CIO claims the firm was fleeing to avoid unionization.

In fact, many data-processing jobs could easily be farmed out to the Third World. One company in Denver hires low-wage employees in Barbados, who sit in front of computer terminals and compute data sent to them from the United States; hiring computer operators in the Third World for two dollars an hour is much less expensive than hiring computer operators in the United States—even the ones who work in home computer sweatshops. Computer jobs could, in fact, be the easiest ones to export, because of the satellite communications that link all points of the world instantaneously.

These scenarios illustrate how changeable the economy is, how vulnerable we are to its dislocations.

THE CONTINUING WAGE SPREAD

Much of the manufacturing that began to move out of the northeast twenty-five years ago and went to the South is now shifting onward to places like Korea and Singapore. Looking at this in a global context, what happened to the northeast might well happen to the entire nation. Stanford economist Clark Reynolds, who describes himself as being in the "militant middle," contends that the American economy has split into two distinct halves: the onshore economy, which includes investments, business, and commerce conducted within U.S. borders; and the offshore economy, the shift of American capital and business into the Third World. He calls these two economies "U.S. 1 and U.S. 2."

Companies who move from big, older cities to rural areas are often taking the first step into the offshore economy, says Reynolds. "One company I consult with moved out of the San Francisco Bay Area and into Colorado and South Carolina because of the cost of labor. If they hadn't moved out of the Bay Area they'd be out of business. So moving to the countryside is one step in the evolution out of the nation. It takes corporate management some years to rethink, so the rural step seems necessary. Now that company is talking about moving to mainland China."

Wage spreading is, in large part, a product of this process; and it is creating an explosive situation. While American executive salaries are zooming (American executives make, on the average, five times as much as Japanese executives), the wages on the bottom are falling rapidly.

In the past, the United States, except for the Deep South, has usually protected its labor: immigrant labor was allowed in only as long as it did not threaten the native-born labor force. By protecting the labor market, wages were kept relatively high. But times change. "The world economy is getting much more competitive, so U.S. business interests assume that, in order to compete, the United States has two choices: move plants offshore, or bring cheap immigrant labor into the United States." The result: the global north/south wage split is gradually becoming internalized within the United States; as wages rise in developing countries, and fall in the United States, the division is blurred. Consequently, the United States is developing a two-tiered labor force: the skilled, professional Postindustrials; and a mix of the traditionally poor, the new poor pushed out of their jobs by the new technologies and by plants moving offshore, and a subterranean economy made up of underground entrepreneurs and undocumented immigrants.

To illustrate the effects of wage spreading, Reynolds tells this story: "I worked in the first Jack-in-the-Box, in the mid-1950s, in National City, California. My son worked last year at a McDonald's in the Bay Area. We had exactly the same job, but his real wage was less than I made years ago. On my wages, I could buy a used car, pay for college and my social life. Today, you couldn't even think about a car or college on a fast-food salary. That's a fact of wage-spreading."

Such wage spreading has happened before, as defined by Nobel Prize–winning economist W. Arthur Lewis, during the decades when the United States was industrializing. Then, immigrants helped build the railroad systems and the auto and plastics industries. Once these labor-intensive tasks were completed, the doors for immigration were held open for several years, then slammed shut, with mass deportations of Mexican laborers, and wages at the bottom began to rise again. Today, it is quite questionable whether we could slam the door shut even if we wanted to. First, the world economy is so interdependent that such an action could cause more problems than it solves. Second, the migration from Latin America has become so institutionalized that shutting the door could cause starvation and revolution in

Mexico. And third, doing so would demand such draconian methods that our civil liberties would be jeopardized.

Wage spreading has been turned around in the past by private and government investment in the nation's industries, and by the efforts of labor unions. Today, however, much of the investment capital is flowing offshore; American workers find themselves helpless as they watch their plants and jobs move overseas, even as their tax dollars are poured into a huge defense umbrella designed to protect those worldwide investments.

Meanwhile, the explosive potential grows. Entrepreneurialism is the escape valve for rising pressure: locked out of traditional jobs, members of the middle class are working for themselves, often in refashioned service jobs, such as franchises of domestic servants who now call themselves "home management experts" and use sophisticated cleaning machines; or in typesetting and word processing at home; or in a great outpouring of imaginative, new, self-made jobs. But even with the growth of entrepreneurialism and the recasting of low-skilled jobs, the frustration grows. "It's a logical linear outcome of this kind of economy," says Reynolds, "that people begin to protect themselves any way they can, to buffer themselves from change, to try to escape or to pull inward, to build new institutions to try to protect themselves. But ultimately, the only solution is a national political solution. The nature of that solution is not preordained. The middle class has an extreme sense of what it deserves, and an incendiary fear of leftists and aliens. There have been precedents. When the wage spread has occurred in other countries, often accompanied by raging inflation, it's resulted in totalitarian governments. Maybe we can escape that." Should that frustration rise too far, though, there will be no place to hide—no walled community or company cult or small town will protect anyone. The middle class, not the poor, could present the greatest danger in America II.

PART SIX

SOMEWHERE OVER THE POSTINDUSTRIAL RAINBOW

Water is important to people who do not have it, and the same is true of control.

—*Joan Didion,* The White Album

In a dying culture, narcissism appears to embody—in the guise of "personal growth" and "awareness"—the highest attainment of spiritual enlightenment. The custodians of culture hope, at bottom, merely to survive its collapse. The will to build a better society, however, survives, along with traditions of localism, self-help, and community action that only need the vision of a new society, a decent society, to give them new vigor.

—*Christopher Lasch,* The Culture of Narcissism

THE TRANSFORMING
CITIES OF AMERICA I

One eventually has to ask what becomes of America I, especially the most easily recognized part, the old industrial cities and the people who live and work in them. These cities are not dying, but transforming. If America II can be considered a force, then it is returning across the land, back to the regions and cities from which it pulled life and people, and it is now also reshaping the older industrial regions and cities of America I. For now, the voices of those public officials who have called for a "reindustrial-ization" of America have been drowned out by those who believe that the best way to compete with America II is to join it. This recasting is both economic and social. In the course of this trans-formation, certain social issues are emerging, not the least of which is what will become of the legions of the less-skilled and poor.

Philadelphia is a good example of a city trying to make the transition to America II. Thacher Longstreth, the longtime presi-dent of the Greater Philadelphia Chamber of Commerce, with a penchant for argyle socks and controversial views and a Philadel-phia line of ancestry stretching back 300 years, has his own sug-gested solutions for the poor—solutions that reflect the opinions of many of the powers that be in Philadelphia. On the morning I visited the tall, white-haired, and excited Longstreth, he paced around his office and leaned over his desk, splaying out his fingers: "This city isn't dying; it's just shifting from a blue-collar work force to a white-collar force. Manufacturing may be leaving, but we now have 20 million square feet of office space—more than Atlanta, second only to New York. We may be down but we're not out; and we can come back, but it won't be by trying to resurrect the past. There's not a damn thing we can do to get the small entrepreneurs to come back—at least for a while. But in twenty-five years the Houstons and San Diegos will have all the problems we have now, and we'll be in good shape for a reverse wave of business and entrepreneurs."

Longstreth blames the crippling of old cities on "high taxes and crushing unemployment compensation." His approach to urban renaissance would substantially lower business and other taxes in an attempt to compete directly with states such as Arizona, South Dakota, and North Carolina, which have attracted so many of the expanding industries by offering extremely favorable, virtually tax-free business climates. But the tax situation, as he sees it, is not the only stumbling block.

He stood staring out of his office window. "Now, what I'm about to say, no elected official can say, because it sounds too awful." He leaned out of a window and stared at the city. The sound of jackhammers drifted up from the street. "What we have to do to stop the decay of the northeastern cities is . . . we *have* to relocate a lot of our unskilled people as fast as possible, and start importing skilled workers. We've got to move the unemployed out of here, to places where they can get a job." He pulled his head in, walked over and sat behind his jumbled desk. A raccoon's tail was stuffed into his in box. "Take 250,000 of the unemployed deadwood off our back and we'd do fine. Our economic expansion in the northeast—into high technology, petrochemicals, law, marketing, medicine, higher education—is going to require someone other than uneducated blacks. You see, unless we make it possible for blacks to move, we doom them. There is no possibility that the American people will continue to accept the welfare state. The bitterness of the middle class is increasing. They're going to be saying, 'Let 'em die.' Maybe not publicly or consciously, but *here.*" He pointed to his heart. "They'll be saying, 'Let 'em die.'"

Longstreth's theory, which the *Philadelphia Inquirer*'s editorial writers termed "cryptoracist," enrages the city's black leaders and most of its politicians. Yet, a number of high-powered academicians, and the President's Commission for a National Agenda for the Eighties, have asserted that the federal government should help people move to opportunity. Donald A. Hicks, a University of Texas professor of political economy who helped author the commission's urban policy report, argues that migrating to good jobs has traditionally been a luxury of the affluent. Corporate executives, for instance, are assisted with fat company packages that cover moving expenses and sometimes even help to purchase a new house. Though the Postindustrials have their own national computerized job search networks, those job seekers who are not as skilled find it difficult to look beyond their own localities. Most state employment agencies make no effort to share information on available jobs. The want ads are useful, but many job openings are never listed in newspapers.

European governments that help people move to new regions have determined that to a worker thinking about moving to another city, financial subsidy is not as important as information—for example, what the schools are like. Hicks suggests the federal government set up an interstate job information service, and even offer unemployed Americans a moving assistance stipend. The federal government would be stepping in to help the poor in the same way that corporations help more affluent Americans. The theory is that government could better put our tax dollars to use by helping the poor link up with jobs in healthier regions of the country than by keeping them dependent on government handouts, perpetually locked into slums generation after generation.

The trouble with this theory is that, while it may be workable for those unemployed workers with needed skills, no section of the country wants many more poor, unskilled residents—with the exception of foreign migrants who are more malleable, not as demanding, and, as long as they are within the United States illegally, less of a drain on social services. So less-skilled Americans are gathering in tent cities in Houston and Denver and Southern California, or left behind to fester in the old cities.

Further, it is not at all clear that taxes and poverty are the primary reasons for Philadelphia's lack of economic growth. In the steamy, cramped, and messy newsroom of the *Philadelphia Inquirer,* Larry Williams, the newspaper's young business editor, disputes Longstreth's contention that taxes have killed the city's entrepreneurial spirit. The rich, Williams told me, are more of a drain on Philadelphia than the poor. During the 1970s, Philadelphia lost 143,000 manufacturing jobs and 13.4 percent of its residents. A good portion of the exodus is made up of entrepreneurs ignored by Philadelphia's leading financial institutions. "We started an investigation with the idea that Philadelphia Savings Fund Society—a mutual savings bank, the largest financial institution in the area—might be red lining Philly. But what we found was they were red lining the whole *region,* by investing in the South and West, in multiunit condo and apartment projects. They're loath to invest in their own city's future." A hotly contested study by Corporate Data Exchange, Inc., and the liberal People's Business Commission showed that billions of dollars in big union pension funds are being invested in economic-growth regions, especially in the South and West, often in antiunion companies.

"So the wealth flows out," said Williams. "People leave with the wealth. And the financial institutions won't back entrepreneurs. Small wonder that the small entrepreneurs leave, or never get started."

BUNKER CITIES WITHIN CITIES

Nonetheless, there is plenty of evidence that wealth is flowing into the old cities, but it is not the kind of wealth that employs less-skilled workers or workers with the wrong skills. As in the South and West, this revival is and will be primarily for the Postindustrials.

Whole new cities are growing, pushing up like new crystals within what remains of the older industrial cities. What is happening there looks surprisingly like America II. While thousands continue to leave Philadelphia, the Postindustrials arrive. Philadelphia's skyline is being reshaped by more than a billion dollars' worth of new office buildings. Society Hill, Germantown, and other old inner-city neighborhoods are being rejuvenated, with refurbished, elegant eighteenth- and nineteenth-century homes and high-security, bunker-style condominiums. A whole new nostalgic/high-tech city is growing up inside Philadelphia, an insulated city with no need for the unskilled workers who helped build this twentieth-century metropolis. These cities within the cities are highly compartmentalized by profession, race, and sexual preference.

This transformation, as Longstreth says, is based on the the new economics, not the old. In the past decade, more than 100,-000 manufacturing jobs have been lost in Philadelphia, but a burgeoning service industry has added 15,000 new jobs, most of them in high-technology fields that require highly skilled workers. In Boston, tens of thousands of new jobs have been created since the mid-1970s, but most of these have gone to engineers, computer technicians, managers, an America II gentry who have moved into once decaying areas, displacing the poor and the working class.

New York State is another example of the economic transformation: 1982 marked the first time that more than half of New York's 1.5 million manufacturing workers held jobs directly involving high-technology goods and services. Out of thirteen metropolitan areas in the state, the four with the lowest unemployment rates were those whose economies were linked to high technology. While some older industrial cities, Buffalo, for example, wither (with shipyards and locomotive plants closing, causing a desperate depression), other cities, such as Rochester (the site of Eastman Kodak), have been doing quite well. New York City lost more than 600,000 jobs in the 1970s, chiefly in manufacturing, a net job loss resulting in an estimated tax loss to New York City of almost $500 million—an amount that would have just about covered its 1981 deficit. During this same period, the number of white-collar jobs increased dramatically, though not enough to make up for the loss of blue-collar jobs. However, this shift has changed the social texture of the city.

These transforming America I cities, which only a few decades ago were the magnets for millions of Americans and immigrants seeking entry-level jobs, no longer have much room for those who dream of working their way from rags to riches. The urban renaissance is only for a few. While the gleaming skyscrapers shoot upward, Philadelphia's municipal government battles street vendors, who do not fit the new image, who compete with the chic shops serving the Postindustrials. In the transforming America I city, there is no longer a bottom rung on the economic ladder.

Just as deconcentration is changing the face of rural America and producing new kinds of cities in the West and South, deconcentration is also changing the face of the older industrial cities, making them less dense. True, people are moving back to the old inner cities, buying up brownstones, "gentrifying" neighborhoods. But this movement is not significant statistically, since the urban pioneers are often single and usually childless, and when and if they do marry and have children, they usually move. In 1982, a study by the U.S. Census Bureau in ten major cities showed that in the census tracts where neighborhood renewal had been occurring there was a substantial loss of both white and black residents from 1970 to 1980, and that this decline in the renovated areas was even greater than that for the cities as a whole. Renovation, to the surprise of those who spoke of saving the cities and stopping the out-migration, actually contributed to the out-migration. In Baltimore, which the national newsmagazines often point to as an old industrial city reborn and a model for urban renewal, the study found that the central core was being rebuilt on a much smaller, more prosperous population base than before the renovation.

Downtown Seattle, which in 1960 housed 23,500 people but is now home for only 10,000, with the population continuing to decline, is described by *Seattle Times* reporter Paul Andrews as being "like a bodybuilder with angst. On the outside it is big, gleaming and healthy, endowed with new skyscrapers and hotels and energized by the promise of a convention center. But its heart and soul are suffering. . . . During the day, streets are bustling with shoppers, joggers, and office workers. But in the evening it's as though a neutron bomb had hit, leaving buildings unscathed but people blown away. . . . People do still live downtown. But 85 percent are in low-income, often subsidized units. The remainder are mostly well-to-do professionals living in expensive condominiums."

In Jamaica Plain, an integrated Boston neighborhood, the young professionals have quintupled the prices of some homes since 1969, pushing up rents as much as 70 percent, forcing out a quarter of the neighborhood's Hispanic residents, according to an MIT study. In the same Boston that boasts of an urban renaissance (of young professionals, especially singles, replacing families), arsonists torch an average of nearly two buildings every night. On June 11, 1982, 101 fires were reported in twelve hours.

It is a very strange environment in these older cities, compared to the bustling places of social and economic interchange that they once were. Even Thacher Longstreth, so enthusiastic about the revival, wonders about the edifices going up. "The Detroit renaissance is a joke—one magnificent structure, protected by armed guards with machine guns to keep the locals out!" He exaggerates about the machine guns, but the image sticks.

Urban sociologist William H. Whyte describes the new downtown as being a place of "megastructures" and "blank walls." These walls, the flat facades of much of the new downtown architecture, "are meant to be blank, and they have a message." The message is security first, he says. It is an expression of hostility to the city. The blank walls, as he told a reporter for the *Christian Science Monitor,* are designed to put down and intimidate. Whyte, who has traveled around the country photographing and studying this new walled architecture, says it symbolizes the draining of public life and the rise of private life. He calls this the "double life" of large cities: one life led within these interior environments, one people gathered in cocktail lounges overlooking fountains within the walls; and another people, the "undesirables," outside the walls spiked with iron rods, watched by television cameras. This kind of architecture was given birth by a "whole generation of architects whose idea of a design is based almost entirely on a suburban shopping center."

Some of the older cities are beginning to resist the new architecture. New York, for instance, has zoned against the trend toward blanking out first- and second-story windows. But the "warm and gutty" urban environment of many older cities is giving way to what Whyte calls a "phony Disneyworld" kind of downtown—an America II downtown, which, if it cannot get rid of the undesirables, turns its back on them, fortifies against them, pretends they do not exist.

In the midst of this transformation are the old urban residential neighborhoods, balanced at a pivotal point between evolving into caring, inclusive small towns inside the big cities, or taking on the most disturbing aspect of America II—the exclusive-bunker mentality. The dominant trend is toward the latter. Ironically, the original design of these old neighborhoods is very much what cities such as Phoenix are trying to create in the "new" form of urban village. The basic structure—the neighborhood markets; the jobs nearby; the courts, front steps, and porches; a church or two; a luncheonette; a schoolyard; a baker; the narrow streets—these are the things that make a community, the things that the condo developers and city planners are trying to fabricate out there in the land of shopping malls and office parks.

But slowly the old neighborhoods in the older cities are giving way to a new kind of neighborhood, one that looks very much like the covered malls and high-security walled communities in Houston and San Diego and Miami.

Methods of fortification long used by the urban rich are now commonplace in the gentrified neighborhoods of young professionals. Private guards, hired by neighborhoods to supplement the police, are in vogue. Some New York neighborhood associations are collecting several hundred dollars a year per family for this kind of private protection. The South Bronx Development Organization is building two-story, three-bedroom row houses with driveways and front yards in slum areas already "cleared" by arson, the idea being to repopulate areas of the South Bronx with homeowners rather than with renters. These homeowners, the theory goes, will defend their "strategic hamlets." In Columbus, Ohio, the Metropolitan Housing Authority is building fenced-off, concrete culs-de-sac. In St. Louis, some neighborhoods have bought their streets from the city, blocking them off with iron gates and private guards. They are governing themselves through powerful, incorporated street associations that, by deed restrictions and small-scale democracy, limit the uses of homeowners' property and collect private fees to maintain the common property. These private streets became popular in St. Louis in the 1960s, declined for a few years, and then came back strong in the mid-1970s. There are far fewer urban privatized streets than there are new suburban walled communities, but they operate on the same principle: the idea that safe zones can be created, islands in the dark stream.

Generally, they do give people a sense of safety and community, but too often this safety is defined racially. In St. Louis, the residents of private streets send their children to private schools; in Memphis, white neighborhoods have closed off their streets, rerouting traffic from a predominantly black area of the city around the white islands. (In April 1981, the U.S. Supreme Court upheld the right of Memphis to close streets, with Justice John Paul Stevens arguing that the city's action was "motivated by its interest in protecting the safety and tranquility of a residential neighborhood.")

Even the National Association of Neighborhoods, once a left-leaning activist organization, has taken up the privatization banner. Admitting that the sudden enthusiasm was, perhaps, partially a dance for federal funds in the Reagan era, Marla Anderson, NAN's training director, told me that private neighborhoods were an idea whose time has come. I talked with her at NAN's Washington, D.C., headquarters, in a run-down stucco building off Embassy Row, in a black neighborhood. The modest offices were behind a locked iron gate. The growing interest in private neighborhoods, she said, was a logical extension of the original NAN philosophy, first arrived at in 1975, which stated that neighborhood government was the place where democracy could allow people to gain control over their lives. In Washington, D.C., activists are even talking about gaining for neighborhoods the right to opt out of city government and be reimbursed for the tax money saved by their withdrawal, with the reimbursment being invested in private services contracted by the neighborhood governments. Local urban neighborhoods could, under this system, run their own affairs, contract their own services, zone themselves. This is the same system popularized in Houston, which uses self-regulating covenants as an alternative to conventional zoning, a practice that works especially well in corporation-built private enclaves for the upper middle class.

To be fair, there is a certain amount of idealism at work here. Anderson describes a scenario in which neighborhood associations could use this proposed form of neighborhood revenue sharing—from federal, state, or municipal coffers—to hire unemployed people within the neighborhood to do garbage pickup, park maintenance, et cetera. These local entrepreneurial employees would be cheaper and more accessible to a neighborhood than unionized city employees. With suburbs deciding to run their own bus companies, Washington's metro bus service is teetering on bankruptcy; so an alternative might be that inner-city neighborhood organizations would contract with local people to run small jitney services. The same could be done with neighborhood security forces using, as the NAN training director put it, "former gang members as security guards." Such an approach would, according to theory, produce dramatic savings for citizens who are burdened with the high cost of inefficient municipal services. The problem with all of this, as Anderson admits, is that the poorest neighborhoods are the least likely to organize themselves, and they have the fewest resources to pay for private services. This would further the trend toward two Americas, one that gets the good services it can afford to buy, while the other is left behind, without resources. In an article in the libertarian magazine, *Reason* (which supports privatizing neighborhoods), Theodore J. Gage quotes a skeptical police lieutenant who patrols one of the private streets of St. Louis: "It's true that you have two different worlds a few blocks apart. But as long as you have poverty three blocks away from affluence, you'll have crime. It's tempting to hide in your fortress and simply ignore what is going on outside. But the way to continue the stabilizing process and to strengthen the neighborhood is to reach out and help improve the blighted areas."

Private police and private governments are not the only similarities to America II. Katy Butler, a San Francisco newspaper reporter, writes of the peculiar sterility of some of the gentrified inner-city neighborhoods that house, as she calls it, the "croissant culture":

> We, the gentrifiers, adrift from the towns of our childhoods, create neighborhoods with a character all their own. Sports such as jogging are solitary, and our breakfast places and cappuccino cafés, designed for the single, allow us to be around people without talking to them. Ten-speed bicycles and other grown-up toys move through the childless streets. Distant from friends and relations of other generations, we have made a commodity of the past, fetishistically adoring the Victorian, the brownstone, the carved mantel, and the cobblestone street. There's bought nostalgia for every income level, from $200,000 antique houses to $50 sets of bulbous 1950s kitchenware, full of the dreams of mothers' kitchens from the days when families were whole. Instead of baby shoes, we buy endless fresh flowers, whole roasted coffee beans, croissants, imported wines, and cheeses once reserved for the truly rich. But the price tag of these little luxuries may be higher than we think. Our precious urban neighborhoods are well on the way to becoming as homogeneous as the suburbs we fled.

RESISTANCE

Still, there are those, in the older cities, who resist. Though the city's transitional economy has little room for people too old or too rooted to move, some old ethnic neighborhoods hang on to their traditions. In the Italian neighborhood of South Philadelphia, Gus Denicola told me he considers himself one of the lucky ones, though he's accepted a certain amount of downward mobility: "I'm making the best of it." He was told after twenty-seven years as a supervisor in a gear manufacturing company that the company was leaving Philadelphia. "First they moved to the suburbs, then down to Florida." He leaned over a counter at Talluto's Authentic Italian Food Market, which he now helps manage. "I decided to move back to the Italian section; I just couldn't see going with everybody else down to Florida, with all those golf courses." He almost shuddered at the thought.

It is difficult for those of us without geographic roots to understand the depth of feeling among the people who live in these old neighborhoods, who can't conceive of moving around the country at the behest of a changing economy, or because an image of home is out there. They're already home. They already have what a lot of the rest of us are looking for.

There are other resisters. Though greatly outnumbered by those who represent the impulses of America II, many community organizers and small political and social groups who still believe some of the more idealistic precepts of the 1960s are trying to create alternatives. They're out there, often living in the decaying, older America I cities, involved in community gardens, "sweat-equity" projects, food and energy and child-care co-ops, urban agricultural projects, and a number of other approaches that have as their common denominator a sense of democratic equity, rather than exclusivity and protection. Then there are those few remaining neighborhoods that, with no particular ideology, are trying to hold on to their sense of community without the bunker mentality or the homogenization that comes with gentrification.

Mount Airy, in Philadelphia, is one such neighborhood. Mount Airy almost always had a black middle class, but when blockbusting began in the 1960s, many—but not all—of the whites left. About twenty minutes from the center city, this is a neighborhood integrated in the 1960s that has stayed that way, with a balance of white and black, middle class and poor living in old row houses and stately homes. While every other neighborhood in Philadelphia lost population in the last decade, Mount Airy has remained stable, a remarkable accomplishment considering the odds.

Robin Warshaw, wheeling her aging Toyota down the narrow

streets, likes to point out the landmarks of Mount Airy: old gray, Wissahickon stone mansions that now each house several middle-class families; a lawn near one of them that was the site of a Revolutionary War battle; a cemetery with graves from the 1700s, in a particularly rough block; tiny row houses, once the servants' quarters for the mansions, that have been restored and now house low-income blacks; a boarded-up row house built in 1750, now decorated with graffiti.

"Irish Catholic domestics lived in that one in the 1700s." Robin, in her thirties, is an energetic young member of the Mount Airy community association. She showed me around the neighborhood she grew up in and has stayed in. Her parents moved to Mount Airy, from Boston to Philadelphia, when Robin was a child. They chose this neighborhood because of its mixture of races and economic classes. They wanted their daughter to grow up exposed to different kinds of people.

"You know, I was never scared when I lived on this block, as bad as it might look to you. I didn't see doing this as being any kind of urban pioneer, because this neighborhood is like home. Over in West Philly it's alien to me. It looks just like this, but I *know* this. I'd be terrified over there. Your fear is defined by what you don't know. I know which stores to go to on this block." She laughed. "In fact, I'd be scared to move to the country—too much space.

"What's really something is that Mount Airy is a neighborhood where a lot of white families—from the Midwest, many of them —are moving, and the whites who have lived here aren't moving, and the blacks aren't being pushed out. There's a kind of balance. There's an . . . understanding . . . you know, not to get too fancy, to keep the price down. There's a common feeling of what people want."

She stopped at one of the old mansions and parked, and we walked around back. Eversley Vaughn, a loquacious man who serves on the Mount Airy neighborhood organization and is vice president of the Philadelphia Council of Neighborhood Organizations, was there to meet us. He had forgotten the key. So we waited for a few minutes until Robin's father and mother arrived to unlock the door. We went upstairs to a meeting room used as a volunteer day-care center, lined with children's drawings. Shortly, two other members of the Mount Airy council arrived:

Tom Johnson, an assistant district attorney, and his wife, Mauria Johnson, who had moved here from Columbus, Ohio. Vaughn, who is black, launched into a long introduction to Mount Airy, in which he traced three centuries of history, including a detailed account of Philadelphia's block-busting period and the yellow fever epidemic of 1887. Tom Johnson grinned and pointed out that Eversley "is running for president of the Philadelphia Council this year."

"Well, I've got to practice my speaking voice," he said.

The group talked about Mount Airy lovingly, the way people used to talk about their neighborhoods a long time ago.

"There's a feeling, a common vision here, I guess is how I'd put it," said Johnson. "It's not so much that we have some kind of special neighborhood government setup or ideology, it's the fact that when we talk about Mount Airy we all have the same feeling, we all see the same place. There's a feeling that it's worth . . . planting yourself here, planting your children—in spite of some of the decay you see—planting something that's going to grow. You can't really pin it on anything material.

"There's something about this neighborhood, spatially, that creates the atmosphere that you want to live in. On the street I lived on in Columbus, in the suburbs, the houses had large lawns and you could only physically see one neighbor, who was across the street. You couldn't see anyone else even if you sat on your front porch—and there usually wasn't a front porch, except for a cement block that led to your house. Here, the houses are physically close together. They all have porches where people are constantly sitting, talking to their neighbors. You get to know people. Here, it's the expected thing that you're not just going to *live* on your block, but you're going to get to know your neighbors, you're going to join cooperatives, you're going to participate in block parties, and you're going to have friends. People look at you askance if all you want to do is what people do in the suburbs, if you want to sit in your house and never know who it is that lives on either side of you, and it's not that they resent you for that, it's just that they say, 'Why'd you move to Mount Airy if you don't want to take advantage of it?' "

Like most other older urban neighborhoods, Mount Airy is losing corner shops and local grocery stores. So, a few years ago, the residents got together to form a cooperative market,

Weaver's Way. The cooperative now has a membership of 2000 families, with a long waiting list of people trying to enroll. As a responsibility of membership, the families take turns working behind the cash register or stacking onions.

The community organization has, over time, changed its attitude about business. In the past, especially on those blocks of Mount Airy where the more affluent citizens live, the organization would lobby for zoning rulings favoring residential use. Now, the residents believe, as Robin Warshaw put it, "that if we don't help keep our bucks in our own neighborhood, the bucks are going to go elsewhere," so zoning decisions usually come down on the side of businesses who want to move in. "Which means that if they're putting a locally run convenience store in at the corner of Alice Lane and Germantown Avenue and the people around it don't like it because that's gonna cause more traffic, then that's really too bad. We need that store, we need the jobs, and we need the gas pumps out in front of it, because all our gas stations moved out a long time ago." The organization, though short on funds, is trying to devise some ways to finance entrepreneurs in the neighborhood.

Again and again, the group expressed a deeply felt commitment to a racial and economic mix of residents. I asked them what they thought of Thacher Longstreth's theory that what the city needed was for 250,000 poor blacks to leave. "I would suggest," said Eversly Vaughn, "that they all move next door to Mr. Longstreth."

The people in this neighborhood object to being associated with the croissant culture, even though many of them came here from somewhere else. What they value, they say, is not the chic, but the permanent: those elusive elements that make a community last for a long time. They have no real plan to accomplish this, just a common vision, caught in between America I and America II. So far, by force of will, it seems to be working.

Another town in the Philadelphia area fighting to survive is Chester, which, though now a quite urban neighborhood, was one of the original nineteenth-century suburbs. Here, again, are the fading original symbols of what so many people are trying to re-create in the far reaches of America II: downtown Chester still looks like a postcard from the past, perhaps a Norman Rockwell painting of an idealized 1940s urban America (except that most of the residents are black). Walking down Chester's main street, I was amazed that pedestrians outnumbered the cars. A street cleaner's broom cart was parked next to a fire hydrant, and a big, white-haired Irish cop in an Eisenhower jacket bent over to give a little black girl a touch on her nose. But the edges of this postcard were curling, burning. Haunting old half-burned and empty brick buildings stood off to each side of Chester's main street, their tall Victorian windows dark as freshly dug graves. Tough young men hung out at the corners, drinking from bottles in brown bags.

I was walking through Chester with the district's congressional representative, Bob Edgar. He stopped suddenly and looked at a brick wall on which someone had scrawled, "Go South Sick Bums." The enigmatic message could have been from one street gang to another, or it could have referred to the mass exodus of businesses and residents from Chester. In 1970, Chester claimed a population of 57,000; in 1980, there were 43,000 residents. And the drop meant the loss of a multitude of federal grants, which, in turn, has speeded Chester's decay.

The graffiti, and the idea that America I's salvation is to be found primarily by importing high-tech workers and shipping out the poor, fill Edgar with righteous anger. A Methodist minister and the first Democrat elected in his district since before the Civil War, Edgar is chairman of the Northeast-Midwest Congressional Coalition, a leading defender of the old industrial cities. The coalition includes 212 congressmen who have banded together to stop the economic drain of their districts. He stared at the graffiti for a moment, then turned and walked down the street, past the Chester federal building, the oldest continually inhabited building in America.

We turned into a bank, walked up old marble steps worn down in the middle, and entered a meeting room. Like the streets, the meeting rooms in the government buildings and the banks are smaller than they are out West, and darker, being so often lined with polished wood. The windows were open to the street. Arthur Bean, a black businessman who grew up in Chester, described his feelings: "I managed an electrical supply business in a building that I can remember when I was seven years old," he said. A hurt look came into his eyes. "And it's hard seeing whole streets shut down. . . . Sun Ship Company moved out, and Ford, and Reynolds Metal . . . and the old locomotive plant. All gone. You know, there used to be a time that if you couldn't make a living in Chester, you couldn't make a living anywhere."

Watching all this heritage deteriorate is painful for Bean and Edgar and the residents of Chester. When they talk about this neighborhood, they speak of it with something approaching love. They do not speak of it with the kind of bland satisfaction that I had heard in so many towns and cities and planned communities of America II. In Chester, the people speak of the neighborhood as they would a dying aunt who had been a part of their lives for years, who had once been full of life, and who now had turned a bit nasty from the pain.

Something old and good seems to be seeping out of places like this as people leave the industrial cities, and as these neighborhoods, block by block, either decay beyond recognition or change into places alien to real community. Edgar thinks there's still a possibility for recovery.

Once, when a gang fight erupted on the front lawn of his parsonage, Edgar charged out of his house and chased the gang members down the street, disarming one youth who was carrying a baseball bat studded with nails. With a similar sense of purpose, he has taken out after the federal government, which he says has been mugging America I. According to Edgar, a larger proportion of many city budgets in the South and West is made up of federal aid than is the case in some of the older industrial cities. A study by the Bureau of the Census backs him up: in fiscal year 1978–1979, 10 percent of Philadelphia's total revenue was in the form of federal aid. San Diego, a far healthier city, received 13 percent; Houston, 12.2 percent; and Phoenix, a whopping 22.5 percent.

"Boston loses 40 percent of its fresh water every day because it still has a system partially made up of nineteenth-century wooden water pipes," Edgar points out. "At the same time, the federal government spends billions on the Central Arizona Project, which is going to pipe Colorado River water into Arizona—in part to water lawns in the desert. Since 1824, seventy-five cents out of every dollar spent by the Army Corps of Engineers went to projects in the South and West." The Tennessee-Tombigbee Waterway, Edgar continues, is the largest public works project currently under construction by the Army Corps of Engineers, and is costing nearly twice what the corps is spending in all states of the northeastern United States. And until 1978, the federal tax structure encouraged the building of new buildings rather than the renovation of existing structures. This stimulated more out-migration of businesses to cheap farmland, to southern and western open space, to decentralized cities such as Phoenix. The Northeast-Midwest Coalition was responsible for reversing that tax policy, which Edgar considers one small step in the right direction. "We can't reverse the deterioration overnight," he said, "but we sure can slow it down."

Whether or not that is true remains to be seen. Meanwhile, the transformation of the America I cities continues. Part of this transformation is not just the buildup of high-rises and fortified neighborhoods, but the presence of more desperate urban poor. These two urban Americas, it seems to me, are on a collision course, and people like Robin Warshaw, Arthur Bean, and Gus Denicola will eventually be caught between them.

THE PEOPLE LEFT BEHIND

As the *Philadelphia Inquirer*'s Larry Williams says, "there's nothing intrinsically wrong with letting nature take its course" in terms of the transformation. He adds two large caveats: "an even-handed approach to rebuilding the nation's infrastructures, which means a refocusing of federal money on the northeast and upper Midwest, and a national policy that goes beyond welfare to help those who are left behind." Possibly a guaranteed annual income or guaranteed jobs, he suggests. "Otherwise, you have this vicious cycle of people who can afford to move moving to growth areas, hurting the tax base, causing more movement, leaving a shell of the community populated with the walking wounded." Such changes in policy are, of course, quite unlikely in the current political climate.

Meanwhile, Philadelphia's minority unemployment rate is second only to Detroit's. More than 22,000 houses have been abandoned, largely by whites fleeing the city. More than a third of Philadelphia's residents cannot maintain their houses without government grants, subsidized loans, or other types of financial aid. Parts of Detroit have an infant mortality rate equal to that of Honduras, the poorest country in Central America. According to the 1980 census, though New York City lost more than a million children in the 1970s, it gained 156,000 children living in poverty. The proportion of poor people in the older cities is pushing ever higher. As Peter Morrison of the Rand Corporation points out, the demographic differences between black and white populations will only perpetuate racial separation: in large central cities, 29 percent of blacks are between five and seventeen years of age, compared with only 20 percent of the cities' white residents. These contrasting age distributions "mean that blacks, already disproportionately concentrated in the central cities, will become even more so."

A strange twist in all of this is that Thacher Longstreth may yet get his wish that a big portion of the unemployed simply disappear. In North and West Philadelphia white flight has left some 22,000 homes abandoned. Now some of the city's black population is beginning to leave Philadelphia as well, according to a study released by the Center for Philadelphia Studies at the University of Pennsylvania. The study's authors were amazed to discover that, in some areas of North Philadelphia, almost 30 percent of the black population disappeared in the 1970s, though the study gives no clue as to where they've gone.

Community activists have their hunches, though. Like a lot of Americans, ambitious blacks of North Philadelphia are following their own economic instincts, heading to America II, the suburbs, cities such as Houston, and back to the rural South where poverty is perhaps more endurable than an inner-city slum. Even with this black out-migration, the disparity and dependency increases each year, in part because (as with most migrations), the hardiest, the most ambitious and adventurous, the most entrepreneurial are the ones who have left. And that is the hidden catch in the theory that shipping out the unemployed is a solution to anything. Not only are they unlikely to find work elsewhere, but the people left behind grow ever more desperate, more violent.

What is left in North Philadelphia is a burned-out shell, a dead city section for the ones who are left behind.

"You *walked* through there?" exclaimed a gray-haired cabdriver, after picking me up at the edge of the half-empty, forbidding neighborhood. "My God, my God."

He was black, and he hated North Philadelphia. "Nobody goes in there," he said. "Nobody." He held up an electrical cord, frayed at the end. "See, we don't even have radios anymore.

That's what it's come to. Don't take calls no more. Especially in there."

He paused for a moment. "I came here in 1945. Never would have guessed it'd come to this. It was beautiful," he said. "Beautiful."

THE THIRD ROAD

A few hundred miles south of Philadelphia, down a winding country road, there is a green paradise, a place with the air of exile, of a tribe withdrawing to the hills. It's the ultimate America II settlement, a place that serves as a metaphor and example for much of what is good and what is lost and what could finally be learned in America II.

North Carolina's Research Triangle Park and the surrounding counties contain the largest concentration of Ph.D.'s in the nation. There are no big cities in North Carolina, just a handful of small towns and medium-sized cities, and a dramatically growing number of people living along the farm-to-market roads in trailer parks, in new developments of brick, single-family homes, in condominium communities, and in self-contained settlements for the elderly, off by themselves back in the piney woods. Up these roads, hidden behind the trees, are smooth stretches of trimmed grass and huge monolithic buildings out of some science fiction dream, with pipe railings, metal spiral stairways, tungsten-halogen lamps.

Twenty years ago, they started arriving, all those scientists and engineers, drawn by the dream of a place in America where they could work their technological magic free from urban hassles, a place that valued higher education, a place of refuge. They were drawn by the plans and creations of a handful of forward-looking civic and academic leaders, who marked off an "industrial" park that would truly be a park: a huge triangle of 5500 rolling and pine-covered acres that would be surrounded by universities.

In this new world hidden back in the woods, research scientists are testing coal-to-gas conversion techniques, new contraceptive devices to implant beneath the skin, microprocessor-run devices that will help the deaf read lips, new computer chips, and God-knows-what defense projects. Within a few miles are Duke University, the University of North Carolina, North Carolina State, all in human-scale towns. IBM, Northrop, Data General, TRW, and dozens of other big companies are folded into hills of waving summer grass and buzzing locusts. Right now, this particular region of the country is full of hope and promise, a livable place that draws many people who are sick of congestion, of racial conflict, of pollution—people who want the amenities of both urban and rural living. A national survey found that North Carolina has the highest percentage of people who think their state is the best place in which to live.

But, as in the rest of America II, as more and more people come to North Carolina, the congestion on the country roads grows, the small cities begin to fuse, the countryside begins to fill with buckshot development, the gap between the poor and the high-salaried Postindustrials grows. A report called Project 2000, sponsored by the Triangle Council of Governments, warns: "[Growth] is rolling over the horizon as surely as tomorrow's daybreak. Growth [without planning] can creep across our lives as a pox, choking our highways and scarring the land. Or it can foster an age of progress—better jobs, more parklands, comfortable housing, and convenient transportation."

Just as important is the question of the haves and the have-nots. The report predicts that the region can move toward training and hiring local, mostly black, unskilled workers, or toward importing more high-tech skilled workers, exacerbating the already widening split between those plugged into the new skills and new jobs and those left behind. These are, especially, the migrant and seasonal farmworkers, the elderly, female-headed households, the handicapped, the unskilled, and the illiterate—the rural poor, who "live in poorly heated homes on unpaved roads," isolated by distance and dollars from the "great growth and progress that surrounds them. Without special attention the rural poor will continue to live in the early twentieth century while the rest of us move proudly into the twenty-first." Among this group economically left behind are a growing number of poor, female-headed households. This is the fastest-growing poverty group not only in North Carolina, but in the nation. In North Carolina a staggering 35 percent of all women workers are members, or heads, of households living in poverty. Few people here talk much about the number of smaller, low-wage, labor-intensive manufacturing companies that once came south, and that now have jumped to foreign countries where the wages are even lower. Pretty soon there may not be any low-income jobs left, except in the service industries. This region is rapidly becoming a place for high-salaried workers only. The Triangle report also predicts "more and more use of private police systems."

Over to the side of the road, in the parking lot of a new 7-Eleven, Fred Turnage was waiting for me. Turnage, is mayor of Rocky Mount, one of the little towns in the region that is growing quickly because of the changing economy.

We moved through Rocky Mount, a town and surrounding residential area of 60,000 people that bills itself, in its promotional literature, as a place where "the only surprises you'll encounter . . . are those of the nicest kind." Half of the *Fortune* 500 companies have located offices or plants within driving distance of Rocky Mount. The homes and the streets were bucolic, everything that we seem to want in a town, and yet even this town, to which so many Postindustrials have moved in recent years, is exhibiting some curious symptoms. "See, we built that city administration building there to keep people from deserting the downtown," said Turnage, pointing to a big, white futuristic edifice. And then, on down the road, he pointed to some shops with boarded-over windows. Main Street, lined with American flags, was divided by an old, rusting railroad track, running down the middle of the street. "Sears is even thinking about relocating to a shopping center outside town." Most of the new business development is outside of town. "Well, there's better parking, it's newer, its orderly."

We stopped at what appeared to be an old, restored plantation house, with white pillars outside and plush red carpets and wing-back chairs inside. First, Turnage showed me a slide presentation about Rocky Mount: nice music, nice people, nice little town, a mailbox with a picket fence, the Elmo Pumpkin Farm, memories of Carl Sandburg and Thomas Wolfe, one of the lowest crime rates in the nation, more picket fences, the dream. . . .

Turnage had graciously arranged for me to meet some people

whom he thought were representative of the newcomers. Their stories tell a lot about America in the 1980s. A research pharmacist and his wife came into the room. They did not want me to use their names. He was wearing a short-sleeved white shirt and a tie, and was graying at the temples. He talked very quietly, with his teeth together. The pharmacist described the industrial town in Indiana that had originally been his home:

"We were both born and raised there, and I always thought it would be heaven just to settle down in that part of the country, but it changed, became heavily polluted. There are significant amounts of coal in that area that can be easily strip-mined, and the strippers came in. And of course any time you strip coal you have to have some way of utilizing it, so they started building power plants. And now there's something like fifty power plants within a 100-mile radius of my hometown. There's one county there, that when the strippers are through there will be only one little town left, the county seat. Somebody must have really hated that place. I was a member of the Audubon Society, and I fought a lot of this. Understand, I'm a political conservative, but this had to stop. We had bad water. I had to treat my own water in our house with potassium permanganate—it's a desulfuring agent. Finally it just wasn't safe anymore, none of it: pollution, coming home at midnight and finding men partying on our front lawn, whiskey bottles everywere. So when I got a chance to come down here I grabbed it. We saw the stars at night for the first time."

A representative of the Land Stewardship Council of North Carolina had told me earlier that along the roads near Rocky Mount investigators had found dumps of deadly PCBs, and that throughout this region water and air pollution and the despoliation of the land are on the rise. So I asked the research pharmacist if he was now active in any watchdog environmental groups trying to assure that what had happened in industrial Indiana would not happen here in the postindustrial paradise.

"No, I'm not," he said.

The next fellow who came into the room was black. He was among one of the last groups of Americans who had migrated to America I in search of the dream. His name was George Birth, and he told a remarkable story of how dreams double back upon themselves. He grew up in the North Carolina that had long ago been replaced by the high-tech invasion, a North Carolina of textile mills (now mostly moved to Korea) and tenant farming. George Birth is now thirty-eight and his hairline is moving back on his head. Growing up on a tenant farm, he dreamed of being a professional baseball player.

"We used to work in the field, and we'd drive the car out into the middle of the field to listen to the World Series on the radio," he said. "We used mules then. We didn't go hungry. Really, agriculture back in the 1940s and '50s was very strong. It was really what supported this country over the years until the modern machines came in and took over some of the labor. When the machines came in, it was clear that it was better if you went up to the northern states. When I left the South in 1964, May 15, I'll never forget it . . . my mother and father were there. I did not want to go to New York. I wanted to stay here. But I had no other choice because there was not too much money on the farm and I had to do better than they did. My mother gave me thirty dollars to get to New York, and the bus ticket cost me sixteen dollars. I got about fifty miles down the road from here and I cried like a baby because I did not want to leave my mother and father, knowing that they were not able to work.

"I was nineteen years old and I took the train over to Harlem, and when I stepped off the train I stepped into the first riot I ever seen. It was people throwing bottles, throwing at passing cars, and fights breaking out between the police and blacks. Cops were chasing people and hitting them with sticks. I was meeting my brother there, and he and I had to split up, and we ran."

Birth worked at a candy factory—he made lollipops—and saved his money and went to baseball tryouts. One day a call came from the Bronx Bombers and another day from the Atlanta Braves. He realized his first dream, playing for the pros for a few years, until an old injury flared up. Throughout this period, though, he lived and invested his money in New York, in a record shop, and he nurtured his second dream, to go home in style.

"I knew I was not going to be in baseball for so long. But I knew I couldn't stay in New York, either. You could see what was happening then, the thieves, the higher insurance rates, people moving to the suburbs and the neighborhood falling apart." He knew fellows up in New York who were afraid to come home because they hadn't made it; they had come back for a visit with a big car and fancy clothes to impress everyone, but then would go back to New York to their menial or street jobs, their dead ends. And the decay continued. But then one day George Birth came home. He'd saved his money and he and his new wife, a northerner, bought a clothing store. He's a believer: "Things had changed. People got along better. Your return on an investment might not be as quick as it would in the north, but it lasts longer. We got away from our Southern heritage, you know, into Afro-American stuff, but our real home is in the rural South."

A lot of blacks are coming back, down from New York and Detroit and Philadelphia, but few of them have the kind of experience that George Birth reports. Carole B. Stack, an associate professor at Duke University, is studying the black return, and her preliminary findings show that, as she told me later in the week, "the option to migrate has become a panacea for the unfulfilled aspirations of black people. People come back with more job experience than those who left, and so they get better positions than the people who have not left. But these are still the bottom rung jobs. They're the janitors in the government offices, the cooks at McDonald's, the ones who clean the bright new microelectronics plants of the Research Triangle." This is the last option. The northern cities are no longer a place where dreams can be realized, and so people come home with higher expectations than when they left. Often, they have been laid off from primary sector jobs with relatively good pay and benefits, and now they are coming home to the kind of secondary service sector jobs that offer no avenues of advancement. They accept this, to some extent, because it is good to be home. Some of them escape by becoming self-employed entrepreneurs. But most of them just fester, having been pushed first out of a mechanizing agricultural economy into a northern manufacturing economy, and then pushed out of that.

Mayor Turnage took me home to meet his wife. They live in a rambling ranch house in a pleasant Rocky Mount neighborhood. His wife, Norma, who serves on the State Board of Education, was a relaxed woman with an easy smile. She talked for a while about curriculum and basic skills and other concerns, and then she came to what really concerned her: small-town white flight. Rocky Mount, like many North Carolina towns, is attracting blacks from the rural areas and from the northern cities, and the result is a mirror image of what happened over time in the urban north. "As a result, the upper-middle-class young whites, many of them from the north, are moving to suburban areas that are predominantly white, and which are not in the school district," she said. Not only that, but as efforts are made to draw them back into the school district to keep the black-white balance from shifting further, the young white parents move further out into the country, out to the woods where the buckshot development is spreading, out beyond the reach of towns and their social concerns.

The next day, way out in the woods, beyond any of the little cities surrounding the Research Triangle, I visited a small alternative community of 1960s refugees who, before coming here, became professors and engineers. Their livelihood depends on the huge growth of high-tech industry and the educational institutions that grew along with them. They live in solar houses on common land. They raise some of their own food, take turns driving the tractor, and, during the week, drive their Mazdas and Datsuns and restored 1940s pickups to their jobs at the Triangle or the universities.

I sat for a while with a woman there, an artist who works at home, whose house is lined with her soft sculptures—comical pelicans and a moose made from cloth and stuffing. She gave me a key to understanding so much of what I had seen in the past year. Like so many of the refugees, she and her husband had left a northeastern college town in part because, as she put it, "you'd wake up every morning and say, 'God damn it, it's another gray day.' It was like I needed more sun, needed out of that area. So we moved into an old house that we renovated in Durham." But in Durham, as she tells it, her children were uncomfortable in a predominantly black school. "One of our kids is the kind who, when he encounters a hostile environment, just withdraws and becomes physically sick. And I saw what was happening and took him out and put him in a Quaker school. Then our second child, who's highly peer-group oriented, tried shoplifting, so I took her out. We thought that the white-flight movement would take longer than it did. We'd gambled that we could put our kids in the Durham city schools and it would take three or four years before the ratios would reach the proportion that they reached in the first six months. Our youngest daughter, who is thirteen, went through her first three grades as one of two white children in her class."

So they moved again, this time to the smaller town of Chapel Hill, but at Chapel Hill her children had to deal with the teen drug culture. "You think you're in control of your life, but at a certain point your children begin to control you."

While still living in Durham, she had heard of an alternative community for middle-class professionals starting up out in the woods; two friends had already bought in. "I'd reached the point in my life where I'd made good friends and left them, and made more good friends and left them. Had lost any extended family, had lost any network of friends because of being part of the mobile generation. So I bought this lot with no down payment and $100 a month. At first I had no idea that we were really going to be able to move out here. So I put up a Sioux Indian tepee. It was about twenty-five feet tall and became one of the local historic spots; it had unicorns and frogs and all kinds of things painted all over. We used to camp out in it on weekends. But then the situation in Durham got worse, so we figured this is the last chance. We'd tried everything. So we moved out here. Built this house. My kids have benefited from the move. My son, who's a teenager, knows every inch of the land. He's explored the forest and the hills and started a garden. He was the one who supported my buying here and he loved the tepee and cried when I cremated it because it was too old.

"I'm not sure I consider this my home, but I almost feel like I've been a wanderer for so long that it may take . . ." She stopped for a moment. "If you ask me in another five years if this is home, I'll maybe have a better answer. I love it, though. It's almost like all along I loved it so much I was afraid to say that out loud for fear that it would go away."

Her face grew stiff and her eyes widened. She was staring straight ahead. There was something she wanted to say, but she could barely say it.

"I have a lot of mixed feelings. My husband's first major academic work dealt with the urban riots of the 1960s. I was teaching part time at a community center in Watts called All People's Christian Center. It's like we came from being super idealists in the 1960s, and now at the wise old age of 42, I . . ." She began to cry. "I don't know," she said, "I don't know. . . ."

It's much too easy to judge the individuals who look for refuge, who retreat into private enclaves or into themselves, but when

America II is seen from a distance, it seems only to compound the racial and environmental conflicts that fuel this psychology of buffering.

DOUBLE VISION

On a national level, a kind of double vision is at work. The older industrial cities in the northeast and upper Midwest long viewed the rest of the nation—the South, the West, rural and small-town America—as economic colonies. But the colonies, with rich energy resources, new technology, and plenty of open space, have broken free. Following America's birth, the British resented the successes and excesses of the young United States. So, too, many of the residents of America I are chagrined at the economic growth of North Carolina, Houston, San Diego, Phoenix. The growth, they believe, is happening at their expense. America II, to them, is vaguely threatening, crass, uncultured, and wrongheaded. To the enthusiasts of America II, though, that kind of thinking is probably the result of America I burnout: too many cold winters and too many frozen, outdated concepts. What they see emerging is America's next and best chance: a dispersed, more humane population distribution; a revival of small-scale government in small towns, condominium communities, and the workplace; a blending of rural and urban values; a trust in technology; a sense of being buffered from economic change and social problems.

Indeed, one reason why America can't seem to solve its domestic problems is its elected representatives, business leaders, and academicians are looking at them from two entirely different perspectives. In the coming decades, Americans may well see an ever-widening gap of perspective, based on where people live in part, but, more important, on which American vision they hold —America I, a fading vision, or America II, that peculiar mix of nostalgia, faith in the technological fix, and privatism.

Certainly there are pluses to America II. Deconcentrated, decentralized living may well be more energy efficient than the commuter culture in the older industrial cities. This type of population distribution may mean reduced commuting distances. Particularly in the new country, there is also the promise of residential energy conservation. In the older industrial cities high-density housing precludes widespread use of solar collectors and windmills. And, in the short run, some social stresses are relieved. But not for long. Congestion, crime, and poverty are following the migrants out to the South and the West, out to the small towns. New problems are emerging—a raped environment, water shortages, disappearing farmland—and eventually the bills come due.

Time is running out for the cities of America II, which are suffering new levels of urban blight, crime, poverty. Violent crime in the 1970s in San Diego grew by 211 percent, in large part because of increased population. Though the nation's method of counting crimes is imperfect at best, most experts believe that the rate of violent crime (especially stranger-on-stranger crimes) is rising much faster in cities gaining population than in those losing population. Crime is also rising in small cities, small towns, and rural areas. According to a study by the American Justice Institute in Sacramento, California, while twenty-seven cities report gang problems, only nine of the twenty-seven had a population of more than 500,000, indicating that gang warfare is no longer limited to major urban centers.

More than any other technological development, the freeways have allowed the population to live in dispersed cities far from central urban cores, and in the suburbs and rural regions. But now those freeways are threatened. In 1975, the California State Transportation Plan predicted that by 1983 cars would be banned from the central cities, mass transit would be in place, smog would be reduced by one-half, and electromagnetic people-movers would whisk us around on fixed guideways. None of the predictions have come true. In the major population centers of America II, people see their freeways filling up, becoming more crowded every year. California, the birthplace of the freeway society, is now the forty-ninth state in per capita transportation expenditures. And new residents still are pouring into the state. Projections by the San Diego Association of Government show that San Diego's incoming population is dropping slightly, possibly because of housing prices, but that the region can expect about 30,000 new residents each year until the year 2000. That means more than a million added cars and trucks on San Diego's freeways.

One afternoon, sitting in the dining room of his sunny La Jolla, California, home, Jake Dekema talked of the future of the freeways that he had built. Dekema, retired state Department of

Transportation director for San Diego, was one of the handful of engineers who, in the 1950s, designed the California freeway system, which served as a model for the interstate system. A spidery freeway overpass was named for him. At the time it was the largest concrete bridge in the world. He talks of it wistfully, describing it as "kind of like a cathedral." He helped pave the way, literally, to America II.

"We're only half done with what we'd planned for the San Diego freeway system. There's just enough money to fix the potholes, and that's possibly going to be depleted soon too. I hope we built something more useful than the pyramids," he said, smiling. His jaw looked as hard and straight as a bridge abutment. "Freeway financing is worse now than it was in the 1950s. By 1990, people are going to wish we had done something in 1980. But then again, the worse the traffic gets, the faster the electronic revolution develops. It may well be that mass commuting will no longer be needed. People will be able to stay home and work, or they'll work in small offices, spread out all over the city and the countryside, linked by computers and sophisticated communication systems." And that will mean continued growth of the South and West and the countryside.

The sun was slanting in harder now. A strange look came over Dekema's face—strange for a man of such self-confidence, who had helped oversee one of the greatest public works projects in history. Suddenly he did not look so sure about . . . anything.

Each new technology, he said, plants the seed for its own destruction. "You just can't predict or control these things, can you? They just happen. That's all. They just happen."

As America II expands, seemingly a natural force beyond control, its dispersed cities and small towns cover more and more farmland. The United States has been converting agricultural land to nonagricultural uses at a rate of about 3 million acres per year, according to the National Agricultural Lands Study. By the turn of the century, the amount of land covered over by cement—shopping centers, industrial parks, highways—may double. Calling for more restrictions on the conversion of farmland, the report warns that if current trends continue, not only will American agriculture be unable to feed a hungry world, it will be barely capable of feeding its own nation. The proponents of America II, who believe in the technological fix, are more optimistic. They can produce their own set of figures that show that every year for the past decade the amount of productive cropland actually harvested increased significantly. While some farmland is lost to development, they say, new rural acreage is being created by swamp drainage, desert irrigation, forest reclamation, and the application of new technology. The Great Plains could not be farmed for much of our history because of its tough sod; the plains had to wait for the manufacturing of steel plows before they could be considered prime farmland. Likewise, we are just beginning to see the possibilities of hydroponics, new fertilizing and irrigation methods, and genetic engineering.

But is technology enough? Calvin Beale, who is chief demographer of the U.S. Department of Agriculture and one of the nation's most knowledgeable experts on population dispersal, believes that deconcentration is basically healthy for the nation —if it is accomplished with respect for the land. He finds himself "somewhere between" the enthusiasts of America II and the National Agricultural Lands Study. "There is no doubt," he says, "that we're losing farmland. How much we're losing isn't clear. But we're going to have to come to terms with that before we can really measure the wisdom of population dispersal or the effectiveness of new technologies."

Another factor yet to be fully measured is the effect of our spreading population on water resources. In many cases, the population is moving to those regions of the country with the most vulnerable water tables. Already, vast underground reserves of water, which were deposited over thousands of years, have been seriously depleted. The contamination and the overuse of this ground water continues.

In addition to these unintended consequences, the battle lines have been drawn between the have states and the have-not states. The South and West, because of their vast oil and coal resources, are more immune to rising energy costs than the rest of the nation. The northeast and Midwest pay up to 50 percent more per household for energy than the South and nearly twice as much as the West, according to a new study by the Northeast-Midwest Congressional Coalition. And if certain business interests in the West have their way, the balance of power will shift even more to the West. Energy companies and developers in the eight Rocky Mountain states, which are less populated than New

York City, want to develop federal land reserves amounting to one-fifth of the nation, a whole new frontier for the drilling rig and the bulldozer. Indeed, the energy-producing states, including Alaska (an America II state), are becoming the equivalent of a domestic OPEC, slapping stiff severance taxes on their resources. Montana, for instance, imposes a 30 percent severance tax on coal leaving its state to heat homes in the Northeast. Alaska is taking in so much revenue from its severance taxes that the state has been able to do away with its income tax and business tax. And citizens of Alaska are getting a $50 rebate for every year they have lived in the state. By the year 2000, Alaska will have a minimum of $200 billion in its treasury. This is happening in a state with 400,000 people, fewer people than live in one congressional district in Pennsylvania.

Unless these inequities are faced, states that produce tin or wheat may, in retaliation, begin to put high severance taxes on their own resources, and America will face internal economic warfare. This kind of competition between states is already occurring in the rush to attract high technology. The result: high-tech industry moves around the nation, drawn by special tax considerations, creating better conditions for the Postindustrials, but much worse conditions for the people left outside the postindustrial gates, because in the process, social services are cut, and the nation's people become more insecure about just where their home will be next year or even next month.

The tent cities of Southern California and Houston are testimony that, as the poor leave America I in search of greener economic pastures, they take with them their lack of skills, their unemployability. And eventually, their frustration, like a time bomb shipped from Philadelphia to Houston, will make itself felt. The bomb is already ticking. The Southern Regional Council, an Atlanta-based human-rights agency, warns that in some regions of the South, the economic distance between blacks and whites is wider than it was thirty years ago. No planning is being done, according to the council, to help the South and West avoid the slums of Northern cities. And a Massachusetts Institute of Technology study points out that many of the cities of the South and West are developing ominously compartmentalized growth patterns in which well-to-do whites and well-to-do blacks cluster in one area, poor whites in another, poor blacks in a third and, in some cases, poor Mexican-Americans in a fourth. As a result, the study contends, "the rich and poor live in different worlds. They almost literally never see one another."

After the urban riots of the 1960s, the Kerner Commission on Civil Disorders predicted that if poverty and racism were not relieved, Americans would soon be living in armed camps. That prediction may be coming true, with the growing emphasis in America II on high-security condominium complexes and planned communities with their own private security forces. The obsession with security is understandable, but in this proliferation of security, we are gradually losing the ease and openness of society. One wonders if the cure is as bad as the disease, or if there might be another cure.

We withdraw into our homes, using our new cable television connections to bank, shop, and vote from the privacy of our living rooms. And yet the privacy we think we are getting is diminished by computers that quantify and analyze what we order, what we watch. We move into perfect walled communities to escape government regulation and, as one Rancho Bernardo resident told me, "the riffraff"; and yet, instead of Big Brother, we end up with Little Brother, a system of local government that controls what we plant, what color our curtains are, and potentially how we think. We move to small towns and planned communities and gentrified Victorian neighborhoods to find community, and what we get is more people just like ourselves often living in a peculiar kind of isolation. We pretend that we can find protection in a high-tech, cult company, when no protection is possible in an economy changing as quickly as this one, especially if the pain of change is not shared. We circle the wagons, withdraw into our homes, and the decay continues around us.

Certainly there are those people who have made the best of these new social forms, and many of them have spoken in this book, passionately, eloquently. When I began this project I believed that this new nation emerging was full of promise; I was excited by what I saw at the end of the migrant streams, at the end of the postindustrial rainbow where, it seemed, new life forms were rising. People were taking control of their own lives, working out their own private solutions. And so they are. But as I talked to so many of these pioneers, I began to see a larger picture, to understand the price being paid. The truth is we have confused a few symbols within the dream for the dream itself.

The hungers and yearnings of America II are legitimate. The days of cities that grow forever are over, but that does not mean that in our search for smaller communities we find community, that in our yearning for home we find home. So often, we eventually create the antithesis of what we have sought. Partly, this is because our search was ambivalent from the beginning. We wanted communication without commitment, community without commitment. The reason for this national fractionalization is not just new technology, but the weakening of the national commitment to social justice and shared progress. Ultimately, fractionalism does not solve our problems, it just moves them around. It took the Civil War to establish that the nation was a whole. Now we are moving into new tribes, into condo communities and urban villages and new small towns. The selectivity of these new tribes ultimately means that a few members have the key to the future. The new tribes operate wonderfully for those who can afford, through money or knowledge, to buy into them. But this privilege comes at a price. Andrew Oldenquist, a philosophy teacher at Ohio State University, writes of one result of this approach. In an era of growing crime, he says:

> We can understand "mindless" violence that serves no rational interest—frenzied vandalism, refusing to be taken alive for a traffic citation, pushing strangers in front of subways—as a rage at tribal exclusion. It is the revenge of an innately tribal creature for not being initiated into society and treated as a member. To be a social animal means subjection to rules and being held personally answerable to them in ways in which a mad dog or a virus is not.

America is fragmenting into subsocieties, regions, sections, information-rich and information-poor, instead of defining what we want—security, economic stability, community, home—and then trying to get that for all the people.

The America II pioneers that I interviewed in North Carolina, and so many of the others, yearn for the image of elsewhere, but that image seems always beyond their grasp. What they describe is the seductiveness of the image, how it makes us think again and again that the real American dream can be found somewhere else. There is so much in the society that pushes us consciously and unconsciously in this direction. But the final secret of America II is simple and discomforting. There isn't any place to hide.

A THIRD VISION

America II may well be more of a crossroads than a destination, a chance to begin again in a new direction. With luck, though it is only barely visible on the political or social horizon, a third vision will emerge. This vision would permit us to let go of the old America, to let go of the knee-jerk assumptions that cities should get bigger and that the movement to the countryside is entirely destructive. This vision would suggest that smaller governments and entrepreneurial enterprises are good for the nation. The vision would, however, reject certain destructive aspects of America II: the "let 'er rip" approach to economics, the faith that the free market alone will result in humane housing, a preserved landscape. This vision would allow us to look beyond the fictional technological fix. It would recognize that a democratic nation cannot long endure in which the economic-and-information haves shop in their covered malls, live protected in their walled communities and their neo-Rockwellian small towns and urban enclaves, in which the haves hire their own private cops, bank and shop via television, and work in their protected company cults, seldom having a disorderly encounter with a have-not. The third vision would accept our commonality. The new era is not nearly as cheerfully sure as the Postindustrial priests would have us believe. So we need to enter it together. There is more safety in numbers than in isolation.

This third vision would encourage the resettling of America, if done with a sense of stewardship for the land, if done not just for a few of the lucky, but also for those pushed out of the old cities and old industries. It would encourage small farms and part-time farms and the gradual growth of small towns, while discouraging buckshot development and environmental destruction. It would encourage the trend, so far more wishful thinking than reality, toward urban villages within the anticities—not just for a privileged few, but for a mixture of economic and racial groups. It would discourage the privatization of the public responsibility.

In the older industrial cities, the third vision would recognize the so-called urban revival for what it is, a renaissance for a very few Postindustrials. The current method of pouring millions of dollars into "reviving" downtowns works chiefly to the benefit of those who least need benefits. Rather, the third vision would suggest that aid should go first to those who need it most.

A third vision would also include cross-state federal assistance to help people move to jobs, and massive training programs to ease those people shoved out or left behind by the new economy not only into high-tech jobs, but into entrepreneurial endeavors. Instead of the current competition between states, in which they rush to waive environmental laws and taxes to attract business, a third vision would call for a policy based on the notion that we are one nation, that national tax breaks and a national development bank are more fitting and proper than pitting region against region. This third vision would include laws restricting certain corporate movements offshore, and a recommitment to public employment. The issue here is fairness; a climate in which state competes against state may work to the benefit of a few corporations, but certainly not of people forced to move every few years because of an economy that flits around the country like heat lightning on a summer night.

The alternative to fractionalization is to reestablish our membership in the nation, to recognize that we are all moving into this new era, and if we do this in a way that creates two cultures, then we will all eventually answer to or become part of the rage of tribal exclusion. The third vision would entail sharing the benefits and the detriments of the economic transformation.

Such a sense of national purpose would be healing. It would reduce the tensions that now cause people to feel they must hide away in a small town or walled community, in enclaves surrounded by laser beams. It would create among us a real sense of community, not the illusion of community. The third vision would recognize that we do share a common purpose in our national search for the lost town, but that we need to make this search a conscious one. We need to redefine the way we physically live. Rather than leaving this redefinition up to developers, packagers, and market forces, *we* need to do this.

So many of the false promises and blind alleys of America II arise not from any particular political persuasion, but from our posing. We imagine ourselves yeomen farmers, and create a suburbia that does not work. We imagine ourselves mountain men and mountain women in our mountain condos with computerized sensors in the fireplace, and then wonder why we do not feel fulfilled. We move into a condominium thinking we are leaving our troubles (along with the lawn mower) behind, and then the community association slaps a lien on our airspace because we have infringed on the tribal sensibility. We hire our own police to protect us, to create the illusion of safety, and put walls around our communities, then wonder why all those people are coming over the walls. Sooner or later, our posturing must be sorted out, decisions must be made.

America II is a transitional period, a crossroads, a choice among three directions. The first road is the road behind us, the fading America of smokestacks, giant metropolises, and seemingly unlimited economic expansion.

The second road is the road that much of America is now on. It leads toward organized units that enforce social sameness, a commercialized nostalgia, a perversion of traditional democratic values and American hungers, toward walled enclaves, cults of disposable friends, overorganization, a kind of technological security that gives a false sense of protection while increasing our society's disruption. Down that road are private services for those who can afford them, and not much at all for those who cannot. Down that road is the kind of world Orwell and Huxley warned us against, though it will be much more subtle and pervasive than they envisioned. The road to this particular future is lined with signs, futurists, and fortune-tellers telling us of the wonders and freedom of high tech and the value of escape. Home, they whisper as we pass, home is down this road, don't look back, don't question, don't worry. Home, down there, around that next corner, or maybe the corner after that. Down there is what you want, down there is home. All you have to do is wish. And pretend.

The third road, which looks vaguely like the second, leads to a quite different potential. Down this third road, which is poorly marked, are, indeed, dispersed cities and a new country, but within them is an intensified sense of responsibility, the realization that the farther society disperses physically, the more we need human connections. Down this third road, instead of disposable cults, we form stronger and more lasting bonds of family and friendship; instead of walled enclaves, neighborhoods that reach out; instead of economic and social buffering, a recommitment to racial equality and the sharing of economic troubles. Down this road are communities, cities, and towns that approach some semblance of self-reliance, but in a way that assures a greater degree of equity; instead of a new countrified population that destroys the land it seeks to enjoy, a people who accept their stewardship of the land. At these destinations, which are not so much *out there* as they are within ourselves, we could find our place and touch each other. Down that road lies home.

The following references are listed in the order of appearance. Most are referred to directly in the text, but a few are not—these include articles and papers used as sources for specific statistical material. Also, the authors of some of the following studies were interviewed directly. In these cases, their related publications are listed.

OPENING QUOTE

de Tocqueville, Alexis, *Democracy in America* (New York: Harper and Row, 1966).

Springsteen, Bruce, "Atlantic City" on *Nebraska* (1982).

INTRODUCTION

Bell, Daniel, *The Coming of Post-Industrial Society, A Venture in Social Forecasting* (New York: Basic Books, 1976).

PART ONE—HOME AND PAIN
Quote

Stein, Gertrude, *The Geographical History of America* (New York: Random House, 1936).

Berry, Wendell, *The Unsettling of America* (New York: Avon, 1977), p. 3.

Abbey, Edward, *Desert Solitaire* (New York: Ballantine, 1968), p. 1.

CHAPTER 1—The Image of Elsewhere

Morrison, P. A. and Wheeler, J. P., *The Image of Elsewhere in the Tradition of American Migration* The Rand Corporation, Santa Monica, CA (October 1976).

Davis, Fred, "Nostalgia, Identity and the Current Nostalgia Wave," *Journal of Popular Culture* (Fall 1977), pp. 414–415. (On the origin of the word *nostalgia.*)

Jones, George E., "The Great Nostalgia Kick," *U.S. News and World Report* (22 March 1982), pp. 57–60. (The Ralph Gardner quote.)

Langway, L. with Prout, L. R., "Lauren's Frontier Chic," *Newsweek*, (21 September 1981), p. 115.

Salholz, E. with Resener, M. and Dallas, R., "Here Comes Country Chic," *Newsweek* (16 August 1982), pp. 42, 44.

Unger, Craig, "Attitude," *New York Magazine* (26 July 1982), pp. 24–32. (Regarding new wave nostalgia.)

Naisbitt, John, *Megatrends* (New York: Warner Books, 1982), p. 39.

CHAPTER 2—Fueling Forces

Williams, James D. and Sofranko, Andrew J., "Motivations for the Immigration Component of Population Turnaround in Nonmetropolitan Areas," *Demography*, vol. 16 (May 1979), pp. 239–255.

———, "Why People Move," *American Demographics* (July-August 1981), pp. 30–31.

"Urban Residents' Attitudes Toward Their City and Neighborhood," Gallup Poll (1981).

Paving the Way to America II

Kasarda, John D., "The Implications of Contemporary Redistribution Trends for National Urban Policy," *Social Science Quarterly*, vol. 61, nos. 3 and 4 (December 1980), p. 381.

The Search for Control

U.S. News and World Report (15 Febuary 1982).

Betz, John, "Firm Finds New Housing Market," *Los Angeles Times* (6 July 1980).

Thomas, William V., "A Nation of Stay-at-Homes," Editorial Research Reports Daily Service (1 September 1981).

"America's New Immobile Society," *Business Week* (27 July 1981), pp. 58–62.

Yankelovich, Daniel, "New Rules in American Life: Searching for Self-Fulfillment in a World Turned Upside Down," *Psychology Today* (April 1981), p. 40.

The New Economy

Birch, David, "The Job Generation Process," MIT Project on Neighborhood and Regional Change, Massachusetts Institute of Technology, Cambridge (1979).

Brenner, M. Harvey, "Assessing the Social Costs of National Unemployment Rate," formal statement submitted for testimony before the Subcommittee on Domestic Monetary Policy of the Committee on Banking, Finance, and Urban Affairs, U.S. House of Representatives, Washington, D.C., (12 August 1982).

"Suicides: 'Baby Boom' Males Are Hardest Hit by Loss of Job, Prestige," United Press International, in *The Seattle Post-Intelligencer* (25 October 1982).

CHAPTER 3—The Dispersal of America
Manso, Peter, "Playboy Interview: Ed Koch," *Playboy* (April 1982). "American Graffiti," *Newsweek* (17 May 1982), p. 61. (On George Poulos and the missing bricks.)

Deconcentrated America
"Center of U.S. Population is Missouri Town," *Los Angeles Times* (20 April 1981).

Sawyer, Kathy, "Population Center Marches Across Mississippi River," *The Washington Post* (15 July 1981).

Herbers, John, "Population Wave Washes Back from the Coast," *New York Times* (31 August 1980).

Vining, Daniel R., "Towards a National Urban Policy—Critical Reviews, The President's National Urban Policy Report: Issues Skirted and Statistics Omitted," *Journal of Regional Science*, vol. 19, no. 1, (1979), pp. 69–77. (Regarding testimony by Arthur P. Solomon.)

Stevens, William K., "New Life After the Last Picture Show," *The New York Times Magazine*, (4 April 1982), pp. 43–46.

A New Way of Looking at America
Phillips, Kevin, *The Emerging Republican Majority* (New York: Arlington House, 1969).

Rice, Bradley R., "Searching for the Sunbelt," *American Demographics* (March 1981), pp. 22–23.

Allis, Sam, "America's Penchant for 'Belts,'" *Wall Street Journal* (14 April 1981), p. 25.

Hosken, Fran, "Egypt's Explosive Growth," *Christian Science Monitor* (6 March 1981), p. 16.

Garreau, Joel, *The Nine Nations of North America* (Boston: Houghton Mifflin Company, 1981).

Abbott, Carl, from an article in *Journal of the West* (1979) quoted in Rice, Bradley R., "Searching for the Sunbelt," *American Demographics* (March 1981), pp. 22–23.

Fuchs, Roland J., and Demko, George J., "Big Brother Loses Again," in *Human Behavior* (June 1978) from "Spatial Population Problems in Socialist Countries of Eastern Europe," *Social Science Quarterly*, vol. 58, no. 1 (June 1977), pp. 60–73.

Vining, D. R., Jr., Pallone, R. L., and Yang, C., "Population Dispersal from Core Regions: A Description and Tentative Explanation of the Patterns in 20 Countries," *Working Papers in*

Regional Science and Transportation, no. 26 (Philadelphia: University of Pennsylvania, 1980), pp. 1–16.

PART TWO—LIVING IN THE ANTICITY
Quote

Wright, Frank Lloyd, quoted in Edward Abbey, *The Journey Home: Some Words in Defense of the American West* (New York: Dutton, 1977).

Wells, H. G., *Anticipations* (London: Harper and Row, 1962).

CHAPTER 4—Dreams of the Anticity

Glaab, Charles N., and Brown, A. Theodore, *A History of Urban America* (New York: Macmillan Company, 1967), pp. 67–71. (Thomas Jefferson quote.)

Gordon, David M., *Class Struggle and the Stages of American Urban Development,* p. 76. (On the distribution of labor in preindustrial and industrial cities.)

The Suburban Roots of the Dream

Harlan, Paul Douglas, quoted in Kaplan, Samuel, *The Dream Deferred, People, Politics, and Planning in Suburbia* (New York: Random House, 1976), p. 205.

Kaplan, Samuel, *The Dream Deferred, People, Politics, and Planning in Suburbia* (New York: Random House, 1976), p. 205.

Berger, Bennett M., "American Pastoralism, Suburbia, and the Commune Movement," *Society Magazine* (July-August, 1979), pp. 64–69.

Mumford, Lewis, *The City in History: Its Origins, Its Transformations and Its Prospects* (New York: Harcourt, Brace, and World, 1961), pp. 22, 23.

Morrison, Peter A., *It's Not Overpopulation—It's the People,* Publication P-5004, The Rand Corporation, Santa Monica, CA (May 1973).

The Dream Continued

Mumford, Lewis, "Why Experts Are Wrong in Their Prescriptions for Cities," *The National Observer* (1 May 1967), p. 22.

Leven, Charles, "Economic Maturity and the Metropolis's Evolving Physical Form," in *The Changing Structure of the City* (Beverly Hills: Sage), p. 34.

CHAPTER 5—The Blob Gets a New Image

Hance, Margaret T., "Phoenix—My Kinda Town," *PSA Magazine* (April 1982), pp. 74, 76.

Bracken, Paul, with contributions by Kahn, Herman, "A Summary of Arizona Tomorrow," Hudson Institute, Croton-on-Hudson (April 1980), pp. 1–31.

The Evolution of Sprawl
Leven, Charles, "Economic Maturity and the Metropolis's Evolving Physical Form," in *The Changing Structure of the City* (Beverly Hills: Sage), pp. 34–36.

Looking for the Urban Village
Tsujimoto, Lauren, "Orange County Urban Hub Found?" *Los Angeles Times* (2 August 1981).
Chamberlain, David, "Aurora, Mysterious City to the East," *Rocky Mountain Magazine*, pp. 46–51.
Blundell, William E., "Boon Town, How a City Stretches Tax Dollars by Using Imagination and Energy," *Wall Street Journal* (9 March 1977), pp. 1, 14. (On Scottsdale, Arizona.)

The Skeptics: A Blob Is a Blob Is a Blob
Abbey, Edward, "The Blob Comes to Arizona," in *The Journey Home: Some Words in Defense of the American West* (New York: Dutton, 1977), pp. 146–157.

CHAPTER 6—Laissez-Faire Lifestyle: The Anticity Unchained

The Private City
Lupsha, Peter A. and Siembieda, William J., "The Poverty of Public Services in the Land of Plenty: An Analysis and Interpretation," Berry, D. C. and Watkins, A. J. (eds.), *The Rise of the Sunbelt Cities* (Beverly Hills: Sage, 1977), p. 185.
Ashby, Lynn, quoted in Burd, Gene, "The Selling of the Sunbelt: Civic Boosterism in the Media," in Berry, D. C. and Watkins, A. J. (eds.), *The Rise of the Sunbelt Cities* (Beverly Hills: Sage, 1977). (Regarding good government leagues.)
Thompson, Thomas, *Blood and Money* (New York: Doubleday, 1976), p. 68.
Moran, Tom, *Houston Chronicle* (20 November 1981), p. 19.
Bjornseth, Dick, "Houston Defies the Planners . . . and Thrives," *Reason* (February 1978), pp. 16, 17.

The Blob Moves On
Lupsha, Peter A. and Siembieda, William J., "The Poverty of Public Services in the Land of Plenty: An Analysis and Interpretation," Berry, D. C. and Watkins, A. J. (eds.), *The Rise of*

the Sunbelt Cities (Beverly Hills: Sage, 1977), p. 185. (Regarding the convergence theory.)

PART THREE—THE SHELTER REVOLUTION
Quote
   Robert Frost, "Mending Wall," from *The Poetry of Robert Frost* (New York: Holt, Rinehart and Winston, 1969), p. 33.
   Chamberlain, David, "Aurora: Mysterious City to the East," *Rocky Mountain Magazine* (1982), p. 46.

CHAPTER 7—The Coming of the Shelter Revolution
   "Condomania," *U.S. News and World Report* (17 January 1983), pp. 50–51. (This was the source of some of the figures on the growth of condos; other statistics were supplied by Community Associates Institute in Washington, D.C., and Community Management Corporation in Reston, Virginia.)
   Duncan, Mary and Lerner, Max, "Walled Cities: The Fortress Mentality," *San Diego Magazine* (September 1982), p. 86.
   Byron, Doris A., "Communities for Elderly Come of Age," *Los Angeles Times* (19 May 1981), pp. 1, 3, 18.

The Making of a Revolution
   Jacob, Bernard, "The Down-sized American Dream Home," *Northwest Orient Magazine* (February 1983), pp. 25–29. (On the shrinking American home.)
   Kincher, David M., "Shelter Journal Sees New Housing Boom," *Los Angeles Times* (10 February 1980).

CHAPTER 8—The Rise of Capitalist Communes
Seeds of Revolt
   Glaab, Charles N. and Brown, A. Theodore, *A History of Urban America* (New York: Macmillan Company, 1967), p. 2. (Background on planned towns in American history.)
   Huth, Mary Jo, "A Path to Real Reform," *The Urban Habitat, Past, Present, and Future* (Chicago: Nelson-Hall, 1978). (Material on Ebenezer Howard and Garden Cities.)

Coming Home to America II
   The Woodlands Development Corporation, Multimedia Script, Woodlands, Texas (20 January 1976), p. 1.

CHAPTER 9—The Design and Selling of Condo America
   Francaviglia, Richard V., "Main Street U.S.A.: A Comparison/Contrast of Streetscapes in Disneyland and Walt Disney World," *Journal of Popular Culture* (Summer 1981), pp. 140–156.

Myerhoff, Barbara, "The Tamed and Colonized Imagination in Disneyland: Fun and Peril When Dreams Come True." (To date, this excellent paper has been published only in Japan; an English version is available through Barbara Myerhoff's office at the University of Southern California, Los Angeles.)

Jacob, Bernard, "The Down-sized American Dream Home," *Northwest Orient* (February, 1983), pp. 25–29. (On the use of illusion to disguise the smallness of condos.)

The Emergence of Theme Housing

Byron, Doris A., "Communities for Elderly Come of Age," *Los Angeles Times* (19 May 1981), pp. 1, 3, 18.

Kaplan, Sam, "Privileged Preview of American Demographics," *Los Angeles Times* (15 March 1981), part VI, pp. 1, 14, 15.

Gustaitis, Rasa, "No Room for Youth in Florida's Elderly Ghettos," Pacific News Service, San Francisco (14 August 1979).

CHAPTER 10—Control Thy Neighbor

Huncher, Wendell E., "Elected Local Leadership in Municipal Government," *The Annals of the American Academy* (January 1973), pp. 137–44.

Private Power

Goodkin, Sanford, "Trashing the Condo," *Condominium World* (Winter 1975), pp. 65–69.

Evans Teeley, Sandra, "Homeowners Say Condo Path Will Lead to Paradise Lost," *The Washington Post* (24 July 1982).

King, Florence, "Why Condo Owning is Un-American," Network News, Inc., Washington, D.C. (1 May 1982).

PART FOUR—THE NEW EDEN
Quote

Martin, Russell, "Writers of the Purple Sage," *New York Times Magazine* (27 December 1981), pp. 18, 43.

Rockwell, Norman, *Norman Rockwell, My Adventures as an Illustrator* (Garden City: Doubleday, 1960).

CHAPTER 11—Eden Redux

Davis, Jay, "Retrospect, A General History of Waldo County," *The Republican Journal* (July 1979), pp. 3–12.

Berry, Wendell, *The Unsettling of America* (New York: Avon, 1977).

Beale, Calvin L., *The Revival of Population Growth in Nonmetropolitan America,* Economic Development Division, Economic Research Service, U.S. Department of Agriculture (1975), pp. 3–15.

Fuguitt, Glenn V. and Zuiches, James J., "Residential Preferences: Implications for Population Redistribution in Nonmetropolitan Areas," *Population Distribution and Policy,* vol. 5, U.S. Commission on Population Growth and the American Future (1972), pp. 617–630. (Information on preference for rural versus small-town life.)

———, "Residential Preferences and Population Distribution," *Demography,* vol. 12, no. 3 (August 1975), pp. 491–504.

The Assumption of a New Eden
Kasarda, John D., "The Implications of Contemporary Redistribution Trends for National Urban Policy," *Social Science Quarterly,* vol. 61, nos. 3 and 4 (December, 1980), p. 381.

CHAPTER 12—In Search of Norman Rockwell
Rockwell, Norman, *Norman Rockwell, My Adventures as an Illustrator* (Garden City: Doubleday, 1960).

CHAPTER 13—The New American Gothic
The Force
Wardwell, John M., "Revitalization of Rural America: Patterns and Consequences of Nonmetropolitan and Rural Growth," in Hicks, Donald A. and Glickman, Norman J. (eds.), *Transition to the 21st Century: Prospects and Policies for Economic and Urban-Regional Transformation* (Greenwich, CT: JAI Press, 1983).

"Back to the Country, but Not to the Land," *New York Times* (17 May 1981).

Kasarda, John D., "The Implications of Contemporary Redistribution Trends for National Urban Policy," *Social Science Quarterly,* vol. 61, nos. 3 and 4 (December 1980), p. 381.

Herbers, John, "Can't Keep 'em in the City Once They've Seen the Farm," New York Times News Service (28 April 1980).

The Urbanizing Countryside
Reed, John Shelton, *One South, an Ethnic Approach to Regional Culture* (Baton Rouge: Louisiana State University Press, 1982), p. 187.

Wardwell, John M., "Revitalization of Rural America: Patterns and Consequences of Nonmetropolitan and Rural Growth," in Hicks, Donald A. and Glickman, Norman J. (eds.), *Transition to the 21st Century: Prospects and Policies for Economic and Urban-Regional Transformation* (Greenwich, CT: JAI Press, 1983).

Russell, Cheryl, "All SMSAs Are Not Alike," *American Demographics* (May 1981), pp. 36–37.

Herbers, John, "Can't Keep 'em in the City Once They've Seen the Farm," New York Times News Service, in the *San Diego Union* (20 April 1980), pp. F9, 11, 12.

Doherty, J. C., "The Countryfied City," *American Demographics*, vol. 2, no. 4, (Fall 1981), pp. 7–8.

Hyperculture Comes to the Country

"Home Is Where the Hanger Is," *Time*, (14 September 1981), p. 92. Curry, Bill, "Wood Stove Benefits Go Up in Smoke," *Los Angeles Times* (18 February 1982), pp. 14, 15.

Maloney, Lawrence, "The Mobile Home: A Stepchild No More," *U.S. News and World Report* (12 April 1982), pp. 66–67.

CHAPTER 14—The Price of Eden

Little, Charles E. and Fletcher, W. Wendell, "Buckshot Urbanization: The Land Impacts of Rural Population Growth," *American Demographics*, vol. 2, no. 4 (Fall 1981), pp. 10–35.

Robertson, James and Carolyn, *The Small Towns Book* (Garden City: Anchor Books, 1978), pp. 19, 21.

Chicago Tribune News Service, "As Maine Goes: Downhill," in the *San Diego Union* (5 April 1982), p. A13.

Wardwell, John M., "Revitalization of Rural America: Patterns and Consequences of Nonmetropolitan and Rural Growth," in Hicks, Donald A. and Glickman, Norman J. (eds.), *Transition to the 21st Century: Prospects and Policies for Economic and Urban-Regional Transformation* (Greenwich, CT: JAI Press, 1983).

Curry, Bill, "Wood Stove Benefits Go Up in Smoke," *Los Angeles Times* (18 February 1982), pp. 14, 15.

Berry, Wendell, *The Unsettling of America* (New York: Avon Publishers, 1977), p. 7.

Mayer, Robert, "In the Sun's Shadow," *Rocky Mountain Magazine*, (January-February 1982) p. 42.

Williams, James D. and Sofranko, Andrew J., "Why People Move," *American Demographics* (July-August 1981), p. 31.

Doherty, J. C., "The Countrified City," *American Demographics*, vol. 2, no. 4 (Fall 1981), pp. 7–8.

PART FIVE—WORKING IN AMERICA II

Quote

Johnson, Richard Tanner and Ouchi, William G., "Made in America (under Japanese Management)," *Harvard Business Review* (September-October 1974), pp. 61–69.

Thurow, Lester C., "Expanding Private Welfare," *Newsweek* (3 August 1981), p. 68.

CHAPTER 15—You're on the Bus or You're off the Bus
Getting There
   The following three articles were especially helpful for general
   statistics and background:
Serrin, William, "Worry Grows Over Upheaval as Technology
   Reshapes Jobs," *New York Times* (4 July 1982). (Including quotes
   from Harvey Shaiken.)
Treadwell, David, and Redburn, Tom, "Workplace: Site of Latest
   Revolution, Part I," *Los Angeles Times* (24 April 1983), pp. 1,
   12–14.
Steinert-Threlkeld, Tom, "The Invisible and Pervasive Industry,"
   Fort Worth Star-Telegram (4 October 1981).

CHAPTER 16—The Company as Cult
Efficiency and Community
Ouchi, William G. and Jaeger, Alfred M., "Type Z Organization:
   Stability in the Midst of Mobility," *Academy of Management Review*
   (April 1978), pp. 1–10.
Keyes, Ralph, *We the Lonely People* (New York: Harper and Row,
   1973), p. 75.

Second Thoughts
Thurow, Lester C., "Expanding Private Welfare," *Newsweek*
   (3 August 1981), p. 68.

The Role of Unions
Seligman, Daniel, "Who Needs Unions?" *Fortune* (12 July 1982),
   pp. 54–66.
Serrin, William, "Controller Called Typical of New Breed of
   Worker," *New York Times* (16 August 1981), p. 38.

CHAPTER 17—The Faith of Entrepreneurialism
Comes the Entrepreneurial Revolution
Harwood, Edwin, "The Entrepreneurial Renaissance and Its
   Promoters," *Society Magazine* (March-April 1979), pp. 27–31.
Macrae, Norman, "Intrapreneurial Now," *The Economist* (17 April
   1982), pp. 67–72
"The New America," *Esquire* (May 1983), p. 143. (Regarding the
   research of David Birch.)

Why Entrepreneurialism
Russell, Cheryl, "The Minority Entrepreneur," *American
   Demographics* (June 1981), pp. 18–20.
Cox, William A., "Changing Consumption Patterns," *American
   Demographics* (May 1981), pp. 18–20.

Kleiman, Carol, "Two-Paycheck Home Liberates Husband," *Chicago Tribune* (29 March 1982).

Charboneau, F. Jill, "The Woman Entrepreneur," *American Demographics* (June 1981), p. 21.

Gottschalk, Earl C., Jr., "Promotions Grow Few as 'Baby Boom' Group Eyes Managers' Jobs," *Wall Street Journal* (26 October 1981).

Home Work

Morris, David, *Self-Reliant Cities* (San Francisco: Sierra Club Books, 1982), p. 12. (The historical figures on how many people worked at home.)

Goldstein, Nora, "Need for Networking," *In Business,* (March-April 1982), p. 44.

CHAPTER 18—Winners and Losers

McGahey, Richard, "Higher Tech's Lower Jobs," New York Times Special Features (June 1983).

High-Tech Vulnerability

Lewis, Hunter and Allison, Donald, *The Real World War: The Coming Battle for the New Global Economy and Why We Are in Danger of Losing* (New York: Coward, McCann and Geoghegan, 1982).

"Computer 'Chip' Menaces Third World," United Press International, in the *San Diego Union* (30 November 1979).

PART SIX—SOMEWHERE OVER THE POSTINDUSTRIAL RAINBOW

Quote

Didion, Joan, *The White Album* (New York: Simon and Schuster, 1979), p. 65.

Lasch, Christopher, *The Culture of Narcissism* (New York: Warner Books, 1979), pp. 396–397.

CHAPTER 19—The Transforming Cities of America I

Lyons, Richard D., "Technology Adds Jobs in State," *New York Times* (20 June 1982), pp. 1, 33.

Andrews, Paul, "Downtown Gains Skyscrapers but Loses Heart," *Seattle Times* (3 July 1983), p. A1.

Kay, Jane Holtz, "The Blank Wall," *Christian Science Monitor* (18 March 1983), p. 15.

Gage, Theodore J., "Getting Street Wise in St. Louis," *Reason* (August 1981), pp. 18–26.

Frazier, Mark, "Privatizing the City," *Policy Review* (Spring 1980), pp. 91–108.

Butler, Katy, "Bite by Bite, the Croissant Culture Is Swallowing Up the Ghettos," *Los Angeles Times* (24 August 1980).

Morrison, Peter, "Beyond the Baby Boom, the Depopulation of America," *The Futurist* (April 1979).

CHAPTER 20—The Third Road

Focus on Tomorrow: Report of Project 2000, on the Future of the Triangle J Region, Triangle J Council of Governments, Research Triangle Park, North Carolina (3 February 1982), pp. 1–30.

"Executive Summary, Final Report," National Agricultural Lands Study (1981), pp. 1–25.

Oldenquist, Andrew, "On Belonging to Tribes," *Newsweek* (5 April 1982), p. 9.

Suggested Readings

Abbey, Edward, *The Journey Home, Some Words in Defense of the American West* (New York: E. P. Dutton, 1977).

Archibald, M. (ed.), *The Farm and the City: Rivals or Allies?* (Englewood Cliffs, NJ: Prentice-Hall, 1980).

Bell, Daniel, *The Coming of the Post-Industrial Society, A Venture in Social Forecasting* (New York: Basic Books, 1976).

Berry, Brian J. L. and Silverman, Lester P. (eds.), *Population Redistribution and Public Policy* National Academy of Sciences, Washington, D.C. (1980).

Berry, Wendell, *The Unsettling of America, Culture and Agriculture* (New York: Avon, 1978).

Brenner, M. Harvey, "Assessing the Social Costs of National Unemployment Rate," formal statement submitted for testimony before the Subcommittee on Domestic Monetary Policy of the Committee on Banking, Finance, and Urban Affairs, U.S. House of Representatives, Washington, D.C., (12 August 1982). Available through Johns Hopkins Medical Institution, Office of Public Affairs, 624 N. Broadway, Eighth floor, Baltimore, MD 21205.

Brown, David L. and Wardwell, John M., *New Directions in Urban-Rural Migration,* (Academic Press, 1980).

Butz, W. P., et al, *Demographic Challenges in America's Future,* The Rand Corporation, Santa Monica, CA, (1982).

Coates, Gary J. (ed.), *Resettling America—The Movement Toward Local Self-Reliance* (Andover, MA: Brick House Publishing, 1981).

Corbett, Michael, *A Better Place to Live, New Designs for Tomorrow's Communities* (Emmaus, PA: Rodale Press, 1981).

Duncan, Mary and Lerner, Max, "Walled Cities: the Fortress Mentality," *San Diego Magazine* (September 1982), p. 86.

Garreau, Joel, *The Nine Nations of North America* (Boston: Houghton Mifflin, 1981).

Harris, Marvin, *America Now: The Anthropology of a Changing Culture* (New York: Simon and Schuster, 1981).

Hawken, Paul, *The Next Economy* (New York: Holt, Rinehart and Winston, 1983).

Herbers, John, "Sun Belt Cities Prosper as Those in North Decline," *New York Times* (28 February 1983).

Hicks, Donald (ed.), *Urban America in the Eighties, Perspectives and Prospects, President's Commission for a National Agenda for the Eighties* (New Brunswick: Transaction Books, 1982).

Jacobs, Jane, *The Economy of Cities* (New York: Vintage Books, 1970).

Kasarda, John D., "The Implications of Contemporary Redistribution Trends for National Urban Policy," *Social Science Quarterly*, vol. 61, nos. 3 and 4, (December 1980), pp. 373–400.

Keyes, Ralph, *We, the Lonely People, Searching for Community* (New York: Harper and Row, 1973).

Lamm, Richard D. and McCarthy, Michael, *The Angry West, A Vulnerable Land and Its Future* (Boston: Houghton Mifflin, 1982).

Loomis, Mildred J., *Alternative Americas* (New York: Universe Books, 1982).

Meyer, Ralph C., "The Dictator Syndrome—Heredity or Environment?" synopsis of address on condominiums to the Fourteenth National Conference of the Community Associations Institute, Division of the Social Sciences, College at Lincoln Center, Fordham University, New York, NY 10023.

Morris, David, *Self-Reliant Cities* (San Francisco: Sierra Club Books, 1982).

Mumford, Lewis, *The Culture of Cities* (New York: Harcourt Brace Jovanovich, 1970).

Naisbitt, John, *Megatrends* (New York: Warner Books, 1982).

A National Agenda for the Eighties, President's Commission for a National Agenda for the Eighties, (New York: New American Library, 1981).

National Agricultural Lands Study, Executive Summary, final report (1981), 722 Jackson Place, NW, Washington, D.C. 20006.

Newman, Oscar, *Community of Interest* (Garden City: Anchor Press, 1980).

Nichols, John and Davis, William, *If Mountains Die, A New Mexico Memoir* (New York: Alfred A. Knopf, 1980).

Nisbit, Robert A., *The Quest for Community* (New York: Oxford Press, 1970).

Oosterbaan, John, *Population Dispersal: A National Imperative* (Lexington: Lexington Books, 1980).

Packard, Vance, *A Nation of Strangers* (New York: David McKay, 1972).

Reed, John Shelton, *One South, An Ethnic Approach to Regional Culture* (Baton Rouge: Louisiana State University Press, 1982).

Robertson, James and Carolyn, *The Small Towns Book* (New York: Anchor, 1978).

Robertson, James Oliver, *American Myth, American Reality* (New York, Hill and Wang, 1980).

Sampson, R. Neil, *Farmland or Wasteland, A Time to Choose* (Emmaus, PA: Rodale Press, 1981).

Toffler, Alvin, *The Third Wave* (New York: Bantam Books, 1981).

Vining, Daniel R., "Towards a National Urban Policy—Critical Reviews, The President's National Urban Policy Report: Issues Skirted and Statistics Omitted," *Journal of Regional Science,* vol. 19, no. 1 (1979), pp. 69–77.

Wardwell, John M., "The Reversal of Nonmetropolitan Migration Loss," in Dillman, D. A. and Hobbs, D. J. (eds.), *Rural Locality in the U.S.: Issues for the 1980s* (Boulder: Westview Press, 1982), pp. 23–33.

Weber, Max, *The City* (New York: Free Press Paperback, 1966).

Whyte, William H., *The Last Landscape* (Garden City: Doubleday, 1968).

Williams, James D., "The Nonchanging Determinants of Nonmetropolitan Migration," *Rural Sociology,* vol. 46, no. 2 (1981), pp. 183–202.

————, "Turnaround Migrants: Grubby Economics or Delightful Indulgence in Ruralism?" *The Rural Sociologist,* vol. 2, no. 2, pp. 103–108.

Wolfe, David B., *Condominium and Homeowner Associations that Work, on Paper and in Action,* published jointly by the Urban Land Institute and the Community Associations Institute, Washington, D.C. (1978).

Two excellent journals for further reference are *American Demographics* (Ithaca, New York), and *American Land Forum* magazine (Bethesda, Maryland).

Abbey, E., 62, 188
Abbott, C., 30
Agriculture, disappearing
    farmland, 197–99
Air travel, 13, 17–18
Alger, H., 6–7
America I
    cities, 73, 77
    economy of, 20–21
    shelter, 83–84, 86–88
    transformation of cities,
        267–85
America II
    affiliation, 33–34
    cities, 73–74, 77–78
    downtown areas, 273
    emerging vision of, 293–301
    growth in cities, 270–71
    high-tech security, 120–22
    home ownership, 89
    new directions, 301–304
    new economy, 21–22
    shelter, 85–87
    unions and, 237–38
    zoning rules, 87–88
    See also Rural America.
American Gothic (G. Wood), 181
Americanism, 5
Anderson, M., 274–75
Anderson, S., 149
"Andy Griffith Show," 4

Angelou, M., 15
Anticity, 37–46
    description, 45–46
Apple Computer, 232–33
Apple Computer Supersite,
    219, 233
Arizona, 57–64
    migration to, 47–51
    social aspects, 58–59
    urban villages, 55–57
Arizona Tomorrow, 49, 59
Aronowitz, S., 239
Athens, 31
Aurora, Colorado, 55–56

Babbitt, B., 54, 62–63
Baby boomers, 8
Batten, M., 23
Beale, C., 16, 28, 156, 202, 297
Beaver Creek, Colorado,
    189–90
Berger, B. M., 40–41, 44–45
Berry, W., 151–52, 155, 201
Birch, D. L., 21, 247
Bjornseth, D., 76
Blecksmith, F., 134
Boston University School of
    Management, 238
Bowling Green State University,
    8

Brenner, M. H., 21–22
Browne, R., 8
"Buckshot urbanization,"
    184–86
  farmers and, 198
  urban/rural person and,
    185–86
Byron, D. A., 115

Cairo, 31
California, 11, 45
Canada, 25
Capitalism, entrepreneur and,
    243
Carter, J., 61, 130
Casa Grande, 63–64
Centerville, Iowa, 186
Central Arizona Project, 61
Charboneau, J., 247
Cities
  backwoods cities, 286–93
  ethnic neighborhoods,
    277–82
  gentrification, 271–76
  historical perspective, 37–39
  industrial, 38–39
  Jeffersonian design, 37–38,
    43
  migration to (internationally),
    31–32
  minority groups, 283–84
  polynucleated form, 52
  transformation of, 267–85
Co-op, ownership, 90
Common interest community,
    85
  Rancho Bernardo, 92–96
Communist countries, 32
Community associations,
    128–36
  developers and, 131–32
  legal and social aspects of,
    133–37
  powers of secession, 132–33

"Compa," 227
Company towns, 97–98
Computers
  farmers use of, 209–10
  inequalities created by,
    258–61
  machine monitoring, 250
Condominiums
  ownership, 89–90
  rise of, 84–85
Conservatism, 15
Corbett, M., 138–44
Corporate moves, 18–20
Cottage industries, 246
Counterculture/libertarian
    movement, 15–16
Counterurbanization, 78
Country music, 7
Covenant law, 133
Covenants, conditions, and
    restrictions (CC&Rs), 128
Cox, W. A., 246
Crime, 14–15

Davis, J., 150–51
Davis, South Dakota, 176,
    207
Deconcentration, 65, 78
  of America, 25–29, 33–34
Demko, G., 32
Disney, W., 109
Disneyland, 109–10
Doherty, J. C., 204
Douglas, H. P., 40
Duke University, 291
Durer, A., 97

Economy
  rural, 178–81
  underground, 253–55
Eisenhower Era, 12
Elderly, 16–17
Electronics industry, 224

Ely, R., 98
Emcon, 235–37
Emerson, R. W., 149
Energy, 14
Entrepreneur, classic definition,
    243
Entrepreneurialism, 241–56
    cottage industries, 246
    current expansion of, 244–48
    isolation of, 250–51
    pot farmers, 253
    psychological attraction,
        247
    working at home, 241–42,
        248–51
Epcot, 109
Euclidian zoning, 88
Eureka, 5

Faulkner, W., 149
Federal involvement, planned
    communities, 99–100
Fletcher, W. W., 195
Ford, H., 39
Fordham University, 133, 246
Foulkes, F., 238
Fractionalization, alternative to,
    302
Francaviglia, R. V., 109
Freeways, 295–96
Friedman, J., 142–43
Friedman, M., 142
Fuchs, R. J., 32

Gage, T. J., 276
Garden cities, 98
Garreau, J., 30
"Gated communities," 85
Gays, small-town migration,
    171–72
Gentrification, 271–76
    neighborhood security and,
        274–76

Goodkin, S., 131
Greeley, H., 38
Greenbelt, Maryland, 99
Greendale, 99
Gurwitz, A. S., 260
Gustaitis, R., 118
Gutierrez, A., 47, 60, 62

Hance, M. T., 49
Harris, L., 15
Harwood, E., 244–45
Hayden, T., 233
Helmers, C., 254
Herbers, J., 184
Hewitt, W., 23
Hewlett-Packard, 228–30
Hicks, D. A., 268–69
"High tech/high touch," 8
High-technology, vulnerability
    created by, 260–63
Hohokam civilization, 63
Hollywood, decay of, 4
Home ownership
    in America II, 89
    historical view, 83–84
Homesteaders, 159–64
Houston, 21
    entrepreneurialism, 70–72
    growth of, 66–70
    Montrose section, 69–70
    private services, 74–77
    traffic in, 68
Howard, E., 98
Hucher, W. E., 127–28
Humboldt County, California,
    16

IBM, corporate moves, 18
"Image of elsewhere," 5
Imperial County, California,
    191–92
Interstate highways, 12–13
Irvine, California, 113–14

Jackson, Wyoming, 190
Jackson Hole, Wyoming, 188, 200
Jacob, B., 112–13
Jaeger, A. M., 222, 231
Japanese companies, 224–28
  management style, 231
Jefferson, T., 37, 43, 149
Johns Hopkins University, 21
Johnson, B., 258
Jonishi, A., 224–28, 235–37

Kaplan, B. J., 66
Keyes, R., 222, 247
Klein, D., 120
Koch, E., 24
Kramer, D., 64
Kyocera, 225–28
  Emcon and, 235–37

Laissez-faire lifestyle, 65–80
Lake Ridge, 131–32
Lane, F. K., 98
Laser beams, security systems, 123
Lauren, R., 7
Lautenberg, F., 257–58
"Leave It to Beaver," 4
Leff, S., 41
Leven, C., 52–53
Lewis, W. A., 263
Little, A. D., 217
Little, C. E., 195
Local governments, 127
Longstreth, T., 267–68, 270, 272, 284
Los Angeles, 4–6, 62–63

Machine monitoring, 250
Machlin, P. R., 200
Macrae, N., 244

Maine
  homesteaders, 159–64
  middle-class migrants, 164–69
  migration to, 159–69
  suicide rate, 160
Mammoth, California, 190–91
Management
  Hewlett-Packard, 228–30
  Japanese/American combination, 231
  Kyocera, 225–28
  proponents of Japanese style, 231, 234–35
Manufacturing technology, 13
Massachusetts Institute of Technology, 21, 218, 238, 244, 298
Mayer, R., 202
McConn, M., 71–72
McGahey, R., 256
McGill, W., 23–24, 33, 47
Megalopolis, 43–44
Merrill Lynch, 18
Meyer, R. C., 133–34, 144
Micropolitan small towns, 186–87
Migration patterns
  1970s onward, 10–22
  demographic studies, 10–11
  new economy and, 20–22
  nostalgia and, 3–9
  shifts in population, 23–34
  social forces, 15–19
  technology and, 12–13
Miller, H., 8
Mitchell, G., 100–102
Mobile homes, 190–92
Montgomery County, North Carolina, 184
Mooney, M., 246
Moral Majority, 9
More, T., 97
Morrison, P. A., 5, 42
Mullane, J., 121–25

Mumford, L., 42–43, 53, 88, 91, 144–45
Myerhoff, B., 109–10

Naisbitt, J., 7–8
National Association of Neighborhoods, 274–75
National Association of Working Women, 249
National League of Cities, migration survey, 11
"National hometown," 222
Nature
  demystification of, 201
  in the planned community, 112–13
  value to people, 201
New tribes, 300
New wave, 7
New York State, economic transformation, 271
New York University, 256
North Carolina
  blacks return to, 291–92
  Research Triangle Park, 286
  Rocky Mount, 288–92
Nostalgia, 5–7
  in the planned community, 112–13
Nuclear family, 86–87
Nussbaum, K., 249–50

Ocean County, New Jersey, 118
Ohio State University, 300
Oldenquist, A., 300
Ong, W., 259
Organizations, Types J, A, and Z, 231
Orwell, G., 181
Ouchi, W. G., 222, 231
Our Town (T. Wilder), 169–70

Pennsbury Village, Pennsylvania, 132
Peterborough, New Hampshire, 169–75, 254
Philadelphia
  Chester, 280–82
  decline of, 267–70
  growth in, 270–71
  Mount Airy, 277–80
  South, 276–77
Phillips, K., 29
Planned communities, 88–91
  new towns, 99–100
  rural, 188–91
  theoretical roots of, 97–99
Planned-unit developments, ownership, 89–90
Ploch, L. A., 159, 165
Population deconcentration, entrepreneurialism and, 244–48
Population density, effects on people, 42
"Positive ghettoism," 114–15
Pot farmers, 16, 253
Poverty, 298–99
  rural, 196–97
Private governments, 127–36
Privatization, of services, 74–77
Protective associations, 134
Pullman, G. M., 97

Racism, 298–99
Radburn, New Jersey, 98
Rancho Bernardo, 92–96
Recreation towns, 188
Reed, J. S., 181
Renovation, in cities, 271–72
Research Triangle Park, 286
Reynolds, C., 262–63
Robertson, C., 196
Robertson, J., 196
Robotics, 254
Rockwell, N., 158–59, 173

Rogers, E. M., 257–58
Rosenthal, N., 217–18
Rossmoor Leisure World, 116, 119
Rural America
  assumptions about, 155–57
  buckshot urbanization, 183–86
  continued growth of, 203–11
  demystification of nature, 201
  disappearing farmland, 197–99
  the far suburbs, 182–83
  hyperculture and, 187–94
  micropolitan small towns, 186–87
  migration to, 27–28
  migration to Maine, 159–69
  migration to Peterborough, 169–75
  migration to Sioux Falls, 176–78
  mobile homes, 190–92
  myths of, 202
  personal identity search, 158–59
  planned communities, 188–90
  poverty in, 196–97
  resettling of, 150–54
  resistance to change, 192–94
  the rural economy, 178–81
  urbanization of, 181–94
Rural shelter, 188
Russell, C., 183, 245
Ryan, R. E., 66, 68, 71

San Diego, 5
  Gaslamp Quarter, 6
San Jose, 26
Schaller, D., 57–58
Schaumburg, Illinois, 132
Schumpeter, J., 243–44

Schwartz, R., 246
Scottsdale, 56–57
Secondary oral culture, 259
Security
  in common interest communities, 118–21
  senior citizens and, 119
  Towers of Quayside, 121–26
Senior citizens
  golden-age ghettos, 115–19
  rural migration of, 155–56
  security in condos, 118–19
  "snowbirds," 191–92
Senior zoning, 115–16, 118
Shaiken, H., 218, 238
Shelter revolution, 83–146
  capitalist communes, 92–107
  condominiums, 84–86
  implications of, 89–91
  nature and the community, 112–13
  ownership conflicts, 135–36
  packaging of community, 110–11
  planned communities, 88–91
  private government and, 127–36
  single-family detached homes, 86–87
  theme housing, 113–18
  Village Homes, 137–44
  The Woodlands, 100–107
Shopping malls, 52
Shrank, R., 238–39
Sierra, 5
Silicon Valley, 180, 186, 257, 260
Sioux Falls, South Dakota, 176–78
"The slabs," 191–92
Small Towns Book (J. Robertson, C. Robertson), 196
Small towns, 149. See also Rural America.

Smith, A., 222
Smith, J. E., 116
"Snowbirds," 191–92
Sofranko, A., 156–57, 203–204
Solomon, A. P., 27
South, growth of American, 26
St. Louis, 24–25
Stack, C. B., 291
Stanford University, 257–59,
    262
Suburbia, 40–43
    1950s, 40
    childhood memories, 3
    growth of, 26–27
Sun Belt, 26, 28–30
"Sunshine laws," 135
"Surrogate farms," 165–66

Tamina, Texas, 78–79
Tanenbaum, M., 8
Technological linkages, 14
Technology, migration and,
    12–13
Tent cities, 298
Thailand, 31
The Unsettling of America (W.
    Berry), 151
Theme housing, 113–18
    golden-age ghettos, 115–19
    single-interest
    neighborhoods, 114–15
Thurow, L. C., 233–34
Towers of Quayside, security
    system, 121–26
Trudeau, P., 25
Tweeten, L., 186
Two-paycheck families, 246–47
Type Z organization, 231–32

Underground economy, 253–55
Unemployment, 216–18
Unger, C., 7

Unions
    new management style and,
        234–35
    role of, 237–40
Universal Studios, 4
University of California, Los
    Angeles, 4
University of California, San
    Diego, 40
University of Illinois, 10–11
University of Maine, 165
University of South Florida,
    244
University of Texas, 268
Urban villages, 53–57
    Casa Grande, 63–64
    Scottsdale, 56–57
Urban/rural person, 185–86
Urbanization, the anticity,
    37–46
Utopia (T. More), 97

Veblen, T., 158
Village Homes, 137–44

Wage spreading, 262–64
Waldo County, Maine, 150–51
Walled communities, 85
Wardwell, J., 179, 182, 197
Water resources, 297
"Weighted" voting, 133
West, growth of American,
    25–27
Western Behavioral Sciences
    Institute, 206
Whyte, W. H., 88, 273
Wiggins, J. R., 164
Wilcox, E., 59–60
Wilder, T., 169–70
Williams, W., 111–12, 114–15,
    120
Williamsburg Landing, 117

Winston-Salem, 15
Wolfe, D., 90–91, 116, 135–37
Wood-burning stoves, 200
Wood, G., 181
Woodlands, The, 100–107
Word processing, 241–42
    office conflicts and, 258
Work
    Apple Computer, 232–33
    Emcon example, 235–37
    Hewlett-Packard model, 228–30
    Kyocera model, 225–28
    changes in, 216

company as cult, 224–40
electronics industry, 224
future job markets, 217–19
insular community/company, 222
the workplace, 219–23
unemployment, 216–18
See also Entrepreneurialism.

Yankelovich, D., 18–19

Zoning, senior, 115–16, 118
Zoning theory, 87–88